YEARBOOK IN EARLY CHILDHOOD EDUCATION

Bernard Spodek • Olivia N. Saracho
EDITORS

VOLUME 1
Early Childhood Teacher Preparation
Bernard Spodek and Olivia N. Saracho, Editors

VOLUME 2
Issues in Early Childhood Curriculum
Bernard Spodek and Olivia N. Saracho, Editors

VOLUME 3
Issues in Child Care
Bernard Spodek and Olivia N. Saracho, Editors

VOLUME 4
Language and Literacy in Early Childhood Education
Bernard Spodek and Olivia N. Saracho, Editors

The *Yearbook in Early Childhood Education* is a series of annual publications. Each volume addresses a timely topic of major significance in the field of early childhood education, and contains chapters that present and interpret current knowledge on aspects of that topic, written by experts in the field. Key issues—including concerns about educational equity, multiculturalism, the needs of diverse populations of children and families, and the ethical dimensions of the field—are woven into the organization of each of the volumes.

**YEARBOOK
IN
EARLY CHILDHOOD EDUCATION
VOLUME 3**

ISSUES IN
CHILD CARE

Bernard Spodek • Olivia N. Saracho
EDITORS

**TEACHERS
COLLEGE
PRESS**

Teachers College, Columbia University
New York • London

*To Francisca Villarreal, who gave me life,
and whose love, wisdom, and strength supported me
all these years.*

Olivia Natavidad Saracho

Published by Teachers College Press, 1234 Amsterdam Avenue
New York, NY 10027

Library of Congress Cataloging-in-Publication Data

Issues in child care / Bernard Spodek, Olivia N. Saracho, editors.
     p.   cm. — (Yearbook in early childhood education ; v. 3)
    Includes bibliographical references and index.
    ISBN 0-8077-3204-4 (cloth : alk. paper). — ISBN 0-8077-3203-6
(pbk. : alk. paper)
    1. Children — Services for — United States.   2. Child care services —
United States.   3. Early childhood education — United States.
   I. Spodek, Bernard.   II. Saracho, Olivia N.   III. Series.
HV741.I89   1992
362.7′12′0973 — dc20   92-22919

Printed on acid-free paper

Manufactured in the United States of America

99 98 97 96 95 94 93 92 8 7 6 5 4 3 2 1

Contents

Introduction: Child Care in Early Education

Olivia N. Saracho
Bernard Spodek

The provision of child care services has become an increasingly important part of early childhood education. As Carollee Howes notes in Chapter 3, "Most children in America are enrolled in some form of child care arrangement prior to formal school entrance." Child care arrangements include center care, family day care, in-home care, relative care, and no supplemental care. These are defined as follows:

• *Center care:* Care provided to groups of children in a nonresidential setting for all or part of the day. Centers can be categorized by their legal status and auspices: nonprofit centers, both sponsored and independent; and for-profit centers, both independent and members of a chain. Nonprofit sponsored programs are further categorized by auspices, including those sponsored by Head Start, public schools, religious organizations, or other sponsors such as employers or community agencies.

• *Family day care:* Care provided for a small group of children in the caregiver's home. Often a family day care provider is a mother with children of her own at home. Family day care may be regulated or nonregulated. Nonregulated care includes providers who are not licensed or registered even though they are subject to regulation.

• *In-home care:* Care provided by a nonrelative who comes into the family home. Sometimes the provider brings her own children with her to the home.

• *Relative care:* Care provided by a relative in the child's home or the relative's home.

• *No supplemental care:* Parents provide all the care for their children or use nonparental arrangements on an irregular basis (Willer, Hofferth, Kisker, Divine-Hawkins, Farquhar & Glantz, 1991).

The first two types of arrangements might be considered professional child care. According to Bettye Caldwell (1984), "professional child care is a comprehensive service to children and families which serves as a sub-system of the child rearing system and which supplements the care children receive from their families" (p. 4). Issues related to professional child care are the focus of this volume.

Professional child care is primarily offered in child care centers, although somewhat more children below age three are in family day care than in center care (Hofferth, Brayfield, Deich & Holcomb, 1990). These centers have come a long way from the day nurseries established in the first half of the nineteenth century. These early day nurseries usually provided only minimal forms of care and protection, sometimes offering only inadequate meals to children. Often the same person who cooked and cleaned also supervised large numbers of children. These day nurseries lacked the resources to offer anything more than simple child-minding services — services that would be considered inadequate today. Child care has evolved from a service to meet the needs of poor families with working mothers, through a period where it was viewed as a mechanism to maintain families in need, to a service potentially serving all families with young children (Cahan, 1989).

Professional child care offered in centers today provides educational as well as caring services. The size of children's groups are limited, and teachers in charge of these groups must have at least a minimum of preparation. Health and safety codes must be met, and some form of educational program must be offered. Standards are embedded in state licensing regulations for child care. However, the standards in place today are less than ideal. They do not reflect as high a level of quality as many in the field would like to see. In addition, standards vary greatly from state to state and, like the standards themselves, enforcement is highly variable. Such licensing standards represent a floor below which the quality of child care services should not fall if children are to be protected from harm (Morgan, 1982). A higher level of standards is found in the accreditation standards of the National Academy of Early Childhood Programs of the National Association for the Education of Young Children. These accreditation standards are voluntarily met by centers that wish to demonstrate that they provide higher-quality care.

Child care is provided not only in centers, but in family child care homes as well. These homes also need to provide more than custodial care. Although nutritional meals and snacks, adequate rest, and a safe and healthy environment are basic, educational experiences must also be offered to children in these programs to nurture their psychomotor, cognitive, language, and social development. All child care programs should be designed to integrate children into the smaller social milieu of the peer group as well as into the larger social milieu of the community.

The education and nurture of young children have been a part of early childhood education programs since the creation of the nursery school at the beginning of the twentieth century. However, child care differs from other forms of early childhood education in a basic way: Child care responds to parents' need to care for their children as well as to educate them. The original nursery school operated for the normal hours of a school day, and many nursery schools offer half-day programs today. This is much less than the extended day that is typical of child care centers. Indeed, most early childhood programs — under either public or private auspices — operate from about two-and-a-half to six hours daily. Child care centers typically enroll children for eight hours a day or longer.

The educational content of child care programs should be no different from the content of other types of early childhood education programs. The issues of curriculum for child care centers serving young children differ little from those for other early childhood programs. These issues were addressed in Volume 2 of the *Yearbook in Early Childhood Education* (Spodek & Saracho, 1991). The extended day and the increased responsibilities of these programs, however, raise additional issues and place increased responsibilities on child care personnel. Not only should they be competent in providing an adequate early childhood education program, but they also need to know a great deal about how to support child development broadly — knowledge that includes the areas of health, nutrition, and physical development.

Embedded in the increased acceptance and use of child care by American families and the ways in which child care is provided in the United States are the issues that this volume addresses. When few young children were in organized child care, little attention was paid to these issues, except by the few professionals who where involved in the field. Now these issues have become a national concern.

In the first chapter, Roger Neugebauer identifies five trends that will shape the future of early childhood centers in America. The first trend, which he characterizes as the child care habit, reflects the increased use of child care centers and child care homes. Although the use of both is growing, child care centers have become the prime choice of working parents. The popularity of child care is reflected in the increasing political support that child care is receiving in our country. In addition, public schools are becoming more involved with the care and education of young children. Kindergarten education grew at a tremendous rate in the public schools in the 1970s. Today public school prekindergarten programs are increasing. Although these are primarily part-day programs for children from special populations, many local school systems are contracting with private agencies to provide child care services. The increasing concern for quality in child care is implicit in all the chapters, and the key to quality child care is the teacher. As Neugebauer asserts, "failure to address this issue could yet be the Achilles heel of quality child care."

Any understanding of the present and future of child care in America would be incomplete without a historical overview of the field. In Chapter 2, Alice Sterling Honig begins by identifying child-rearing practices in early times, focusing on the role of philosophy and ideology in establishing these practices. She places the development of child care within the broader field of early childhood education from the earliest times through today. The theorists that influenced early childhood education in general are seen as having influenced child care practices as well. Primary among these are scholars in child development, both theorists and empirical researchers. Honig also identifies the economic and political bases of child care trends. Important among these are the need to respond to teacher unemployment in the 1930s, the need to serve the war effort in the 1940s, and the need to deal with concerns about children in poverty in the 1960s. Honig identifies the current dilemma in child care as the attempt to establish a balance between the needs of families, society, and dual-career families and the requirements for optimal child development.

Because so many children are enrolled in child care programs today, the consequences of their enrollment have become an increasing concern of early childhood practitioners, child development specialists, parents, and the public in general. Carollee Howes reviews what we know about child outcomes of child care in Chapter 3. The major focus of this research has been the relationship between indicators of quality and child outcomes. These indicators include elements of structural quality, such as class size or the training of caregivers, and elements of process quality, including the quality of programs and interpersonal relationships. Differences that have been found in quality indicators and child outcomes are related to the sponsorship of child care programs and the regulatory climate of child care centers. Based on her review, Howes concludes that "the child is likely to have positive and pleasant experiences in care when child care is regulated, when it is not-for-profit, and when it is of high quality."

In Chapter 4, Ellen Galinsky and Bernice Weissbourd identify a significant shift toward family-centered child care. In such child care, parents and teachers learn from one another in community centers where parents' adult needs are met through center programs and links with community services. The authors describe the influences on this innovative approach to child care, the barriers to establishing family-centered child care, and the principles underlying it. They also present examples of centers that provide such care. They conclude with the fact that family-centered child care, although more expensive than traditional child care, has both economic and psychological benefits. The focus on prevention and the linkages to service agencies are essentially cost-effective. Perhaps most important, family-centered child care represents a different way of thinking about, feeling about, and interacting with families in child care.

As more and more young children are enrolled in child care programs, these programs find themselves serving an increasingly diverse population of children. The next two chapters in this volume address the issue of diversity in child care. In Chapter 5, K. Eileen Allen identifies the range of special populations in child care. Among those who need child care are children with health and orthopedic problems, children with vision and hearing problems, children with speech and language problems, and children with behavior disorders, conduct disorders, and developmental disorders. Increasing numbers of victims of child abuse, of maternal substance abuse, and of AIDS/HIV are among those served by child care. Each of these populations of children needs special services and programs. Special programs must also be provided to gifted children.

Patricia G. Ramsey, in Chapter 6, discusses the increased diversity of backgrounds found among children enrolled in child care. This diversity includes racial differences, cultural differences, socioeconomic differences, and differences in family composition. Child care personnel need to respond to this diversity by integrating a multicultural perspective in the programs they design and by responding to each child individually. Ramsey concludes that we can support the move toward a truly multicultural and egalitarian society through such responses.

Just as the population being served by child care has become increasingly diverse, so have child care services themselves. Often when we think of child care we visualize preschool children in a child care center. A large number of young children are served by family day care homes, the approach Susan Kontos characterizes as the "other" form of care in Chapter 7. Such care is provided for small groups of children in the homes of caregivers. Kontos discusses issues related to the regulation of such child care and the characteristics of family child care providers and users. Since family day care occupies a niche between the formality of the center and the intimacy of the home, Kontos questions whether it can best be characterized as a "home away from home" or as a small child care center. Reviewing the research on center care versus family day care, Kontos concludes that there is no basis for a blanket assertion that one form of care is superior to the other.

The need for child care does not end when children enter elementary school. Since the full school day is considerably less than the period of the day when working parents are absent from home, the need for child care continues. This before- and after-school child care is reviewed by Michelle Seligson and Ellen Gannett in Chapter 8. They assert that the majority of young school-age children remain regularly unsupervised and are considered "latchkey children." These children, especially those who are young, live in inner-city neighborhoods, and are out of contact with their parents, experience more negative effects than their supervised counterparts. A number of responses have been created to the problem of latchkey children, including serving children in public libraries. A number of city and local agencies as well as public schools have also responded to the need for before- and after-school care. Seligson and Gannett identify the developing knowledge base for school-age child care, the new initiatives that are being established, and the new partners engaged in financing the expansion of this service. They believe that creativity, spontaneity, nurturance, mentoring, and role modeling should serve as priorities for the new programs that are being developed.

The quality of the teaching staff and the quality of the educational setting are two of the most important elements that determine the quality of a child care program. Issues related to these elements are discussed in the next two chapters of this volume. Paula Jorde Bloom addresses staffing issues in Chapter 9. She presents arguments for well-trained teaching and administrative personnel in child care, in spite of the fact that child care regulations reflect the assumption that child care is unskilled work. She identifies issues relating to in-service and preservice teacher training and profiles the levels of education and preparation of current child care personnel. She also describes the current conditions of employment in child care. Bloom presents a vision of the future that could assure a stable and high-quality program staffed by competent personnel and identifies what professional organizations, states, and center directors can do to make that vision a reality. Bloom asserts that it will take the efforts of all these groups and individuals to meet the personal and professional needs of chid care staff.

Thelma Harms, in Chapter 10, deals with a number of issues relating to the design of child care settings. She explores the relationship between the physical setting and child outcomes related to safety, health, and development. Building on the research presented, she offers a set of recommendations for the creation of child care settings. Such flexible, pleasant, and functional settings should allow children and staff to express themselves and communicate the values of sound child care programs.

In the final chapter in this volume, Bernard Spodek and Olivia N. Saracho look to the future of child care in America. Programs of child care have changed rapidly in recent decades. These changes have reflected the evolving needs of young children and families in a changing social context. Needs for child care will continue to evolve, as will the mechanisms that are created to meet those needs. We need to build on the knowledge we have today — knowledge of children, knowledge of parents, and knowledge of practice — to create the kinds of child care programs that will serve the needs of children, parents, and communities in the future.

REFERENCES

Cahan, E. D. (1989). *Past caring*. New York: National Center for Children in Poverty.

Caldwell, B. M. (1984). What is quality child care? *Young Children, 39*(3), 3–12.

Hofferth, S. L., Brayfield, A., Deich, S., & Holcomb, P. (1990). *The national child care survey 1990*. Washington, DC: Urban Institute.

Morgan, G. (1982). Regulating early childhood education programs in the eighties. In B. Spodek (Ed.), *Handbook of research in early childhood education* (pp. 375–398). New York: Free Press

Spodek, B., & Saracho, O. N. (Eds.). (1991). *Issues in early childhood curriculum. Yearbook in early childhood education, vol. 2*. New York: Teachers College Press.

Willer, B., Hofferth, S. L., Kisker, E. E., Divine-Hawkins, P., Farquhar, E., & Glantz, F. B. (1991). *The demand and supply of child care in 1990: Joint findings from the National Child Care Survey 1990 and a profile of child care settings*. Washington, DC: National Association for the Education of Young Children.

CHAPTER 1

Child Care 2000

FIVE TRENDS SHAPING THE FUTURE
FOR EARLY CHILDHOOD CENTERS

Roger Neugebauer

In a time of gloom and doom about U.S. schools, early-childhood education is something different, a cauldron of fresh and innovative approaches.

These are not the words of a motivational keynote speaker at an early childhood conference. Rather, they are taken from a headline in a *Newsweek* magazine article brimming with good news about developments in the early childhood world (Kanfer, 1991). The article contends:

Preschools are bright and inviting; so are the teachers and staffs. They have to be. Close to 60% of U.S. mothers with children under age six are out of the house and on the job. Child care has had to grow up fast.

Child care has indeed grown up fast. In 20 years it has developed from a struggling social service for disadvantaged children to an accepted part of the American scene for all working families. But though it has developed, it has not matured. Child care in this country has not yet matured into a stable, predictable system. The infrastructure of child care in America is still evolving, with forces acting on it from a variety of spheres.

In order to predict what the world of twenty-first-century child care will look like, the best we can do is take some cues from the major trends influencing its development today. Five trends in particular promise to having a lasting impact.

1

THE CHILD CARE HABIT

In the 1980s, child care centers were the fastest growing form of care for children of working parents. From 1977 to 1985, the number of working mothers using child care centers increased by 215% (Neugebauer, 1989). During this same period, their use of family day care centers increased by 60%, nannies by 35%, and relatives by 39%.

By the end of the 1980s, child care centers were the most popular form of nonrelative child care. In 1977, 30% of working mothers placing their children in care outside the family used child care centers, compared to 54% using family day care homes and 16% using nannies. By 1985, 48% of working mothers were taking advantage of centers, 42% of family day care homes, and 10% of nannies (Neugebauer, 1991).

Several factors are commonly cited when explaining the tremendous growth of centers in the past decade. The rise in the number of preschool children (the mini-baby boom) and the surge of women into the work force are the two best known explanations. Between 1977 and 1985, these two factors resulted in a 67% increase in the number of working mothers with children under the age of five (Neugebauer, 1989). But none of the demographic and employment indicators can explain why center care grew at a rate three times faster than the overall demand for child care. The missing factor in the equation has been tagged by Ross Sackett, editor of the vendor newsletter *Six Months to Six Years*, as "the child care habit" — the propensity for parents to select centers over other types of care. According to Sackett, it is the growth of the child care habit that accounts for the magnitude of the surge in demand for center care.

All indications are that the child care habit will continue to grow. Centers will grow in popularity as the prime child care choice for working parents. By 2000, if current trends prevail, nearly 50% of working mothers with preschool children will enroll them in child care centers.

POLITICAL APPLE PIE

The October 1988 issue of *Child Care Information Exchange* had a unique collage on the cover. It featured pictures of George Bush and Michael Dukakis on the campaign trail visiting child care centers. Although neither candidate looked particularly comfortable, the fact that both of them perceived their visits to centers as critical photo opportunities demonstrates what a long way child care has come as a political issue. In previous presidential campaigns, the issue of child care seldom emerged beyond a few sentences in the platform of the Democratic party. But with child care being used more and more by middle-class voters, politicians sensed the need to at least give child care lip service in their campaigns. In the 1980s child care became an "apple pie" issue for politicians.

Political support for child care was translated into positive action early in the 1990s. Authorizations for Head Start funding reached record levels in 1991. In addition, new funding for child care was approved in the form of the Child Care and Development Block Grant—the first significant new funding legislation for child care in over two decades.

It is not certain that politicians have acquired a long-lasting child care habit. Although campaigns for state and national elections still reverberate with acclamations about the value of the early years, child care may be an issue whose time is past. Advocates pushing for funding increases are now encountering the attitude, "We've already done our thing for child care." With the emergence of the elderly as a significant voting block, it is possible that elder care, not child care, will be the social issue of the 1990s.

PUBLIC SCHOOLS DISCOVER EARLY CHILDHOOD

A recent magazine advertisement for the National Education Association (NEA), the largest trade association of public school teachers, asked, "How Long Does It Take a Five-Year-Old to Get Ready for School?" The answer, in part, read:

> Getting a child ready for school doesn't happen in a single morning. How ready children are to learn depends on how well they've been cared for in their preschool years. . . . If we are to succeed as a nation, we must provide every child with the best start possible, by expanding prenatal, nutritional, health, and child care programs to protect and heal all of America's children.

The fact that the NEA would invest its precious advertising dollars to demonstrate its interest in the early years is a strong indicator of how public schools are directing their attention toward preschool children. Responding to concerns about the failures of public schools—the increasing dropout rates and the decreasing skill levels of high school graduates—public school advocates have indicated that it is in the lower grades where public schools start to lose children. They are now concluding that the solution lies in getting off to a good start in the preschool years.

Whether the "discovery" of early childhood is a self-serving passing of the buck or a real conviction about the importance of the early years, the result is a surge in preschool programs in the public schools. By the fall of 1990, 33 states had adopted and funded preschool programs through the public schools (Brady & Goodman, 1991).

The amount allocated to these programs is not insignificant. For fiscal year 1991, state legislatures in the 33 states allocated nearly $444 million for preschool programs. Although this allocation is still well below the $1.9 billion allocated by the federal government to Head Start programs, it does represent a substantial increase from the less than $200 million allocated by 28 states in 1988 (Brady & Goodman, 1991).

Public school involvement in preschool programming is viewed with alarm by child care providers. In late 1990, *Child Care Information Exchange* surveyed the 500 largest providers of child care in the country about the major threats their organizations would confront in the next two years. By a substantial margin, leaders in both private for-profit centers and private nonprofit centers identified the "funding of early childhood programs by public school systems" as the number-one threat (Neugebauer, 1991).

What private providers fear is a scenario in which the public schools take over the provision of all early childhood services for four- and five-year-olds. Indeed, some early childhood advocates, most notably Edward Zigler, actively advocate shifting all funding for child care to local public school systems (Zigler & Lang, 1991). Under this scenario, private providers would be restricted to caring for infants and toddlers, the two age groups that require the most expensive levels of staffing. This scenario would work only if all federal and state dollars now directed to child care services for all age groups were redirected to subsidize the care of infants and toddlers—not a likely eventuality.

A closer look at recent trends in public school involvement in early childhood indicates that a public school takeover of the care of four- and five-year-olds is not likely. In a study of 1990 and 1991 preschool enactments by states, Joanne Brady found that few school systems are expanding their involvement in preschool programs beyond part-day programs serving only disadvantaged children (Brady & Goodman, 1991). In addition, Brady observed a clear shift away from state funding for programs operating totally in public school systems and toward mechanisms that allow local school systems to subcontract with private providers for child care services.

In all likelihood, the diverse child care system of 1990 will remain a diverse child care system in 2000. If current trends hold, independent centers, operated on a nonprofit or for-profit basis, will continue to dominate the delivery system. Important roles will continue to be played by churches, employers, YMCAs and YWCAs, hospitals, the military, and national for-profit chains. Public schools will become one player among these many others.

PARENTS AS CONSUMERS

The cover of the November/December 1990 issue of *Child Care Information Exchange* featured a painting of Isabella Graham, the founder of the first child care organization in the United States. The founding of this organization, currently operating in New York City as the Graham-Wyndham agency, says a great deal about the early role of parents in child care centers.

In 1806, Graham, with the help of other volunteers including Mrs. Alexander Hamilton, DeWitt Clinton, Peter Stuyvesant, and Jennie Lind, established the Orphan Asylum Society (Neugebauer, 1990). This organization sought to care for orphaned children, who were often forced to work for food and shelter under harsh and exploitative circumstances. As New York City grew, these concerns broadened to include, according to an early Graham-Wyndham fact sheet, the children of "poor but worthy parents" who needed "to go to their daily labors" knowing that their children "would be trained for some practical, useful course of life" and "taught their duties and responsibilities as members of society." As a result, in 1835, the Society for the Relief of Half Orphan and Destitute Children was opened to meet the child care needs of working parents.

This concept of child care centers serving "half orphans," or children orphaned by their parents for half the day, influenced the way early advocates viewed the relationship between parents, children, and providers. The providers were seen as dedicated to raising the children for the parents.

Child care programs initiated during the War on Poverty of the 1960s and 1970s had a similar focus. These programs were designed to save poor children from their disadvantaged environments. More often than not, parents were viewed as part of the problem. Advocates often saw child care programs as protecting children from their neglectful parents.

Practice was often out of sync with promise in this regard. The literature of early childhood consistently proclaimed the virtues of par-

ent involvement. Parents and providers were described as partners in
the child-rearing process. Although it is true that parents were allowed
more active involvement in child care centers than they would later
experience in public school settings, by and large parents were not
viewed as capable partners. There is a strong tradition, therefore, behind child care programs seeing the child as the customer. The duty of
providers was to look after the best interests of the child on behalf of,
and sometimes in spite of, the parents.

During the 1980s this perspective began to shift due to several
factors. To begin with, large numbers of middle-class families began to
use child care centers. These parents were imbued with a growing sense
of consumerism, and they took their responsibilities as consumers of
child care seriously. At the same time, scary headlines about alleged
sex-abuse incidents in child care centers caused parents to become extra
cautious in selecting and monitoring their child care arrangements.
Centers were forced to adjust to increasingly assertive parents. During
the 1980s centers gradually came to see parents as the customers. Providers began to care about keeping parents satisfied.

This new perspective is not always an easy one. Sometimes parents'
expectations conflict with the providers' values. For example, parents
may ask a center director to exert more forceful discipline with their
children than the director believes is appropriate, or parents may want
the center to teach children academic skills when the center's curriculum downplays academics. In these cases, providers need to exercise
tact in explaining why they are uncomfortable carrying out the parents'
requests. By and large, however, the goals of providers and parents
are in close agreement. What both parties want is for the children to
flourish.

The trend toward child care centers viewing parents as their customers does not appear to be a passing fad. Rather, as the year 2000
approaches, parents will likely play an even greater role as key players
in child care arrangements.

FOCUS ON QUALITY

For the past five years the runaway best-seller of the National
Association for the Education of Young Children (NAEYC) has been its
guide, *Developmentally Appropriate Practice* (Bredekamp, 1987). This
book has sold over 250,000 copies since its publication. The success
of *Developmentally Appropriate Practice* reflects a growing emphasis
throughout the early childhood arena on the need to deliver appro-

priate services for children. Parents looking for caregivers they can trust, center directors trying to build their enrollments, employers hoping to solve the child care needs of their employees, and advocates seeking to build a better world for children all share an interest in improving the quality of child care.

The fact that interest in quality is high by no means guarantees that services for children are actually improving. Nor is there any practical, scientifically sound means of ascertaining whether quality is rising. All we can be sure of at this time is that there is a growing awareness of, and support for, certain practices that are generally accepted as determinants of quality.

As we approach the year 2000, this commitment to developmentally appropriate practices will be increasingly important. In April 1991, President George Bush unveiled *America 2000*, his administration's plan for improving the performance of America's schools. The primary goal of this plan is that "All children in America will start school ready to learn" (*America 2000*, 1991). Not only is this an ambitious goal, but it is also one that is subject to various interpretations. Some advocates and enlightened state officials will use this initiative to bolster their efforts to promote the growth of developmentally appropriate services for preschool children. Others will see this as a call to push academically oriented curricula into the preschool years.

Whether *America 2000* will promote or abuse the best interests of young children will depend in large measure on the commitment of early childhood professionals. There is a tremendous need to educate new players entering the early childhood arena on developmentally appropriate practices. In addition, there is a tremendous opportunity for providers to demonstrate how the current delivery system can, if properly supported, play a key role in preparing all children for success in school.

ONE MISSING TREND

Many of the current trends support an optimistic forecast for child care in the year 2000. It is not too hard to imagine a diverse and thriving system, with all parties working together with parents to provide developmentally appropriate environments for children.

The one missing element in this utopian vision is the thriving teacher. The one additional trend that is critical to the success of this vision—improving wages and working conditions for preschool teachers—is not yet in evidence.

For all the talk about the importance of teachers and their need to earn worthy wages, there has been little movement in upgrading the low wages now paid to teachers. Failure to address this issue could yet be the Achilles heel of quality child care. Unless wages are improved, child care centers will not be able to attract and retain the caliber of teachers needed to implement high-quality programs for our children.

REFERENCES

America 2000: An educational strategy. (1991). Washington, DC: U.S. Government Printing Office.

Brady, J., & Goodman, I. F. (1991). *Lessons learned: Head Start's experience with state activities.* Boston: Educational Development Center, Inc.

Bredekamp, S. (Ed.). (1987). *Developmentally appropriate practice in early childhood programs serving children from birth through age eight.* Washington, DC: National Association for the Education of Young Children.

Kanfer, S. (1991). Good things, small packages. *Newsweek,* July 29, 54–55.

Neugebauer, R. (1989). Surveying the landscape: A look at child care '89. *Child Care Information Exchange,* March/April, 13–16.

Neugebauer, R. (1990). Child care's long and colorful past. *Child Care Information Exchange,* November/December, 5–9.

Neugebauer, R. (1991). Status report #2 on nonprofit child care. *Child Care Information Exchange,* March/April, 16–19.

Zigler, E. F., & Lang, M. F. (1991). *Child care choices: Balancing the needs of children, families, and society.* New York: Free Press.

CHAPTER 2

Historical Overview of Child Care

Alice Sterling Honig

During the long history of human evolution, child care has been predominantly the responsibility of family and kin. Yet the further back one goes historically, the more likely it is that children were physically and sexually abused, terrorized, or abandoned (De Mause, 1974). Child sacrifice was a common practice in ancient civilizations such as the Sumerian, Mayan, and Canaanite. The Theodocian code (about A.D. 322) was drawn up to "restrain the hands of parents from infanticide and turn their hopes to the better" (Osborn, 1991, p. 14). By the early fifteenth century, half the abandoned children in Florence were of poor parents, a third were of household slaves and high-ranking men, and more than two-thirds were girls. By the eighteenth century, one in every three or four children in some European cities was a foundling, and in some foundling hospitals only 13% of the children lived to the age of six (Boswell, 1989).

Abandonment was not the only method by which families escaped obligation to care for children themselves. "During the Industrial Revolution, working mothers often left their newborn children with wet nurses who were actually hired for the purpose of disposing of infants" (Osborn, 1991, p. 15). Rich families traditionally made use of wet nurses and nannies to rear their children. Such child care practices could have either detrimental or positive effects. In a touching poem, written in older manhood, Robert Louis Stevenson, who had been a very sick child, paid tribute to the extraordinary devotion of his childhood nurse.

Despite horrific child care practices common until the early twentieth century, such as severe flogging of young schoolchildren in England, children *were* cherished by families, even in prehistoric times. The tomb of a young Neanderthal child has yielded microscopic pollen samples, which reveal that the five-year-old had been carefully garlanded with flowers at the time of burial.

CULTURE AND CARE PRACTICES

Over the ages, cultural beliefs and values have deeply affected the child-rearing decisions of families. In ancient Greece and Rome, a father had the absolute right of life and death over his family. In some societies, infants were abruptly sent away from parents. For example, Ainsworth (1967) studied attachment among the Ganda in Africa, whose custom was to send toddlers to far villages to be reared by kin when their mothers became pregnant again. In ancient societies high-born male children were often sent to be reared and educated at the court of a royal person allied with their own kingdoms.

Some "educational" practices of even a few centuries ago resulted in less education and more relief for parents from caring for their children. In the Middle Ages, some parents sent their youngsters off with a youth (called "old hand") to be educated in a community that had a school. But instead of escorting the "greenhorn" to the school, the older youth often "led a vagabond life from one town to the next, living either by thieving and scrounging, or by the begging of the greenhorns who went singing in the streets and taverns" (Aries, 1962, p. 324).

Child Care: The Role of Ideology

Radical variations in ideology about the value of the lives and well-being of children or the best education for them shape caregiver goals and have led to markedly different practices. Baumrind (1977) reports that parents discipline children based on three main ideologies: authoritarian ("Do as I say because I say so"), permissive, or authoritative (genuine commitment to the child's welfare, with firm, clear rules and explanations and much love). Authoritative parenting has been found to produce more adaptable, persistent, and enthusiastic learners, who show the least inimical long-term effects from family crises such as divorce.

Ideological and theoretical differences also split the educational world. Should the goals of early childhood education be drill oriented, purely academic, or cognitive-developmental? Should the goals of early child care programs focus on social skills and children's mental and physical health? Even when the ideological and theoretical foundations of a child care program are well specified, the degree to which they are implemented in practice may vary greatly. For example, the least implemented of the three Head Start Planned Variation experiments (pre-academic, cognitive, and discovery) was the discovery approach (Bissell, 1973).

Over the centuries, different ideologies have been particularly linked with various philosophical movements, cultural biases, social class status, demands of rapid industrialization, and religious affiliation.

Philosophy.   Today, early enrichment programs for poor children are championed vigorously. Yet a few centuries ago, even as brilliant a thinker as Voltaire thought that "the lower classes should be guided, not educated" (Aries, 1962, p. 311).

Philosophers who advanced more enlightened ideas about education often showed inconsistency between their personal practices and their pronouncements about children. Locke proposed the view, novel for 1690, that a child is not condemned by heredity, but is a *tabula rasa* (blank slate). Therefore, caregiver practices can have a powerful impact. Locke disapproved of the practice of corporal punishment, but he believed that "crying is a fault that should not be tolerated in children . . . an open declaration of their insolence or obstinacy" (Greven, 1973, p. 40). He advocated icy baths and strict toileting practices that would be considered far from enlightened today (Cleverley & Phillips, 1986).

Rousseau is often proclaimed as the first philosopher to propose a gentle tutorial relationship in child rearing. Yet he was virulently sexist in his distinction between the carefulness with which *Emile* should be reared and educated compared with *Sophie*, since girls were to be brought up to serve males. His idea, farsighted in 1762, was that youths should have freedom of movement and opportunities to solve *practical* problems, such as figuring out how to search for a log and construct a bridge over a stream. Rousseau, though, did not believe that until adolescence boys should learn to read or play with peers, whom the philosopher considered bearers of the corruptions of society (Kessen, 1965). Rousseau also boasted that he had consigned his own five babies to orphanages soon after birth.

Social Class and Industrialization.   So firmly were social class differences entrenched in people's thinking that society accepted as normal slavelike conditions of employment for poor children that precluded any nurturing or educational opportunities. In 1842, in an impassioned plea to the British House of Commons, the Earl of Shaftesbury tried unsuccessfully to encourage legislation to limit children's hard labor (often 14 to 16 hours a day) in Welsh coal mines (Kessen, 1965, p. 49).

Religion.   In the early history of the United States, Puritan religious beliefs shaped the early conceptualization of children as inherently evil. From such philosophical views flowed rigorous child-rearing methods that today would be labeled child abuse. Greven (1973) cites early Calvinist writings on child care: "The root and foundation of misconduct in children is human depravity; depravity in the parent, and depravity in the child" (p. 105). In 1797, the president of Princeton College wrote letters counseling that one must establish entire and absolute authority over children. The Calvinist prescription for education was to "teach the children habits of obedience, both to Divine and parental authority; and for this purpose give them lessons in self-denial in the ways of sin. . . . Let every parent make it his inflexible determination, that he will be obeyed—*invariably* obeyed" (Greven, 1973, p. 105).

Despite the severity of prescriptions for child rearing, there was a clear belief that a parent was religiously obligated to take an active part in child discipline and moral education, although in well-to-do homes servants undoubtedly were responsible for major child care chores. Susanna Wesley, at the request of her son, John Wesley, the founder of Methodism, wrote in 1732 on the child-rearing practices she herself had carried out. Although she spelled out a philosophy of strict obedience to parents, intolerance of any crying, and inflexible child care practices, Wesley also advocated literacy for girls and no physical punishment for children if they confessed their misdeeds (Greven, 1973).

PROVISION FOR EARLY EDUCATION

New conceptualizations of the value of children swept the United States in the early 1800s:

> Men and women like Bronson Alcott, Emerson, Henry David Thoreau, Elizabeth Peabody, and Margaret Fuller admired the child, or, rather, their image of the child, because it exhibited none of the greedy materialism or spineless conformity that characterized its elders. The secret of education was, therefore to protect the innocent child from corruption and allow its innate divinity to unfold. Condescension toward childhood, so characteristic of Enlightenment thought, now gave way under the Romantic impulse to reverence. (Strickland, 1982, p. 324)

One of the early responses to the need for early childhood education and care was to send children of assorted preparation and ages off to the "common" school. Such schools were "relentlessly dedicated to strict discipline and to the narrow acquisition of reading, writing, and arithmetic" (Strickland, 1982, p. 326). Because such environments were unsuitable for very young children, from the mid 1850s onward, school authorities in many cities began to exclude children under five or six years of age.

Robert Owen, an English cotton mill industrialist influenced by the Swiss educator Pestalozzi, envisioned the transformation of society by proper child care practices. Owen opened his "Institution Established for the Formation of Character," which specifically included infants from one year old:

> The children were trained and educated without punishment or any fear of it, and were while in school by far the happiest human beings I have ever seen. (Owen, 1971, p. 135)

Thus, in the early to mid 1800s, utopian visions provided a powerful impetus for new modes of child care and education. The goals of the reformers were much like the goals of child care today. Many believed that "proper schools for supplying a judicious infant training would effectually prevent much . . . vicious depravity of character" and "relieve in great measure, many indigent parents, from the care of children" so that the parents could become gainfully employed (Strickland, 1982, p. 328).

By the mid-nineteenth century, a cult of domesticity arose that emphasized the crucial role of mothers' influence in the moral and religious upbringing of their children (Pence, 1980). Mothers were urged to provide good models for children and establish bonds of trust and love. Rather than physical punishment, withdrawal of affection was counseled. For the children of the poor, access to these enlightened new maternal concerns and involvements, which depended on a certain level of material ease, was often nonexistent. Yet the importance of maternal teachings in the formation of children's character was so emphasized, "that not until the decades after World War II did most American women begin to decide that they could safely share the education of their little ones with others" (Strickland, 1982, p. 337).

MODERN CONCEPTS OF EARLY EDUCATION

The boundaries between child care and childhood education have blurred more and more during the past decades. Earlier, day care was traditionally described as protective, or as a service focused on the children of "destitute widows and those with sick husbands" (Fein & Clarke-Stewart, 1973, p. 26). Yet Caldwell (1986) urges:

> There is a false dichotomy between early childhood education and child care. . . . Child care operated within a social service orientation; the mother was the client. In early education programs, the client was the child. But the two fields have not been developing on parallel tracks; rather they have been on converging tracks . . . the resulting service is both educational and protective, and the client is the family unit. (pp. 7–8)

Nonfamilial child care models with varying degrees of educational components have arisen in the past hundred years. These have ranged from family day care models with minimal educational emphasis (Clarke-Stewart, 1982) to compensatory half-day and full-day educational programs. The first child care program in the United States began in 1854 and was called Nursery for the Children of Poor Women in the City of New York (*Encyclopedia Americana*, 1967). Children from six weeks to six years were left for as long as twelve hours a day by their wage-earning parents. Thus, the term "custodial" care, which has come to be synonymous with low-quality, noneducational care, was at first a term used to describe the fact that early child care centers took "custody" of children while their mothers were employed.

Early efforts toward enhancing the care of children across social classes arose in conjunction with other movements toward exploring the world of early childhood. Along with the rise of educational institutions for young children was a parallel rise in interest in children as subjects for scientific research. The study of early childhood in our own century has gone hand in hand with applications of research and theory to the implementation of more optimal child care situations in the early years (Sears, 1975).

Kindergartens and Nursery Schools

The first American kindergarten was German speaking and was begun in 1856 by Mrs. Carl Schurz, a former student of Friedrich Froebel. Innovators such as Elizabeth Peabody worked as early as 1860 to found free English-speaking kindergartens that would provide education and not merely custodial care. In England, Susan Isaacs (1929) advanced public understanding about the distinctive educational needs of young children.

Public nursery schools, first begun in 1919 (Mayer, 1960) and regarded as a supplement to rather than a replacement for home child care, grew between 1920 and 1930 from 3 to 262 (Chittenden, Nesbitt & Williams, 1949). The first documented parent cooperative nursery was formed by Cambridge, Massachusetts, parents in 1923 and, as the child guidance movement flourished, so too did the number of nursery schools.

Important centers for child study operated model early childhood programs. These centers included the Gesell Child Guidance Nursery at Yale (about 1920), the Merrill-Palmer Institute in Detroit (1920), Bank Street College (1919), and the Iowa Child Welfare Research Station at the University of Iowa (Braun & Edwards, 1972; Evans, 1975). In 1923, the Laura Spelman Rockefeller Memorial Foundation began support of child study and parent education, which enhanced the interplay of research and program provision. Because of the laboratory nature of some of these early nursery schools, staff training was highly emphasized, and nursery schools maintained much closer ties to parents than did kindergartens (Vandewalker, 1907).

Montessori schools, initiated for poor children in Italy, were transplanted to the United States as early childhood centers gained popularity among middle-class families. Emphasis is on a set of specific materials, an ideology that stresses the importance of sequenced and orderly use of materials and the importance of teacher observations. Montessori centers serving culturally disadvantaged children have proven effective in increasing attention span, concentration for work, and IQ (Kohlberg, 1968). In contradistinction to Montessori's reality orientation and opposition to fantasy play, Smilansky's work in Israel (Smilansky & Sheftaya, 1990) emphasizes the facilitative nature of teacher-supported sociodramatic play as a medium to enhance the cognitive development of disadvantaged youngsters.

Theorists' Influences in Modern Child Care Programming

Psychoanalysis. The rise of nursery programs in this century was often tied to the ideas of analytic and neoanalytic theorists. Freud's ideas promoted the concept of freeing children's libidinal energy for work and positive family functioning rather than using repressive measures that would increase neuroses. Erikson's (1963) dialectic theory profoundly influenced educators in the realization that the foundations for good mental health were laid by child care practices carried out in the earliest years. If adults encouraged positive ratios of trust to mistrust, confidence in autonomous functioning (versus shame or doubt about abilities), child initiatives, and industriousness (rather than guilt and feelings of inferiority), then children's mental health and learning capacity would flourish. Indeed, early childhood education/care proponents have always emphasized mental health and family life education as important goals to ensure success in early childhood (Frank, 1962).

Prominent among influential pediatricians who espoused psychoanalytic theories that children need to grow more in accordance with their own developmental timetables and styles were Gesell, Spock, and Brazelton. Gesell (1923), despite his emphasis on the primacy of maturational factors for development, believed that the preschool period was the most important for an individual, and that it influenced all subsequent development.

Influential Educators. Pestalozzi and Froebel are prominent among the early educators who tried to change the repressive ways in which child care had been conceptualized in Europe for centuries (Hewes, 1990). Froebel (1782–1852) lived in Germany during the Napoleonic Wars, and his philosophy was centered on the creation of a loving community of persons in cooperative rather than competitive classrooms. He reasoned that positive social values would accrue from many of the "plays" of childhood: "The plays of childhood are the germinal leaves of all later life, for the whole man is developed and shown in these, in his tenderest dispositions, in his innermost tendencies" (Froebel, 1889, p. 55). Froebel's kindergarten philosophy can be considered the first to introduce humanistic ideas of early childhood education and teacher training into the United States.

Dewey was an early exponent of a philosophy of how young children learn best: through self-chosen and self-initiated interactions as well as manipulation of materials, questioning, comparing, and making judgments. Dewey (1916) blazed new conceptual pathways for early childhood education almost a century ago by insisting on the importance of child-initiated *play* for early learning. He also believed in the continuity between home and school life, thus presaging today's strong emphasis on the importance of parent-educator partnerships in child care (Honig, 1990a, 1990b, 1990c). In 1897 Dewey wrote:

> I believe . . . school life should grow gradually out of the home life; that it should take up and continue the activities with which the child is already familiar in the home . . . that education is the fundamental method of social progress and reform. (cited in Peters, Neisworth, & Yawkey, 1985, p. 18)

Piaget and the Cognitive-Developmentalists. Jean Piaget (1950, 1952), a Swiss developmental epistemologist, strove to understand and elucidate the complexities of cognitive transformations from infant sensorimotor schemas to fully flexible formal operational thinking. Piaget stressed the importance of children's active engagement with materials and peers as well as their initiations of their own learning experiences in order for equilibration and new intellectual restructuring to occur.

Hunt (1961) was an early champion of Piaget's ideas, particularly the notion of the critical importance of matching the presentation of learning situations with the cognitive capabilities a young child already possesses. Hunt's seminal book provided inspiration for caregivers to interpret and apply Piagetian equilibration theory to problems of how to stimulate children's cognitive development just as, earlier, Freudian and Eriksonian theory had stimulated new ways to interact socially with young children to promote their emotional well-being. Cognitive-developmental or constructivist curricula have provided the basic theoretical underpinning for early childhood programs across the world. Developmentalists, many of whom have combined the best of British infant school philosophy (Plowden, 1967; Weber, 1971) with Piagetian ideas, have been in the vanguard of the fight to keep purely academic and rote methods from encroaching on early childhood territory. Yet "the choice of an appropriate cognitive curriculum, or an academic one of isolated skill development, remains a matter of values" (Seefeldt, 1990, p. 25).

Sigel's "distancing hypothesis" (1970) affirms that with Socratic questioning the caregiver challenges a child cognitively to construct new ideas, whether of arithmetical relationships or peer relationships. But caregivers may not promote the divergent thinking skills required to energize new learning (Wittmer & Honig, 1991).

Indeed, a troubling issue is that preschool programs, despite goodwill, may not be implementing the theoretical and pragmatic philosophies that research has found to be most facilitative of optimal child development. Goodlad, Klein, and Novotny (1973), in an observational study of 201 representative American nursery schools, suggested that staff operated mostly in isolation from professional and intellectual theory and activity within the early education field. They reported "a frequent lack of critical self-evaluation and continual efforts at program improvement among staff, even though staff are dedicated to child care. Stated goals and program emphases often are incongruent as well" (cited in Evans, 1975, p. 400). Low salaries and high staff turnover (about 45% in child care centers nationally) may be responsible for the gap between knowledge of optimal interactions and provision of more custodial care (Whitebook, Howes & Phillips, 1990). The history of child care is replete with theoretical conceptions that are subtle and difficult to implement appropriately without intensive training. Even today, exponents of Piagetian equilibration theory or of the Montessori method can disagree on their interpretations of the functions of teachers in the classroom, their differential emphases on curricular topics, and their methods of education.

LONGITUDINAL STUDIES OF CHILD DEVELOPMENT: A RESOURCE FOR CHILD CARE KNOWLEDGE

Except for baby diaries kept by eminent men such as Darwin, there was no truly longitudinal research until after World War I. Terman's 1925 study of gifted children (followed for over half a century) was the first such study. In 1928, Jean McFarlane directed the Berkeley Guidance Study of 248 infants, designed to find out whether a great deal of parental guidance, for part of the sample, would reduce the number and severity of behavior pathologies during the first six years of life (Honzik, 1967).

The Berkeley Growth Study of a nonrandom group of 74 mostly middle-class children contributed a great deal to our knowledge of children's mental abilities (Bayley, 1949). The Fels Institute study, begun in 1929 (Sontag, Baker & Nelson, 1958), looked at the outcomes of parental care practices. McGraw's landmark study (1935) of two infant twins, one of whom was trained in motoric and problem-solving skills (including learning to swim and roller skate by two years) contributed to renewed awareness that routine child care is not good enough. Early skill building has the potential to enhance an infant's grace, agility, reasoning, and, more importantly, motivation to attempt and persist at difficult tasks. Decades later, the trained twin still demonstrated superior competence and confidence in the difficult motoric task of climbing a ladder to the roof of McGraw's home.

Skeels (1966) placed some orphaned retarded infants in a home for mentally retarded women and left others in the orphanage. Thirty years later he followed up on the children. Those who had been doted on by the institutionalized women had sharply increased IQs as toddlers and had been subsequently adopted. As adults they became productive citizens. Those left in the orphanage received impoverished custodial care and, as adults, were on welfare or in institutions. An early responsive caregiving environment had made a marked difference in the children's lives.

Werner's (1989) 32-year study of at-risk infants born on the island of Kauai highlights the protective importance of nonparental, high-quality infant care. Children with employed mothers and inadequate substitute care during the first 20 months of life were more likely to grow into adults with coping problems and delinquencies. In contrast, those who turned out to be resilient had had at least one significant caregiver from whom they had received a great deal of positive attention and nurturing during the first year of life.

FEDERAL SUPPORT FOR CHILD CARE PROGRAMS

Child care provisions differ in their economic and political bases, whether private for-profit, private not-for-profit, private industry, or public child care (generally under the auspices of state, county, or municipal governments). In 1863 a day care center was opened to children whose mothers made clothing for Civil War soldiers or were employed in hospitals (Whipple, 1929, cited in Salkever & Singerman, 1990), and by 1929 there were about 12 industrial day care programs in America.

Nurseries established by the Federal Emergency Relief Administration and the Works Progress Administration under President Roosevelt were justified as a source of jobs for unemployed teachers during the Great Depression. They were also expected to improve educational outcomes and thus enhance life opportunities for educationally disadvantaged children (Miller, 1990) — much the same reasons given for founding the Head Start program 30 years later. Program supervision was provided by the National Association for Nursery Education, the Association for Childhood Education, and the National Council on Parent Education (Frank, 1962).

During World War II, the need for women's employment became urgent. Inadequate care and latchkey children fueled the 1942 passage of the Lanham Act, which provided federal funding for full-time child care centers. In the Kaiser Portland Shipyards:

> As mothers entered the yard, they left their children with teachers and nurses. When a mother picked up her child, she was able to buy dinner, at cost, to take home. The centers were open 24 hours a day, 364 days a year. In each center was an infirmary to care for sick children. (Salkever & Singerman, 1990, p. 45)

The Lanham Act day care centers signaled the beginning of a national policy shift toward the idea of governmental and societal responsibility for child care. Yet at peak use these centers served only about 100,000 children, meeting less than 10% of the estimated need (Miller, 1990, p. 259). Six months after the war many of these centers were dismantled, though some were retained under other auspices.

Conflicts of purpose and philosophy mark the spurts and fallbacks along the road toward national implementation of high-quality, publicly funded, educationally enriching child care facilities that represent true partnerships with parents. But the trend of this century has been steadily, if unevenly, toward support for child care, as can be seen even in early publications by the Office of Economic Opportunity (Grotberg, 1971).

For poor children, new child care initiatives arose in the 1960s. The need for these initiatives was made eloquently clear in a nationwide survey by the National Council of Jewish Women that found child care services to be largely inadequate (Keyserling, 1972). Day care centers had already been characterized in the past as having a drab appearance, no organized program, poor equipment, large group size, untrained staff, and passive parents who *had* to send their children. In contrast, nursery schools had trained staff, well-designed equipment, and an emphasis on educational experience, with parents as active partners who chose to send their children (Osborn, 1991, p. 19).

Legislative innovations for poor children began in the 1960s, including Head Start, Title VII of the 1965 Housing and Urban Development Act, and the 1965 Model Cities Act. For the middle class, tax credits and deductions for child care as a business expense were created in the 1970s.

Senator Walter Mondale introduced comprehensive child care legislation in 1971. Passed by both houses of Congress, the bill was vetoed by President Nixon, who claimed that it would commit "the vast moral authority of the national government to the side of communal approaches to child rearing over and against the family-centered approach" (Zigler & Goodman, 1982, p. 345). In 1990, President Bush signed Public Law 101–508, the Federal Child Care Bill. This bill provides $2.5 billion for new federal child care, block grant funds, and provisions to protect children in child care, as well as moneys and tax relief to help low-income working families purchase child care. Along with the early childhood provisions of Public Laws 94-142 and 99-457, this action bolsters the optimistic view that legislators and voters are committed to early childhood care and education for all young children.

The Role of Pioneer Demonstration Programs

A flowering of demonstration programs during the 1960s and 1970s provided remarkable evidence of the efficacy of theory-based, research-informed child care models and programs to enhance the intellective and positive social skills of young children. Exemplary centers and programs proliferated (see Abt Associates, 1971; Day & Parker, 1977; Weber, 1970). Some, like the Amalgamated Child Day Care and Health Center, were sponsored by unions. Some, like the Greely Parent-Child Center, funded by the Colorado Migrant Council, provided care for children of migrant workers and included bilingual and bicultural education. Some, like the Child Development Center of the Atlanta Residential Manpower Center, provided "care, love and supportive services" for mothers who were Job Corps trainees (Cohen & Brandegee, 1974, p. 134). Some, like the Parent-Child Development Centers (PCDCs), promoted a strong parent involvement component as the major thrust in delivering quality care to infants and toddlers. A wide variety of delivery systems and many innovative techniques for enhancing parental child care practices were initiated (Honig, 1979).

Research funds and longitudinal data collection for some of the projects, such as the Perry Preschool Project, provided data on the educational and financial efficacy of programs (Berrueta-Clement et al., 1984; Schweinhart & Weikart, in press). In Syracuse, New York, the Children's Center provided the first evidence that the provision of high-quality, part-time infancy care for the first year, and then full-time day care for toddlers and preschoolers, could boost children's IQs without detrimental effects on mother-child attachment (Caldwell, Wright, Honig & Tannenbaum, 1970). However, concerns have been raised about full-time, non-university-based infant care during the first year of life as a risk factor for insecure attachment to mother and for later increased child noncompliance or aggressivity (Belsky, 1988, 1989, 1990; Park & Honig, 1991).

Head Start (1990), which began under the Johnson administration in 1965, saw its largest authorization for program increases under the Bush administration in 1990. It serves about half a million children of poverty annually. Impressively, 99% of Head Start children complete medical screening, and virtually all who need medical treatment receive it. Over the next decade, the Administration for Children, Youth, and Families will be developing strategies to aid children in making the transition from Head Start, a part-time care and education program, to kindergarten (Horn, 1990).

Funding Fluctuations for Child Care Support

During the Reagan administration, cuts in federal funding for child care were made by decreasing funds through many avenues, including Title XX, so that one-third fewer poor children were being served at the end of the 1980s than at the beginning. Additionally, Title XX no longer requires states to have quality standards (Children's Defense Fund, 1988, 1990). In 1990 Head Start was serving fewer than one in six eligible poor youngsters, and in 1987, Chapter I, which provided for compensatory education for disadvantaged children, served about one-half of the children who needed remediation (Children's Defense Fund, 1990).

Many innovative child care programs lost their funding entirely. For example, one long-term omnibus program that closed was the Family Development Research Program (FDRP) in Syracuse, New York, which had provided home visitation and child care for children of low-income, teenaged, high-school-dropout parents from infancy to age five. Yet FDRP graduates showed, in comparison with controls, marked decreases in rates and severity of juvenile delinquency and higher academic achievement for females 15 years later (Lally, Mangione & Honig, 1988). Many of the research-based longitudinal demonstration projects with at-risk families and children have shown unequivocal gains in educational attainment and self-sufficiency, as well as lowered rates of special education, welfare, and delinquency (Honig, 1989; Lazar, Darlington, Murray, Royce & Snipper, 1982; Levenstein, 1989; Ramey & Gowan, 1986).

Variations in Child Care Personnel Preparation and Status

The quality of child care depends crucially on caregivers, their level of training, their stability of employment in a facility, and the number of children assigned per adult. In France, a teacher in the Ecole Maternelle sometimes cares for up to 50 five-year-olds. In an Israeli kibbutz infant house, a few young toddlers may be cared for by a trained *metapelet* (child care worker) and an aide. Many states require little or no preparation for employment, and the boundaries are blurred for describing child care personnel. Teacher, nurturer, caregiver, nanny, nursery nurse — who is the child care worker? And how should she or he be trained? Caldwell (1986) has urged that the terms *early child care* and *education* be considered interchangeable, and that perhaps we should coin a new term, *nurcherer*, to signify the integration of teaching and nurturing functions. Whitebook et al. (1990) note that "this debate about nomenclature reflects strong differences of opinion related to philosophical and functional dimensions of the services provided by child care workers. Depending on how the service is envisioned, different ideas about preparing practitioners emerge" (p. 131).

Some child development specialists consider the informal pathway of female socialization a sufficient qualification for caregivers of the very young (Kagan, Kearsley & Zelazo, 1978). Yet Haldopoulos & Copeland (1991) found that at least 10% of the women who sought child care employment by enrolling in a comprehensive screening and training program were at high risk for child abuse and violence. At the other extreme, some policymakers demand that caregivers obtain four-year college teaching certificates. Yet many states still require few if any educational or child development credits for licensure or certification of family day care workers or center personnel beyond safety and health requirements. However, nowadays the requirement of two years of college training in early childhood education or child development is becoming more widespread.

Despite radical differences throughout history in what constitutes quality child care in families (and current differential emphases on the relative importance of creativity, sociodramatic play, behavioral modification techniques, and so on in early childhood classrooms), today there is more professional agreement than disagreement (Beardsley, 1990; Griffin, 1982; Honig, 1987; Spodek & Saracho, 1990). Quality has been succinctly described by Mitchell (1989):

> Quality in an early childhood program consists of five essential elements: small group size; favorable staff/child ratios; well-trained staff; a thorough understanding of theories of child development and of principles of early childhood education, coupled with direct experience working with young children; curriculum — a clearly communicated philosophy of education that is based on theories of child development and that is supported by training and good supervision; and strong parent participation. (p. 669)

Monitoring Quality in Child Care

Definitions of quality child care are clearly supported by the findings of practitioners, researchers, and theorists. But establishing a national political agenda to support high-quality child care has been more problematic.

Standards for Child Care.   Minimal standards for child care licensing in many states do not promote quality child care. In 1974, the
U.S. Office of Child Development, after holding forums on licensing,
proposed that the Federal Interagency Day Care Requirements
(FIDCR) be attached to federal child care legislation. Bitter opposition
arose—the mandated ratios (one adult to ten children of nursery age)
exceeded the ratio requirements in most states at the time. After a
large-scale research study of child care in 1974 (Ruopp, Travers, Glantz
& Coelen, 1979), the U.S. Department of Health, Education, and
Welfare (1980) recommended support for small groups of children—16
children with two adults—and mandatory child-related educational
training for caregivers (to be made available by the states). These requirements were shelved as too costly.

Recently, despite such setbacks for licensure, support for voluntary
accreditation has been growing. The National Association for the Education of Young Children (NAEYC) has been at the forefront of forging
a professional consensus about developmentally appropriate practices
(Bredekamp, 1987, 1990). The National Academy of Early Childhood
Programs, an NAEYC initiative, administers the only professionally
sponsored voluntary accreditation system for early childhood centers
and schools in the United States.

HISTORY: PROLOGUE TO FUTURE CHILD CARE POLICY

The need to balance child care choices to serve the needs of family,
society, dual-career parents, and optimal child development has become an acute political as well as personal issue today, especially as
citizen support for quality caregiving becomes more widespread and
articulate. Social policy experts who are child advocates are beginning
to address the complex task of providing quality care for all America's
children that meets these needs (Galinsky, 1990; Lande, Scarr & Gunzenhauser, 1989; Zigler & Lang, 1990). Yet knowledge about the political, economic, educational, staffing, training, licensing, and parent
involvement components that are necessary to succeed at this complex
task is not new. Decades ago, Harrell (1972) surveyed issues for child
care and delivery systems, such as the 4-C (Community Coordinated
Child Care) programs. Ironically, he noted that federal and state rules
are generally devised to meet the needs of bookkeepers rather than the
needs of programs. He believed that "child care cannot be sensibly
placed in a procrustean bed—a single mold. . . . Day care systems
should not become junior ghettos. A system should be able to blend

funds from public and private sources and be so attractive as to recruit children from every social class in the community . . . to serve the whole community's needs" (p. 39).

Congressman George Miller (1990) has eloquently summed up the historical imperative for high-quality child care for citizens of the future:

> Child care that is affordable and safe, and enhances the social and cognitive development of young children improves the ability of families to provide for the economic security of their children. At the same time, it prepares young children for adulthood, allowing them to perform effectively in the labor market and to establish stable families of their own. (p. 271)

Such a credo documents changing values and beliefs not only among early childhood advocates but among legislators and administrative personnel as well. We have begun to travel a new road — one that signals willingness to make commitments to ensure optimal nurturing and educational care for young children.

REFERENCES

Abt Associates. (1971). *A study in child care. 1970–71* (Vols. 11A and 11B). Cambridge, MA: Abt Associates.

Ainsworth, M. D. S. (1967). *Infancy in Uganda*. Baltimore: Johns Hopkins Press.

Aries, P. (1962). *Centuries of childhood: A social history of family life*. New York: Random House.

Baumrind, D. (1977). Some thoughts about childrearing. In S. Cohen & T. J. Comiskey (Eds.), *Child development: Contemporary perspectives* (pp. 248–258). Itasca, IL: Peacock.

Bayley, N. (1949). Consistency and variability in the growth of intelligence from birth to eighteen years. *Journal of Genetic Psychology, 15*, 165–196.

Beardsley, L. (1990). *Good day, bad day: The child's experience of child care*. New York: Teachers College Press.

Belsky, J. (1988). The "effects" of day care reconsidered. *Early Childhood Research Quarterly, 3*, 235–272.

Belsky, J. (1989). Infant-parent attachment and day care: In defense of the strange situation. In J. S. Lande, S. Scarr & N. Gunzenhauser (Eds.), *Caring for children: Challenge to America* (pp. 23–47). Hillsdale, NJ: Erlbaum.

Belsky, J. (1990). Developmental risks associated with infant day care: Attachment insecurity, noncompliance, and aggression? In S. S. Cherazi (Ed.),

Psychosocial issues in day care (pp. 37–68). Washington, DC: American Psychiatric Press.

Berrueta-Clement, J. R., Schweinhart, L. J., Barnett, W. S., Epstein, A. S., & Weikart, D. P. (1984). *Changed lives: The effects of the Perry Preschool Program on youths through age 19.* Ypsilanti, MI: High/Scope Press.

Bissell, J. (1973). Planned Variation in Head Start and Follow Through. In J. Stanley (Ed.), *Compensatory education for children, ages 2 to 8* (pp. 63–108). Baltimore: Johns Hopkins Press.

Boswell, J. (1989). *The kindness of strangers: The abandonment of children in Western Europe from late antiquity to the Renaissance.* New York: Pantheon Books.

Braun, S., & Edwards, E. (1972). *History and theory of early childhood education.* Washington, OH: Charles A. Jones.

Bredekamp, S. (Ed.). (1987). *Developmentally appropriate practice in early childhood programs serving children from birth through age 8.* Washington, DC: National Association for the Education of Young Children.

Bredekamp, S. (1990). Achieving model early childhood programs through accreditation. In C. Seefeldt (Ed.), *Continuing issues in early childhood education.* Columbus, OH: Merrill.

Caldwell, B. (1986). Professional child care: A supplement to parental care. In N. Gunzenhauser & B. M. Caldwell (Eds.), *Group care for young children: Considerations for child care and health professionals, public policy makers, and parents* (pp. 3–13). Skillman, NJ: Johnson & Johnson Baby Products.

Caldwell, B. M., Wright, C. M., Honig, A. S., & Tannenbaum, J. (1970). Infant care and attachment. *American Journal of Orthopsychiatry, 40,* 397–412.

Children's Defense Fund. (1988). *A children's defense budget FY 1989: An analysis of our nation's investment in children.* Washington, DC: Author.

Children's Defense Fund. (1990). *Children 1990: A report card, briefing book, and action primer.* Washington, DC: Author.

Chittenden, G. E., Nesbitt, M., & Williams, B. (1949, January). The nursery school in American education today. *Education Digest, 46–51.*

Clarke-Stewart, A. (1982). *Daycare.* Cambridge, MA: Harvard University Press.

Cleverley, J., & Phillips, D. C. (1986). *Visions of childhood: Influential models from Locke to Spock.* New York: Teachers College Press.

Cohen, D. J., & Brandegee, A. S. (1974). *Day care 3: Serving preschool children.* DHEW Publication No. (OHD) 74-1057. Washington, DC: U.S. Department of Health, Education, and Welfare; Office of Child Development.

Day, M. C., & Parker, R. K. (Eds.). (1977). *The preschool in action: Exploring early childhood programs* (2d ed.). Boston: Allyn & Bacon.

De Mause, L. (1974). *The history of childhood.* New York: Psychohistory Press.

Dewey, J. (1916). *Democracy and education.* New York: McMillan.

Encyclopedia Americana. (1967). s.v. "nursery schools."

Erikson, E. (1963). *Childhood and society* (2d ed.). New York: Norton.

Evans, E. D. (1975). *Contemporary influences in early childhood education* (2d ed.). New York: Holt, Rinehart & Winston.

Fein, G., & Clarke-Stewart, A. (1973). *Day care in context.* New York: Wiley.

Frank, L. (1962). The beginnings of child development and family life education in the 20th century. *Merrill-Palmer Quarterly, 8,* 207–227.

Froebel, F. (1889). *The education of man.* New York: Appleton.

Galinsky, E. (1990). I have seen the beginnings of a transformation in attitudes. *Young Children, 45*(6), 2–3, 77.

Gesell, A. (1923). *The preschool child: From the standpoint of public hygiene and education.* Boston: Houghton-Mifflin.

Goodlad, J., Klein, M., & Novotny, J. (1973). *Early schooling in the United States.* New York: McGraw Hill.

Greven, P. J. Jr. (1973). *Child-rearing concepts, 1628–1861: Historical sources.* Itasca, IL: Peacock.

Griffin, E. F. (1982). *Island of childhood: Education in the special world of the nursery school.* New York: Teachers College Press.

Grotberg, A. (Ed.). (1971). *Day care: Resources for decisions.* Washington, DC: Office of Economic Opportunity.

Haldopoulos, M. A., & Copeland, M. L. (1991). Case studies of child care training volunteers found to be at risk for abuse. *Early Child Development and Care, 68,* 149–158.

Harrell, J. A. (Ed.). (1972). *Selected readings in the issues of day care.* Washington, DC: Day Care and Child Development Council of America.

Head Start. (1990). *Head Start: A child development program.* Washington, DC: U.S. Department of Health and Human Services.

Hewes, D. W. (1990). Historical foundations of early childhood teacher training: The evolution of kindergarten teacher preparation. In B. Spodek & O. Saracho (Eds.), *Yearbook in early childhood education, Vol. 1: Early childhood teacher preparation* (pp. 1–22). New York: Teachers College Press.

Honig, A. S. (1979). *Parent involvement in early childhood education* (2d ed.). Washington, DC: National Association for the Education of Young Children.

Honig, A. S. (1987). How to spot top-notch day care. *Working Mother, 10*(1), 72–73.

Honig, A. S. (1989, Winter). Longitudinal effects of quality preschool programs: Research review. *Day Care and Early Education, 17*(2), 35–38.

Honig, A. S. (Ed.). (1990a). *Early parenting and later child achievement.* London: Gordon & Breach.

Honig, A. S. (1990b). Infant/toddler education issues: Practices, problems, and promises. In C. Seefeldt (Ed.), *Continuing issues in early childhood education* (pp. 61–105). Columbus, OH: Merrill.

Honig, A. S. (Ed.). (1990c). *Optimizing early child care and education.* London: Gordon & Breach.

Honzik, M. P. (1967). Environmental correlates of mental growth: Prediction from the family setting at 21 months. *Child Development, 38*, 337–364.

Horn, W. F. (1990). Head Start: Facing new challenges. *Children Today, 19*(3), 4–5.

Hunt, J., M. (1961). *Intelligence and experience.* New York: Ronald Press.

Isaacs, S. (1929). *The nursery years.* London: Routledge.

Kagan, J., Kearsley, R. B., & Zelazo, P. R. (1978). *Infancy: Its place in human development.* Cambridge, MA: Harvard University Press.

Kessen, W. (1965). *The child.* New York: Wiley.

Keyserling, M. D. (1972). *Windows on day care: A report based on findings of the National Council of Jewish Women on day care needs and services in their communities.* New York: National Council of Jewish Women.

Kohlberg, L. (1968). Montessori with the culturally disadvantaged: A cognitive-developmental interpretation and some research findings. In R. D. Hess & R. M. Bear (Eds.), *Early education: Current theory, research, and action* (pp. 105–118). Chicago: Aldine.

Lally, J. R., Mangione, P., & Honig, A. S. (1988). The Syracuse University Family Development Research Program: Long-range impact of an early intervention with low income children and their families. In D. Powell (Ed.), *Parent education as early childhood intervention: Emerging directions in theory, research, and practice* (pp. 79–104). Norwood, NJ: Ablex.

Lande, J. S., Scarr, S., & Gunzenhauser, N. (1989). *Caring for children: Challenge to America.* Hillsdale, NJ: Erlbaum.

Lazar, I., Darlington, R. B., Murray, H., Royce, J., & Snipper, A. (1982). Lasting effects of early education: A report from the Consortium for Longitudinal Studies. *Monographs of the Society for Research in Child Development, 47* (2–3, Serial No. 195).

Levenstein, P. (1989). *Messages from home: The Mother-Child Home Program and the prevention of school disadvantage.* Columbus, OH: Ohio State University Press.

Mayer, F. (1960). *A history of educational thought.* Columbus, OH: Merrill.

McGraw, M. (1935). *Growth: A study of Johnny & Jimmy.* New York: Appleton-Century.

Miller, G. (1990). The expanding federal role in child care. In S. S. Chehrazi (Ed.), *Psychosocial issues in day care* (pp. 257–274). Washington, DC: American Psychiatric Press.

Mitchell, A. (1989). Old baggage, new visions: Shaping policy for early childhood programs. *Phi Delta Kappan, 70,* 664–672.

Osborn, K. (1991). *Early childhood education in historical perspective.* Athens, GA: Daye Press.

Owen, R. (1971). *Life of Robert Owen (1857–58)* (reprinted). London: Charles Knight.

Park, K., & Honig, A.S. (1991). Infant care and later teacher ratings of preschool behaviors. *Early Child Development and Care, 68,* 89–96.

Pence, A. R. (1980). *Preschool programs of the nineteenth century: Towards a history of preschool child care in America.* Unpublished doctoral dissertation, University of Oregon, Eugene.

Peters, D. L., Neisworth, J. T., & Yawkey, T. D. (1985). *Early childhood education: From theory to practice.* Monterey, CA: Brooks/Cole.

Piaget, J. (1950). *The psychology of intelligence.* London: Routledge & Kegan.

Piaget, J. (1952). *The origins of intelligence in children.* New York: Norton.

Plowden, Lady (Chairman). (1967). *Children and their primary schools: A report of the Central Advisory Council for Education (England).* London: Her Majesty's Stationery Office.

Ramey, C., & Gowan, J. W. (1986). A general systems approach to modifying risk for retarded development. In A. S. Honig (Ed.), *Risk factors in infancy* (pp. 9–26). London: Gordon & Breach.

Ruopp, R., Travers, J. Glantz, F., & Coelen, C. (1979). *Children at the center: Final report of the National Day Care Study, Vol. 1.* Cambridge, MA: Abt Associates.

Salkever, M., & Singerman, J. (1990). The origins and significance of employer-supported child care in America.

Schweinhart, L. J., & Weikart, D. P. (in press). The High/Scope Perry Preschool Study, similar studies, and their implications for public policy in the U.S. In D. Stegelin (Ed.), *Early childhood education: Policy issues for the 1990s.* Norwood, NJ: Ablex.

Sears, R. (1975). *Your ancients revisited: A history of child development.* Chicago: University of Chicago Press.

Seefeldt, C. (1990). Cognitive and appropriate: The kindergarten curriculum. *Early Child Development and Care, 61,* 19–25.

Sigel, I. (1970). The distancing hypothesis: A causal hypothesis for the acquisition of representational thought. In M. R. Jones (Ed.), *Miami symposium on the prediction of behavior, 1968: Effects of early experiences.* Coral Gables, FL: University of Miami Press.

Skeels, H. (1966). Adult status of children with contrasting early life experience. *Monographs of the Society for Research in Child Development, 31* (3, Serial No. 105).

Smilansky, S., & Sheftaya, L. (1990). *Facilitating play: A medium for promoting cognitive, socio-emotional and academic development in young children.* Gaithersburg, MD: Psychoeducational Publications.

Sontag, L. W., Baker, C. T., & Nelson, V. L. (1958). Mental growth and personality development: A longitudinal study. *Monographs of the Society for Research in Child Development, 23* (No. 2).

Spodek, B., & Saracho, O. N. (Eds.). (1990). *Yearbook in early childhood education, Vol. 1. Early childhood teacher preparation.* New York: Teachers College Press.

Strickland, C. E. (1982). Paths not taken: Seminal models of early childhood education in Jacksonian America. In B. Spodek (Ed.), *Handbook of research in early childhood education* (pp. 321–340). New York: Free Press.

Terman, L. M. et al. (1925). Genetic studies of genius: 1. Mental and physical traits of a thousand children. Stanford, CA: Stanford University Press.

U.S. Department of Health, Education, and Welfare. (1980, March). HEW day care regulations. *Federal Register, 45*(55), 17870–17885.

Vandewalker, N. (1907). The history of kindergarten influence in elementary education. In *NSSE Yearbook*. Chicago: University of Chicago Press.

Weber, E. (1970). *Early childhood education: Perspectives on change.* Belmont, CA: Charles A. Jones.

Weber, L. (1971). *The English infant school and informal education.* Englewood Cliffs, NJ: Prentice-Hall.

Werner, E. (1989). High-risk children in young adulthood: A longitudinal study from birth to 32 years. *American Journal of Orthopsychiatry, 59*(1), 72–81.

Whitebook, M., Howes, C., & Phillips, D. (1990). *Who cares? Child care teachers and the quality of care in America. Final report of the National Child Care Staffing Study.* Oakland, CA: Child Care Employee Project.

Wittmer, D. S., & Honig, A. S. (1991). Convergent or divergent? Teachers' questions to three-year-old children in day care. *Early Child Development and Care, 68,* 141–148.

Zigler, E. F., & Goodman, J. (1982). The battle for day care in America: A view from the trenches. In E. F. Zigler & E. W. Gordon (Eds.), *Day care: Scientific and social policy issues* (pp. 338–350). Dover, MA: Auburn House.

Zigler, E. F., & Lang, M. E. (1990). *Child care choices: Balancing the needs of children, families and society.* New York: Free Press.

CHAPTER 3

Child Outcomes of Child Care Programs

Carollee Howes

Most children in the United States are enrolled in some form of child care arrangement prior to formal school entrance. Therefore the issue of child outcomes of child care programs is an important one for schools and for society as a whole (see Zigler & Lang, 1991, for an excellent treatment of the societal implications of children's development as a consequence of child care). Despite its importance for American society there is no national child care system. Unlike most other industrialized countries, the United States lacks a coherent and organized system of child care service delivery (Phillips, 1990). Since there is no national child care system, child care services are patchwork, provided by a variety of agencies and auspices, and without standard regulations. Therefore it is impossible to summarize the literature on child outcomes of child care programs except by saying that child outcomes are as diverse as the child care delivery system itself.

Child care outcomes are heavily influenced by family factors. Whether or not a child will have a good experience in child care is related to the level of family income and stress, parental knowledge of child development, and family child-rearing values and practices (Hayes, Palmer & Zaslow, 1990). Parents who have the most resources are able to find the best child care. Even if families have reasonable incomes and are knowledgeable about and motivated to find high-quality child care, their success in finding it depends in part on luck—the length of the waiting lists when their children are born—and in part on the supply of high-quality care in their communities. Child development outcomes for children in this country are increasingly polarized by family income and organization (Hayes et al., 1990). A recent study of representative center-based child care programs—the National Child Care Staffing Study (NCCSS)—found that middle- and low-income parents were less likely than high-income parents to have children in high-quality child care centers (Whitebook, Howes & Phillips, 1990). In this study, families with the lowest incomes and no subsidized care had children with the most problematic outcomes (Voran & Whitebook, 1991).

Child outcomes from child care programs are, not surprisingly, as variable as child outcomes as a function of family care. Depending on the national mood and economy, we seem willing to tolerate a wide range of child outcomes in this country. For example, societal indicators of child development, including high dropout, teenage pregnancy, and infant mortality rates, do not result in universal remediation programs. Even when there appears to be consensus on the value of helping families in need—for example, with preventive educational or health programs such as Head Start—only a relatively small percentage of families who qualify for the service actually receive it. Similarly, Americans appear willing to accept a wide range of child outcomes from child care programs. When states regulate child care programs, the level of regulation is most often at the threshold rather than the optimal level. That is, regulation is designed to prevent programs that harm children rather than promote programs that enhance development. Because the states' authority to regulate child care relates to their police power, they can only apply regulations that protect children from harm.

Fortunately, it is possible to identify meaningful variations in child care programs that are associated with child outcomes. These include the quality of the child care program, the function of the program, the legal auspices of the program, the regulatory climate of the program, and, to a lesser extent, the age of the child served and the age at which the child entered child care. Although the form of child care—center care versus family day care—is an easily recognized child care variation, child care forms are not associated with child outcome (see Howes & Hamilton, in press, for a review of this literature). Within child care programs of all forms we can identify particular aspects of relationships with adults and peers that may influence child development. The remainder of the chapter examines these variations.

CHILD CARE QUALITY

Parents, state legislators, child care practitioners, and child care advocates often declare that it is difficult to define child care quality or that definitions vary with child care consumers. Not all families need the same kind of child care services, nor do families agree on child care values.

The research community has had more success in developing a consensus on the definition of child care quality. The research literature is drawn primarily from the larger field of developmental psychology. Child care researchers within this tradition are usually interested in applying basic child development theory to children in child care (Fein & Fox, 1990) or in understanding child care as a subset of the study of environmental influences on child development (McCartney, 1990).

Researchers conceptualize child care quality as either structural quality or process quality. Structural quality generally refers to variables that can be regulated, including adult-child ratio, group size, and the education and training of adult caregivers. Such variables are aspects of child care that a state or federal government can regulate fairly easily. Process quality refers to the provision of developmentally appropriate activities and to warm, nurturing, and sensitive caregiving within the child care arrangement. It is more difficult to regulate process quality. For example, most people would agree that a child care teacher should be sensitive to the social bids of the children in her care. But it is difficult to imagine how such sensitivity could be assured with a hiring requirement.

Fortunately, structural quality is not independent of process quality. Structural quality variables are often markers or stand-in variables for process quality variables. For example, although it is difficult to measure or enforce a requirement that teachers be sensitive, research suggests that teachers with more years of formal education are, as a group, more sensitive (Whitebook et al., 1990). Therefore, a requirement of formal education may be intended to assure that teachers are sensitive. As might be expected, process aspects of child care are generally better predictors of children's outcomes than structural aspects because they are more proximal to children's development. For example, adult-child ratio, a structural variable, does predict children's attachment security with teachers. However, the predictive power of teacher-appropriate caregiving, a process variable, is greater than the predictive power of adult-child ratio for attachment security (Howes, Phillips, & Whitebook, in press). Theoretically this is true because a more reasonable adult-child ratio allows a teacher to provide more appropriate caregiving. A teacher who is more appropriate is more likely to facilitate a secure attachment relationship with a child.

Relations between Quality and Children's Development

Adult-Child Ratio. Adult-child ratio is simply the number of children cared for by each adult present in the classroom. Because of the greater caregiving requirements of younger children, it is assumed that the younger the children are, the fewer will be cared for by each adult. Adult-child ratio affects children because as the number of children an adult cares for increases, the opportunity for sensitive or appropriate interaction between the adult and each child decreases. As adults care for larger and larger numbers of children, group management also becomes a potential problem. Some adults, particularly highly educated and well-trained teachers, appear to use routines, rituals, and peer cohesiveness to manage large numbers of children without compromising the quality of adult-child interaction (see Howes & Marx, 1991, for examples within the French child care system). For other adults, caring for large numbers of children leads to restrictive and harsh practices, including leaving children in cribs for long periods, requiring children to stand in lines without talking or wiggling during transitions, and using teacher-led circle times to take up most of the day.

Researchers report that infants and toddlers in centers or family day care homes with more favorable adult-child ratios have more highly developed self-regulatory systems (Howes & Olenick, 1986) and exhibit more play behaviors (Howes & Rubenstein, 1985; Howes & Stewart, 1987). When adults care for large numbers of children, these infants are found to be less persistent at tasks (Howes & Olenick, 1986) and more distressed and apathetic (Roup, Travers, Glantz & Coelen, 1979). More favorable adult-child ratios are associated with more gestural and vocal imitation (Francis & Self, 1982) and with more overall vocalizations (Howes & Rubenstein, 1985). A more favorable adult-child ratio is also associated with more elaborated play (Bruner, 1980) and higher frequencies of peer interaction and fantasy play (Field, 1980) in preschoolers.

As we would expect, adult-child ratio is associated with stronger differences in teachers' behavior than in children's behavior. In infant and toddler classrooms, teachers were more restrictive and controlling when they had more children to care for (Ruopp et al., 1979; Howes & Rubenstein, 1985; Whitebook et al., 1990). In family day care homes, providers with fewer children per adult were more sensitive (Howes, 1983). Similar influences are apparent for preschoolers. Teachers in classrooms with more children per adult rate their jobs as more exhausting, and they spend more time controlling children, than those in classrooms with fewer children (Smith & Connolly, 1981). Teachers who have fewer children to care for engage the children in more conversation (Bruner, 1980; Smith & Connolly, 1981).

Group Size. Group size is defined as the number of children cared for in a child care group. The group may be all the children in a family day care home or all the children in a child care classroom. Infants and toddlers in smaller groups express more positive affect (Cummings & Beagles-Ross, 1983) and engage in more talk and play (Howes & Rubenstein, 1985). Those in larger groups are more apathetic and distressed (Ruopp et al., 1979). Preschool children in small groups not only play more but engage in more fantasy and pretend play (Bruner, 1980; Smith & Connolly, 1981). They may also be more creative and cooperative than children in larger groups (Ruopp et al., 1979). The higher amounts of play in smaller groups may be linked to the fact that children in smaller groups seem to know one another better (Smith & Connolly, 1981), are more cooperative (Ruopp et al., 1979), are more socially competent with familiar peers, and rated higher in social cognitive measures (Clarke-Stewart & Gruber, 1984) than children in larger groups. Most studies of group size have looked only at the effects of too many children, but Clarke-Stewart and Gruber (1984) also report the effects of too few children. Their results indicate that infants and toddlers enrolled in family day care with either too few (less than three) or too many (more than five) children were less socially competent than their peers.

The influence of group size on caregiver outcomes is not surprising given the added demands of caring for a larger group. The teacher must not only monitor more children but may also have to monitor and supervise additional adults. These increased demands seem to lead to an increase in restrictive management techniques (Howes, 1983; Ruopp et al., 1979) and a decrease in social interaction and language stimulation in infant and toddler classrooms (Smith & Connolly, 1981). Preschool teachers may not be as sensitive to the effects of group size, perhaps because their roles involve less direct caregiving. However, Ruopp and colleagues (1979) did find that preschool teachers with larger groups engaged in less social interaction with the children, which may be related to the lack of gains in verbal measures of children enrolled in larger groups (Ruopp et al., 1979).

Teacher Characteristics.   The most important ingredient of quality in child care is probably the teacher. Teacher characteristics fit into both structural and process aspects of quality. The structural aspects of teacher characteristics include the amount and kind of formal education, experience in child care, and length of service. Generally both formal education and specialized training in child care appear to influence a teacher's ability to engage in developmentally appropriate behavior with children (Whitebook et al., 1990). The literature on formal education and specialized training is difficult to interpret because the level of formal education of the child care work force has changed over the last decade. Although it is still a relatively well educated work force, there are currently both fewer teachers with only high school diplomas and fewer teachers with bachelor or graduate degrees than a decade ago (Whitebook et al., 1990). As the number of highly educated (bachelor's degree or higher) teachers in the field declines, research studies find formal education to be a better predictor of effective teaching than specialized training. The exception to this trend is infant and toddler teachers. For teachers of younger children, both specialized training and formal education appear to predict effective teaching. These advantages of formal education seem true for family day care providers as well as center teachers (Stallings & Porter, 1980).

The studies on experience in child care and on caregiver stability present a clearer picture. Experience appears to have little association with child outcomes (Clarke-Stewart & Gruber, 1984; Whitebook et al., 1990). In contrast, increased stability in child care arrangement is linked to positive child outcomes in both the short and long term. Infants and toddlers may be particularly susceptible to the effects of caregiver stability because they are in the process of forming attachment relationships. Cummings (1980) found that infants and toddlers were more positive in their interactions with stable caregivers. Clarke-Stewart and Gruber (1984) found that infants and toddlers did better on cognitive tests when they retained the same caregiver. Howes and colleagues found that children had higher self-regulation scores (Howes & Olenick, 1986) and higher levels of play when they had had more stable child care (Howes & Stewart, 1987). Howes and Hamilton (1991) found that children aged 18 to 24 months who experienced a change in caregiver were less likely to have stable caregiver attachments than those who experienced changes later. Finally, both infant/toddler and preschool age children enrolled in child care centers with more staff turnover spent more time aimlessly wandering and had lower language scores (Whitebook et al., 1990). With at least 40% of teachers leaving their child care jobs in center care and even higher estimates of turnover in family day care, stability of child care teachers is an increasingly serious problem.

Process Quality. Process quality is operationalized in many child care research programs as either a rating scale such as the Early Childhood Environmental Rating Scale (ECERS) (Harms & Clifford, 1980) or a combination of indicators such as adult involvement (Anderson, Nagle, Roberts & Smith, 1981). Process quality in infant and toddler classrooms and family day care homes is associated with higher levels of object and social play (Howes & Stewart, 1987) and with an increase in attachment behaviors directed toward the caregiver (Anderson et al., 1981). Preschoolers in higher-quality centers were rated as more considerate, intelligent, task oriented, and sociable by their teachers (Phillips, McCartney & Scarr, 1987), had higher intellectual and language test scores (McCartney, 1990), and were more socially competent (McCartney, Scarr, Phillips, Grajek & Schwarz, 1984; Vandell, Henderson & Wilson, 1988). Children in lower-quality programs were more likely to rate themselves lower in self-esteem (Vandell, Henderson & Wilson, 1988) and were more likely to engage in solitary or unoccupied activities (Vandell & Powers, 1983).

In summary, child care quality is strongly associated with children's child care outcomes. If children are fortunate enough to have high-quality care, we can predict that they will also have optimal child development outcomes. If children are enrolled in low-quality care the reverse is true.

In our discussions of child care we have not included comparisons of children in child care and children cared for primarily by their mothers. These comparisons are of relatively little value because both mother care and child care are extremely heterogeneous environments. The most comprehensive comparison study of mother care and child care is the Chicago study (Clarke-Stewart & Gruber, 1984). In this study, 150 children aged two to four years were cared for in extremely diverse environments. Child care environments were classified into seven different care arrangements ranging from mother and one child to center care. Children farther along the continuum toward center care scored higher on a battery of measures of social and cognitive development.

FUNCTIONS OF CHILD CARE

Child care arrangements serve several functions. They provide care for children while adult family members work, they provide opportunities for children to socialize with peers, and they may also serve as intervention programs. There is an extensive literature on the child outcomes of child care programs that serve an intervention function. Reviews of Head Start and other early intervention programs for disadvantaged families (Harrell, 1983; McKey, Condelli, Ganson, Barrett, McConkey & Plantz, 1985; Lazar, Darlington, Murray, Royce & Sniper, 1982) have found that these types of programs enhance children's cognitive competence not only during the time the child is in the program but also throughout the first three to four years of elementary school. Beyond elementary school there are less consistent findings. However, some studies show that early intervention may continue to have some positive influences on academic achievement and school performance throughout the elementary years (Gray, Ramsey & Klaus, 1981; Beller, 1983).

High-quality community-based programs may also serve an intervention function, although they are not specifically designed to do so. In a study comparing low-income Black children enrolled in either high-quality government-supported child care programs or lower-quality private child care centers in Bermuda, McCartney and colleagues (1985) found that children who attended the government program had better language skills and were rated as more considerate and sociable than the children enrolled in the private centers. In a study of low-income children assigned to a highly successful intervention program, researchers found that the children enrolled in Title XX community child care programs as opposed to no child care had higher IQ test scores and more secure maternal attachment relationships (Burchinal, Lee & Ramey, 1986; Burchinal, Bryant, Lee & Ramey, 1986). Finally, in a heterogeneous SES sample, children who attended stable and high-quality child care before attending a laboratory elementary school had higher school adjustment scores than children with low-quality child care experiences (Howes, 1988).

Many relatively advantaged families enroll their children in preschool child care to prepare them for formal school. The research literature on the advantages of child care attendance for such children has been mixed (Clarke-Stewart & Fein, 1983). A recent study (Larsen & Robinson, 1989) suggests that preschool attendance was a positive influence on later school achievement for boys, but not for girls. In Sweden, where child care quality is very high, children who enter child care as infants and thus have the greatest amount of exposure also have the highest socioemotional and cognitive ratings as elementary school children (Andersson, 1989). It appears that child care can serve an enhancement function even if it is not designed as an intervention program.

CHILD CARE AUSPICES

Because there is no national child care system in the United States, child care centers operate under a number of legal auspices—private and public, for-profit and not-for-profit. Public centers include those sponsored by state or federal government or by school systems. Relatively few public centers serve children full time. Private centers can be for-profit or not-for-profit. For-profit centers are either single centers, often referred to as "Mom and Pop" centers, or local or national chains. In a chain more than one center is under a single administration. Chains can be franchised or under central control. Not-for-profit centers can be church sponsored or independent. Independent not-for-profit centers can be freestanding or part of a larger agency, such as the YMCA. Some independent not-for-profit centers are physically located in church buildings but are independent of the church.

In contrast to center-based care, most family day care homes have private for-profit status and are considered small businesses. The few family day care homes that are not private for-profit are those that are part of a network administered by a nonprofit agency such as a child guidance center.

It is difficult to get good estimates of the proportion of child care centers that operate under different auspices. States, not the federal government, maintain registries. Some states do not list the auspices of centers. Other states do not require some centers, such as those that are church sponsored, to register or be licensed. A 1989 nonempirical estimate suggests that independent for-profit centers constitute 46% of all licensed centers, with for-profit chains accounting for an additional 7% (Neugebauer, 1989).

A recent nationally representative study of center-based child care (the NCCSS) examined the influence of auspices on child care quality and child outcomes (Whitebook, et al., 1990). Thirty-seven percent of the NCCSS centers were nonprofit, nonchurch centers; 16% were sponsored by religious organizations (referred to as church-sponsored nonprofit); 39% were independent for-profit; and 8% were for-profit national or local chains. The NCCSS research design included extensive interviews with the center directors and representative staff, classroom observations, and child assessments.

Differences in Quality of Care

Nonprofit (as opposed to for-profit) center teaching staff had higher levels of formal education and more specialized training in child development. Nonprofit centers also had better adult-child ratios and were more likely to have two teachers in a classroom and to overlap teacher shifts so that teachers could exchange daily information about the children. For-profit centers were more likely than not-for-profit centers to have staff that "floated," as opposed to being assigned to a single group of children. For-profit centers were also more likely to use accordion groupings of children — with children changing classrooms throughout the day. With accordion grouping, children commonly start the day in one large group, break into smaller groups between 9 a.m. and 5 p.m. (sometimes changing groups more than once), and form a large group in the late afternoon when preparing to leave. This practice allows centers to maintain a smaller teaching staff during the hours when there are fewer children. The disadvantage of accordion grouping is that children can be stressed and otherwise disadvantaged by the confusion of shifting rooms and adults throughout the day.

Nonprofit centers received higher process quality scores (as measured by the ECERS) than for-profit centers. Teachers in independent for-profit centers were rated as more harsh and less sensitive in their teaching than teachers in centers with other auspices.

Differences in Children

European-American children were disproportionately enrolled in independent for-profit, church-sponsored, or other not-for-profit centers. African-American children were enrolled primarily in for-profit chains. Middle-income children were disproportionately enrolled in for-profit chains. Low-income and high-income children tended to be enrolled in not-for-profit centers. When these family differences were statistically controlled, children enrolled in not-for-profit centers were more likely than children enrolled in for-profit centers to be securely attached to their teachers. Children in for-profit centers also spent more time aimlessly wandering. Children in not-for-profit centers were rated as more competent with their peers and were more likely to have Peabody Picture Vocabulary Test scores above the median.

Accounting for the Differences

Kagan and Newton (1989) suggest that not-for-profit centers are higher in quality because they receive government funds. Therefore, quality of care was compared in for-profit and not-for-profit NCCSS centers receiving and not receiving government funds. Not-for-profit centers, whether or not they received government funds, had higher ECERS quality scores than for-profits. In contrast, centers — both for-profit and not-for-profit — that allocated a greater percentage of their budgets to teaching staff salaries and benefits had higher ECERS scores.

Finally, the NCCSS centers were used in a multiple regression procedure to assess the relative strengths of four predictors of quality of care (ECERS scores): auspices, voluntary compliance with Federal Interagency Day Care Requirements (FIDCR), accreditation by the National Association for the Education of Young Children (NAEYC), and government funding. Auspices of the centers were the strongest predictor of quality. The second strongest predictor for infants and toddlers was FIDCR compliance. The second strongest predictor for preschoolers was NAEYC accreditation. Government funding had little predictive value. Thus meeting standards of quality, rather than receiving subsidies, seems to be what distinguishes for-profit from not-for-profit care.

REGULATORY CLIMATE OF CENTERS

As suggested in the introduction to this chapter, the lack of a coherent national child care system means that the regulation of child care in the United States is a function of state governments and thus is diverse. Attempts to achieve a national system of child care have resulted in consensus among experts and advocates but not within the legislative or executive branches of government. Thus, for example, the revised Federal Interagency Day Care Requirements (FIDCR) were briefly adopted and then rescinded. The FIDCR remain a nationally accepted level of regulation that centers can voluntarily meet.

The National Child Care Staffing Study asked whether centers that voluntarily met three provisions of the FIDCR (ratio, group size, and teacher training) differed in teacher and child behaviors from those that did not meet the FIDCR provisions. Teachers in centers meeting the FIDCR provisions were rated as more sensitive, less harsh, and engaged in more appropriate caregiving and more developmentally appropriate activities than teachers in the centers not meeting FIDCR provisions (Whitebook et al., 1990). Children in centers meeting FIDCR provisions spent less time aimlessly wandering, engaged in higher-level peer play, had higher Peabody Picture Vocabulary scores, and had higher self perceptions of competence (Whitebook et al., 1990).

Some critics of child care regulation have suggested that establishing regulatory standards will not lead to higher quality child care. They argue that no one can replace or regulate a warm, loving caregiver and to add regulations leads to institutional care. The findings above suggest otherwise. When centers voluntarily met regulatory standards teachers were more sensitive and appropriate, and children benefited.

AGE OF ENTRY INTO CHILD CARE

More infants and toddlers are entering child care than any other age group. Infants as young as six or eight weeks are entering the child care system. Belsky (1988) has suggested that children who enter child care before their first birthdays may be at risk for future developmental difficulties. He bases this argument on an examination of the maternal attachment relationships of infants whose mothers worked out of the home more than 20 hours a week during their children's first year of life. Although these infants are more likely to be securely attached than insecurely attached to their mothers, they are also more likely than infants whose mothers do not work to be insecurely attached. This finding is replicated within the literature on maternal employment (Fein & Fox, 1990).

Knowing that a mother works a certain number of hours a week does not provide information about who is caring for her children and under what circumstances. The literature on children's child care outcomes based on the child's age when enrolled and the type of child care presents a different picture than that presented in the literature on maternal employment. The age at which a child enters child care is generally a less powerful predictor of social and emotional development than the quality of care the child experiences. However, quality of care appears to be particularly influential when children enter child care before their first birthdays. Thus, in a study comparing four groups of children entering high- or low-quality care before or after their first birthdays, the children who had the most difficulty as kindergartners were those that entered low-quality care before their first birthdays (Howes, 1990).

Our societal beliefs about child rearing make the age at which a child enters child care a particularly potent issue (Howes & Sakai, in press). There is a pervasive belief that babies belong at home with their mothers, and there is a great deal of resistance to the idea of mothers of babies working. In this context it is noteworthy that the United States is one of the few industrialized countries without a parental leave policy.

The realities are, of course, that mothers of infants are employed outside the home and that infant and toddler child care is difficult to find. Moreover, infant and toddler center-based care is generally of lower quality than preschool care (Whitebook et al., 1990), and there is mounting evidence that family day care for toddler-age children is also of lower quality than family day care for preschoolers (Howes & Sakai, in press).

To balance this depressing picture, there is evidence that excellent care for infants and toddlers exists. When children experience this care they are indistinguishable from (Howes, 1990) or better off than (Howes & Olenick, 1986; Ramey & Haskins, 1981) children cared for at home. In summary, the optimum age for a child to enter child care is perhaps the most difficult issue to resolve in discussing child outcomes of child care programs. If infancy is a particular vulnerable developmental period, then there is a certain logic to making sure that child care environments for infants are of particularly high quality. Instead, our nation both denies parents leave after the birth of a baby and provides the poorest quality out-of-home care to the youngest children.

CONCLUSION

Children in child care are not aware that child care varies in form, function, quality, auspices, or regulatory climate. What makes a difference for the children in child care are relationships with teachers and peers. These relationships make child care either a positive and pleasant experience or a dismal and damaging one. From experience with others in child care children may trust their teachers to keep them safe. Children may feel mastery and self-confidence because their teachers create meaningful learning experiences and extend the children's explorations by monitoring their activities and intervening at teachable moments. Children may enjoy their encounters with peers, feel accepted by them, and have friends. Or they may spend their hours in child care feeling lonely and frightened, bored, passive, or overpowered by detached or harsh teachers and out-of-control children. The evidence suggests that the nature of children's experiences in child care is influenced by identifiable variations in child care programs. Children are most likely to have positive and pleasant experiences when the child care is regulated, when it is not-for-profit, and when it is of high quality.

REFERENCES

Anderson, C., Nagle, R., Roberts, W., & Smith, J. (1981). Attachment to substitute caregivers as a function of center quality and caregiver involvement. *Child Development, 57,* 53–61.

Andersson, B. E. (1989). Effects of public day care: A longitudinal study. *Child Development, 60,* 857–866.

Beller, E. K. (1983). The Philadelphia study: The impact of preschool on intellectual and socioemotional development. In Consortium for Longitudinal Studies, *As the twig is bent . . . Lasting effects of preschool programs*. Hillsdale, NJ: Erlbaum.

Belsky, J. (1988). The effects of infant day care reconsidered. *Early Childhood Research Quarterly, 3,* 235–272.

Bruner, J. (1980). *Under fives in Britain*. Ypsilanti, MI: High/Scope.

Burchinal, M. R., Bryant, D. M., Lee, M., & Ramey, C. (1986, August). *Does early day care affect infant-mother attachment levels?* Paper presented at the annual meeting of the American Psychological Association, Washington, DC.

Burchinal, M. R., Lee, M., & Ramey, C. (1986, August). *Day care effects on poverty children*. Paper presented at the annual meeting of the American Psychological Association, Washington, DC.

Clarke-Stewart, A., & Gruber, C. (1984). Daycare forms and features. In R. C. Ainslie (Ed.), *Quality variations in daycare* (pp. 35–62). New York: Praeger.

Clarke-Stewart, K. A., & Fein, G. (1983). Early childhood programs. In P. Mussen (Ed.), *Handbook of child psychology* (pp. 143–167). New York: Wiley.

Cummings, E. (1980). The effects of stability of caregivers on social development in infant daycare. *Developmental Psychology, 16,* 31–37.

Cummings, M., & Beagles-Ross, J. (1983). Towards a model of infant daycare: Studies of factors influencing responding to separation in daycare. In R. C. Ainslie (Ed.), *Quality variations in daycare* (pp. 158–162). New York: Praeger.

Fein, G., & Fox. N. (1990). *Infant child care*. Norwood, NJ: Ablex.

Field, T. M. (1980). Preschool play: Effects of teacher:child ratio and organization of classroom space. *Child Study Journal, 10,* 191–205.

Francis, P., & Self, P. (1982). Imitative responsiveness of young children in day care and home settings: The importance of the child to the caregiver ratio. *Child Care Journal, 1,* 119–126.

Gray, S., Ramsey, B., & Klaus, R. (1981). *From three to twenty: The early training project*. Baltimore: University Park Press.

Harms, T., & Clifford, R. (1980). *Early childhood environmental rating scale*. New York: Teachers College Press.

Harrell, A. (1983). *Preliminary report: The effect of the Head Start program on children's cognitive development*. Washington, DC: U.S. Department of Health and Human Services.

Hayes, C. D., Palmer, J. L., & Zaslow, M. (1990). *Who cares for America's children: Child care policy for the 1990s*. Washington, DC: National Academy Press.

Howes, C. (1983). Caregiver behavior in center and family day care. *Journal of Applied Developmental Psychology, 4,* 99–107.

Howes, C. (1988). Relations between early child care and schooling. *Developmental Psychology, 24,* 53–57.

Howes, C. (1990). Can the age of entry into child care and the quality of child care predict adjustment in kindergarten? *Developmental Psychology, 26,* 292–303.

Howes, C., & Hamilton, C. E. (in press). Children's relationships with their caregivers. *Child Development.*

Howes, C., & Hamilton, C. E. (in press). Child care for young children. In B. Spodek (Ed.), *Handbook of research on the education of young children.* New York: Macmillan.

Howes, C., & Marx, E. (in press). Raising questions about improving the quality of child care in the United States and France. *Early Childhood Research Quarterly.*

Howes, C., & Olenick, M. (1986). Family and child care influences on toddlers' compliance. *Child Development, 57,* 202–216.

Howes, C., Phillips, D., & Whitebook, M. (in press). Thresholds of quality implications for the social development of children in center based child care. *Child Development.*

Howes, C., & Rubenstein, J. (1985). Determinants of toddlers' experience in day care: Age of entry and quality of setting. *Child Care Quarterly, 14,* 140–151.

Howes, C., & Sakai, L. (in press). Family day care for infants and toddlers. In D. Peters & A. Pence (Eds.), *Family day care: Current research for informed public policy.* New York: Teachers College Press.

Howes, C., & Stewart, P. (1987). Child's play with adults, toys and peers: An examination of family and child care influences. *Developmental Psychology, 23*(2), 423–430.

Kagan, S. L., & Newton, J. W. (1989). For-profit and non-profit child care: Similarities and differences. *Young Children, 45,* 4–10.

Larsen, J. M., & Robinson, C. C. (1989). Later effects of preschool on low-risk children. *Early Childhood Research Quarterly, 4,* 133–144.

Lazar, I., Darlington, R., Murray, J., Royce, J., & Sniper, A. (1982). Lasting effects of early education. *Monographs of the Society for Research in Children Development, 47,* (1–2, Serial No. 194).

McCartney, K. (1990). *Child care and maternal employment: A social ecological approach.* San Francisco: Jossey-Bass.

McCartney, K., Scarr, S., Phillips, D. A., & Grajek, S. (1985). Day care as intervention: Comparisons of varying quality programs. *Journal of Applied Developmental Psychology, 6,* 247–260.

McKey, R. H., Condelli, L., Ganson, H., Barrett, B. J., McConkey, C., & Plantz, M. C. (1985). *The impact of Head Start on children, families, and communities: Final report of the Head Start evaluation, synthesis, and utilization project.* Washington, DC: CSR Incorporated for the Head Start Bureau, Administration for Children, Youth and Families, U.S. Department of Health and Human Services.

Neugebauer, R. (1989, April). Surveying the landscape: A look at child care '89. *Child Care Information Exchange, 66,* 13–16.

Phillips, D. (1990). Day care for young children in the United States. In E. Meluish & P. Moss (Eds.), *Day care for young children: International perspectives* (pp. 161–184). London: Tavistock.

Phillips, D. A., McCartney, K., & Scarr, S. (1987). Child care quality and children's social development. *Developmental Psychology, 23*, 537–543.

Ramey, C., & Haskins, R. (1981). The cause and treatment of school failure: Insights from the Carolina Abecedarian Project. In M. J. Begab, H. C. Haywood & H. L. Garber (Eds.), *Psychosocial influences in retarded performance: Strategies improving competence* (pp. 135–151). Baltimore: University Park Press.

Ruopp, R., Travers, J., Glantz, F., & Coelen, C. (1979). *Children at the center: Final report of the National Day Care Study.* Cambridge, MA: Abt Associates.

Smith, P., & Connolly, K. (1981). *The behavioral ecology of the preschool.* Cambridge, England: Cambridge University Press.

Stallings, J., & Porter, A. (1980). *National day care home study.* Palo Alto, CA: SRI International.

Vandell, D. J., Henderson, V. K., & Wilson, K. S. (1988). A follow-up study of children in excellent, moderate and poor quality day care. *Child Development, 59*, 1286–1292.

Vandell, D. J., & Powers, C. (1983). Day care quality and children's free play activities. *American Journal of Orthopsychiatry, 53*, 293–300.

Voran, M. J., & Whitebook, M. (1991, April). *Inequity begins early: The relation between day care quality and family social class.* Paper presented at the biennial meeting of the Society for Research in Child Development.

Whitebook, M., Howes, C., & Phillips, D. (1990). *Who cares: Child care teachers in America.* Oakland, CA: Child Care Employee Project.

Zigler, E., & Lang, M. (1991). *Child care choices: Balancing the needs of children, families, and society.* New York: Macmillan.

CHAPTER 4

Family-Centered Child Care

Ellen Galinsky
Bernice Weissbourd

An important historical shift is occurring in child care. Increasingly, a concept termed family-centered child care is achieving prominence. The traditional focus on the child as the client in child care is being redirected to the parent-child relationship. Likewise, the concept of parent involvement in child care is being changed to family support. Predicated on the principles of the family support movement, family-centered child care moves from a deficit to a strengths approach, from remediation to prevention. As such, the child care center becomes a community center in which parents and teachers learn from one another and in which parents' adult needs are met through programs at the center as well as through linkages to community services.

This chapter discusses the historical trends that have led to the concept of family-centered programming, describes the research base and philosophical underpinnings of this movement, enumerates and analyzes the barriers to family-centered child care, and describes several programs that illustrate this concept.

THE ANTECEDENTS OF
FAMILY-CENTERED CHILD CARE

A view of the past often elucidates the present. So it is with family-centered child care. The lessons learned from a rich past of parent education and parent involvement programs have gradually led to the conviction that parents should be recognized as an integral component of the child care setting.

The Research Basis for Family-Centered Child Care

Research on parent education programs throughout the 1970s indicated that good programs were having significant effects: improvement in children's language development (Barbrack & Horton, 1970; Mann, 1970; Sandler, Dokecki, Stewart, Britton & Horton, 1973), greater sensitivity of mothers to their children's individual characteristics (Andrews, Blumenthal, Bachs & Weiner, 1975; Gordon & Guinagh, 1974; Kogan & Gordon, 1975), and a more optimal learning environment at home (Andrews et al., 1975; Gordon & Guinagh, 1974; Leler, Johnson, Kahn, Hines & Torres, 1975). In some programs there were sustained gains in children's cognitive functioning for up to three years after the intervention, indicating the potential of such programs to improve the capability and well-being of children before their entrance into elementary school (Gordon & Guinagh, 1974; Levenstein, 1974).

Likewise, the research on child care indicated that when a family's well-being is a focus of an early childhood program, the program's effect can be more lasting. For example, the Syracuse Family Development Research Project concluded that the children in its experimental child care program had more success in life and had higher self-esteem than those in the control group. The researcher, Ron Lally, and his colleagues saw a link between the children's subsequent achievement and the fact that the program focused on parents as well as children. After participating in the program, the parents had a more proactive approach to life and believed that one can take steps to reach one's full potential. This stood in contrast to the control-group families, who tended to emphasize merely surviving or getting by. Similarly, the parents in the program placed a higher value on education and on the family unit. Lally and his colleagues state: "It seems clear that our original notion to involve parents as intervention agents paid off. One hypothesis that could be generated for the long-range difference between the samples (children in the intervention program versus the control group of children not in the program) is the lasting impact on the parent and the parent-child relationship" (Lally, Mangione & Honig, 1987, p. 28).

Another influence in elevating the role of parents in child care settings came from a shift in the field of human development research. An ecological viewpoint began to take hold in which children's development was studied in the context of the family and the community (Bronfenbrenner, 1979).

One of the major antecedents of family-centered child care was Head Start. Since its beginning in 1965, this part-day early childhood program has required parent participation in program planning and policy. In fact, a major ongoing purpose of Head Start has been to provide opportunities for parents to develop their adult skills as decision makers and, ultimately, as advocates.

A second but equally powerful influence has been the family support movement. In the 1970s and 1980s these programs began to proliferate. Their ultimate purpose was to help children, but in order to do so, an ecological perspective was necessary. Therefore, family support programs held that (1) the child cannot be viewed as separate from the family, (2) the family cannot be seen as distinct from the community in which it lives, and (3) children and families cannot be considered apart from the policies and institutions of the larger society that either enhance or restrain families' ability to function.

The principles underlying family support programs emphasize that:

1. The most effective approach to families emanates from a prevention orientation promoting health and well-being. This approach requires that programs become involved with families as early as possible in order to provide parents the support they need to create an optimal environment for their children. It dictates an approach that builds on strengths and solutions instead of deficits and problems, therefore preserving parents' integrity and increasing opportunities for growth and change (McCubbin & Patterson, 1981).

2. The capacity of parents to raise their children effectively is influenced by their own development. As a distinct, evolving, ever-changing stage of life, parenthood is shaped by relationships, life experiences, and knowledge (Benedek, 1970). Parents' sense of confidence and competence emerges out of these dynamics, influencing who they are as people and, consequently, how they parent their own children (Unger & Wandersman cited in Littell, 1985).

3. Child-rearing techniques and values are influenced by cultural and community values and mores. Effective professional involvement with families demands an understanding of and appropriate responsiveness to cultural, individual, and community traditions and values (Spiegel, 1982).

4. Social support networks are essential to family well-being. Social support networks provide parents with the concrete and psychological resources that are essential if they are not to become overwhelmed by their responsibilities (Gottlieb, 1983).

5. Information about child development enhances parents' capacity to respond appropriately to their children. Informed parents are better equipped to solve problems, more confident of their decisions,

and more likely to respond sensitively to their children's developmental needs (Wandersman, 1987).

6. Families who receive support are empowered to advocate on their own and their children's behalf.

Demographic Antecedents

Although family-centered child care represents a convergence of these historical trends with the principles underlying the family support movement, it is also a response to the rapid and unsettling changes in family structure and community life. Family life today is characterized by a dramatic increase in the number of mothers entering the work force. In fact, the fastest growing segment of the work force is mothers of infants and toddlers (Galinsky & Friedman, in press). Because there are so few role models for two-parent employed families and single-parent families, many have reached out for support and information from one another. Concurrently, the disappearance of communities as places for mutual aid, friendships, and social support results in a pervasive sense of isolation and, again, the desire for the means to overcome this sense of aloneness (Weiss, 1979).

Although social conditions have changed, the premise that the family has primary responsibility for children's development remains deeply embedded in American culture. The family is considered the guardian of children's health and safety, the nurturer, and the source from which children's social and moral values are derived. In order for families to function well in their expected roles, it has become evident that they need — and deserve — support. Although the numbers of women in the work force created an increased demand for child care, the lessons from research and from the family support movement have led to a new vision of what child care ought to be.

WHAT IS FAMILY-CENTERED CHILD CARE?

With the traditional parent involvement/education approach, child care staff view activities for parents as having two major purposes: involving parents — bringing them into the life of the center — and educating parents — instructing them about their children's development and informing them how the child care curriculum teaches their children.

This approach differs substantially from a family-centered orientation in numerous ways. From the parent involvement/education point of view, families are seen as discrete, independent units whose strength emanates from within. The family-centered orientation, in contrast, views families in the context of their community, which plays a significant role in promoting or curtailing a family's strengths. The more traditional perspective defines parents primarily in terms of their child-rearing role and sees parenthood as synonymous with adulthood, the culminating stage of human development. The family-centered perspective defines parenthood as one of several developmental stages of adulthood, reinforcing a multidimensional concept of parents as individuals with many roles and responsibilities, one of which is parenthood (Galinsky, 1987). The parent involvement/education model defines information about child development, attitudes about and toward children, and knowledge about parent-child interaction as the principal factors that shape parental behavior. Although family-centered advocates believe that these factors are significant and influential, they believe that factors of parental self-esteem, cultural and family background, socioeconomic status, and the community context are of prime influence as well.

In terms of program planning, parent involvement/education advocates take the "teacher-as-imparter-of-knowledge" approach and place major emphasis on content, curriculum, and the intellectual growth of individual parents. Programmatically, the family-centered model equates the values of process and content and targets the overall development of parents as individuals, while acknowledging the vital role of community action in promoting social change. Its format is broad. It includes the teacher as the imparter of knowledge, but acknowledges that teachers learn from parents as well. The family-centered framework values parent interaction and modeling, and thus strongly encourages social interaction among parent participants.

Despite widespread advances in a theoretical understanding of child-parent-community relationships in the early childhood field, programs exemplifying these practices remain at the edge of the child care system. The prevailing mode of child care still conceives the child as separate from the family and sees the teacher as focusing on the child, at times even making up for the deficits of the family (the term "day-care reared" has appeared in the literature). Often careful limits are set on teachers' involvement with parents. Implementing the concept of family-centered child care, therefore, requires an expanded vision on the part of the child care teacher, a change in mind-set. Teachers are no longer "child savers" taking the place of or even protecting children from the less competent child-raising patterns of their parents. Nor are teachers concerned solely with their relationships with the children in their care, even when informed by more frequent contact with the children's parents. The children and families together become the concern of the staff. Building relationships with families that foster children's growth is as important as providing a healthy center environment. In order to do so, the teacher's task is to develop strong relationships with both children and parents for the purpose of strengthening the only enduring relationship in this triangle, that between parent and child. Enhancing children's development while improving the interaction between parents and children becomes the teacher's goal.

Components of a Family-Centered Model

In family-centered programs, teachers collaborate with parents in planning and setting policy for the center. They establish relationships with parents based on the recognition of each other's expertise — the teachers contributing their broad background and knowledge of child development, and the parents bringing the knowledge of their own particular children, their goals for their children, and a commitment to the family's cultural tradition.

The culture and traditions of families served are important considerations in teachers' planning so that activities and approaches are compatible and sensitive to family values. In daily interactions with parents, teachers are conscious of not undermining the parents' sense of competence. For example, if a child begins to fuss at pickup time, the teacher avoids saying something like, "She didn't fuss all day with me," which implies that the teacher knows how to care for the child better than the parent. In contrast, a teacher who says, "Children always save up their frustrations for the people they feel the safest with — their parents," is reinforcing the importance of the parental role. Likewise, when a teacher in a family-centered setting has a classroom problem to discuss with a parent, she or he is careful to do so within an atmosphere of trust and to elicit the parent's ideas on how to solve this problem in the classroom: "When your child gets upset at home, what strategies are the most helpful in settling him?" Goals for the child are, therefore, mutually established and are reinforced both at home and at the center.

A critical difference in family-centered programming is the attention given to meeting the parents' adult needs. Such attention is reflected in small and large ways. For example, center meetings might not be scheduled at 8:00 in the evening because parents would have to rush through dinner, say good-bye to their children, and return to the center. Family-centered programs might instead hold parent meetings at the end of the day, providing child care for the children and dinner for all. Furthermore, the topics of such meetings often extend beyond the traditional child-centered ones, including programs on managing the stress of work and family life, cultural awareness, and job skills. Finally, family-centered programs either offer comprehensive services or have good links with community services so that there is a sound process for referrals when family problems arise.

It becomes apparent that teachers functioning in these ways assume many roles in addition to that of classroom teacher. The teacher is a facilitator, resource, advocate, model, coworker with parents, and adviser. Family-centered child care promotes a new definition of the teacher. As the role of the teacher shifts in relation to the family, the role of the center also changes in relation to the community. The center is no longer a place to drop off children, nor is it a place where parents feel welcomed but uninvolved. The center becomes a place in which parents have a sense of ownership and belonging. The center becomes the family's community place, the hub of community activity.

The staff's understanding of the importance of social networks for families results in planning and programs that are designed to encourage peer relationships and support, which offer both material and emotional assistance to families. Baby-sitting cooperatives or clothing exchanges can make daily life much easier, and developing friendships with other families can reduce the isolation that is so debilitating to family functioning (Weiss, 1979; Garbarino & Sherman, 1980). Peer support groups have demonstrated effectiveness in enhancing parenting behavior and parent-child interaction (Boukydis, 1982; Slaughter, 1983).

When the child care center is a community hub that is closely linked to other agencies, it provides parents with the opportunity to become advocates for improved services for their children. By virtue of being together, sharing mutual concerns, and building skills, parents become empowered to act on their own behalf (*Parent Post*, 1990).

BARRIERS TO FAMILY-CENTERED CHILD CARE

In reality, teacher-parent relationships can be clouded with difficulty. In conferences for child care personnel, problems with parents are frequently mentioned as a source of tension. The research literature to date reveals that many teachers harbor negative feelings about parents. "It appears that negative perceptions of parents by caregivers and teachers may be the norm" (Kontos, 1987, p. 93). This negative stance has been called "judgmentalness" (Kontos, 1987), "parentism"—like racism or sexism (Galinsky, 1988), and "creative tension" (Lightfoot, 1975).

There is a growing body of research confirming that difficulties often pervade parent-teacher relationships. One of the first research efforts to explore the nature of this tension was conducted by Kontos, Raikes, and Woods (1983). The results of their study revealed that early childhood staff were critical of American parents in general and, although to a lesser degree, of the parents in their centers. A follow-up study revealed that staff and parents agreed about the criteria for good parenting and agreed that most parents today fail to meet these criteria. Parents, however, saw themselves as much closer to the standards for good parenting practice than did staff (Kontos, 1984).

The Parent/Teacher Study by Galinsky, Shinn, Phillips, Howes, and Whitebook (1990) also explored the tension between parents and teachers. In this study, teachers were asked to rate the mothers at their centers based on whether they were better, the same as, or worse than the "realistically good mother" on a number of indicators of parenting skill. This measure asked about the "realistically" good mother as opposed to the "ideal" good mother. The teachers in this study were more positive about the parents than those in the Kontos study. On average, between three-fifths and three-fourths of the teachers saw the parents as better or about the same as the realistically good mother. Two in five teaching staff felt that mothers rushed, overindulged, and pushed their children. Were these assessments unrealistic? Without research observations, of course, one cannot say, but it is interesting that analyses of the mothers' questionnaires revealed that 55% reported that their patience with their children was sometimes negatively affected by their jobs, and 50% experienced work-family conflict at least some of the time.

Class and Ethnic Differences between Staff and Parents

Kontos, Raikes, and Woods (1983) found that staff most likely to report positive attitudes toward parents were college educated, parents themselves, over age 30, and had at least five years of teaching experience. The Parent/Teacher Study found that teachers who were less educated and had lower hourly wages viewed parents as worse clients. On every other indicator of tension, however, the characteristics of staff background were not significant in the Parent/Teacher Study. It was the difference between the teachers' and the mothers' backgrounds that was most salient. Teachers rated mothers' parenting skills more

favorably when the mothers were older and more educated than themselves. Teachers rated mothers who were wealthy as better mothers,
and black teachers rated white parents more positively.

The Parent/Teacher Study also investigated whether parents experienced positive support from the teachers. Thirty-eight percent of the
mothers said that teachers often shared ideas; 27% said teachers helped
them figure out how to solve problems; 64% felt that teachers were
understanding or sympathetic with them. Again, ethnic differences between parents and teachers were important. When a greater proportion
of the teachers were black and the parents white, mothers felt more
support from the teachers.

Mothers in the Parent/Teacher Study were more satisfied with
teachers' relationships with their children when the teachers were older
than the mothers. Likewise, the older, wealthier, more educated white
parents reported fewer negative interactions with teachers, and teachers also saw these parents as relating to the center in more positive
ways. Not surprisingly, mothers who were less wealthy experienced
more envy toward teachers.

It is clear from these findings that parents especially in need of
support, those coping with difficulties such as poverty or minority status, are the least likely to receive it. It is especially sad that when
parents are more advantaged they are the beneficiaries of better relationships. These issues must be addressed to achieve family-centered
programming.

Teachers' Attitudes

There were several attitudes on the part of teachers in the Parent/
Teacher Study that differentiated how judgmental they were of parents. These included teachers' job commitment, their belief that it is
important to work with parents, and their approval of maternal employment. When teachers were more committed to their jobs, they
were more likely to feel positive about parents. Teachers who were
more committed to their jobs also reported that parents were more
willing to interact with them, and they saw the parents as better clients.
When teachers felt that working with parents was an important aspect
of their jobs, mothers were somewhat less jealous of and competitive
with teachers. Although very few parents (9%) directly reported being
jealous of teachers, more than a third (36%) said that they were envious
of teachers because they got to see their children do new things. It is
often said that individuals who gravitate toward the early childhood

field may do so, in part, because they are more comfortable with children than they are with adults. This is also a barrier to family-centered programming.

It was striking, but not surprising, that teachers in the Parent/Teacher Study who thought that mothers should not work were more judgmental about the mothers in their classes. Overall, 24% of the teachers were staunchly against mothers working. Interestingly, very few mothers suspected this—only 6% of the mothers reported that teachers were critical of their efforts to combine work with family life.

Many mothers were also guilty about their employment: 25% felt that it is better for children to be cared for at home by their parents, and 68% of the mothers thought that they should work less and spend more time with their children. However, 44% felt that they were better parents because they were not with their children all day, and only 22% thought that their children were unhappy in child care.

Overall, the teachers' attitudes about whether mothers should work and the mothers' own feelings of guilt suffused their relationships with each other. The Parent/Teacher Study makes it clear that although the world has changed in terms of the rapid increase in the number of employed mothers, attitudes have not quite kept pace. If teachers and parents do not support the notion that mothers should work, it stands to reason that they will have more ambivalent feelings about each other's roles and their relationships with each other. A self-perpetuating cycle seems to take place—teacher disapproval of mothers' employment is linked to a more negative judgmental stance, which is, in turn, linked to a poorer relationship with the mothers. These are clear barriers to family-centered child care.

Two other aspects of teachers' attitudes that the Parent/Teacher Study did not investigate often surface in teacher training workshops and conferences when these issues are discussed. First, there are some teachers who come to feel that their job is to save or rescue children. This can be strongly felt by teachers who disapprove of mothers working. As one teacher put it, "If she is going to abandon her child, then I'll be there for him. I'll try to make it up." This is a barrier to family-centered programming. Second, when a teacher has had an especially difficult day with a child, strong feelings can be aroused. It may be harder for the teacher to direct those feelings toward the child, with whom the teacher has to work day after day, than the parents, especially when the teacher's only contact with the parents is at dropoff or pickup time. However, if these attitudes fester, they can inhibit the development of family-centered child care.

Parents' Attitudes and Behavior

Using teachers as the informants on parental behavior revealed that between one-fourth and one-half of the teachers in the Parent/Teacher Study felt that substantial numbers of the parents in their groups did not relate to them or to the center in positive ways. For example, 57% of the teachers felt that half or fewer of the parents in their classrooms saw the teachers as partners, and 66% said that only a few of the parents in their groups used the center as a resource. This finding indicates that teachers may be more willing to accept the concept of family-centered child care than parents. Parents may not want the program to interfere in their private family lives. The Parent/Teacher Study found that when teachers felt that parents did not use the center as a resource, there was more tension in the parent-teacher relationships. Similarly, Kontos and Wells (1986) found that parents held in lowest esteem by teachers were those who did not expect to receive any personal benefit from child care and those who did not use the program to gain knowledge about their children's development.

The Parent/Teacher Study also revealed that those parents most likely to use the center as a resource for themselves thought teachers' work was very important. When parents value the teachers' work and role, the relationship with teachers is more constructive. Likewise, when teachers value working with parents, the relationship is better.

Funding

If centers are to provide comprehensive family-centered programming, it will be expensive. Yet funds allocated to centers, whether through governmental sources, foundations, or parent fees, seldom include resources for such programs. As a result, the family support programs that are springing up across the country rarely include early care and education for children; if they do, it is usually for emergency care or parent-child workshops. As family-centered child care gains prominence, moneys will have to be found. In the meantime, some programs are seeking less costly ways to change their focus from the child to the family, and others are becoming more entrepreneurial in raising funds.

Partnerships

Bringing together the concept of family support and early education and care in a community or state will require the development of co-equal partnerships by primary prevention/family support professionals and early childhood educators. Experience reveals that turf issues are not easily overcome, but when partnerships are successful (often through the provision of technical assistance in working together and skilled leadership), they are powerful forces for change.

EXAMPLES OF FAMILY-CENTERED PROGRAMS

The Carole Robertson Center

The Carole Robertson Center for Learning in Chicago* is a non-profit, parent-controlled program serving low-income, minority, and single-parent families. It provides a variety of programs for families: child care for children ages 3–14, including early childhood; before- and after-school programs; adult and family recreation; and parent support, such as programs on parenting skills, children's development, discipline, tenants' rights, crime, and taxes.

The center began in September 1974 as an after-school child care program in an alternative school and now shares space with other state agencies in two state-owned buildings. The family support programs began informally in response to the needs identified by parents using the child care facilities.

Child care and family support programs are now offered from before 6:00 a.m. to 8:00 p.m. They include recreational and social activities; literacy; leadership development; parenting workshops on stress, taxes, tenants' rights, crime, and the arts; and development issues such as teaching children about sex. Family Health Days address issues of family health care, such as sickle-cell screening day.

On the weekends, family activities include card parties, picnics, and other recreational activities. One weekend a year, there is an adult camp in the country for the parents to attend alone. The fee for this program is approximately $30. The center's operating expenses are provided from the following sources: government funding, parent fees, United Way, local fund-raising, and private and corporate foundations.

The purpose of the program is to provide a comfortable, safe, fun, and stimulating place for children and youth to learn and to grow,

---

*The addresses for the three programs described in this section are at the end of this chapter.

and to support their families to the fullest extent possible. The Carole Robertson Center serves the entire community, from young children to adults. It is the hub of these families' community lives as well as a path to other services. The biggest obstacle to providing this type of program is the lack of financial support. Executive Director Gail Nelson and her staff have to spend a great deal of time fund-raising.

Addison County Parent/Child Center

Addison County (Vermont) Parent/Child Center provides center-based services — two child care centers, family support programs, and parent education; outreach — home visiting of families, school-based services, and organized parent-child play groups; and a service network for families with young children.

The idea for the child care and family support programs grew out of a 1978 meeting of children and family service providers sponsored by the Vermont State Department of Mental Health. Each county formed an ongoing task force, and the Addison County task force conceived of the idea of the Parent/Child Center. It applied for and received a $140,000 start-up grant from the Office of Adolescent Family Life to provide services for teen parents. The program's annual budget has grown to $750,000. It has 27 major funding sources: A third of the support comes from federal grants, a third from state grants and contracts, and a third from local money, fees, fund-raising, private donations, and United Way.

A parent training program hires teen parents to work 20 hours a week at the center either with the children or in other areas of the program. Parents are trained to work as classroom aides, in food service, building maintenance, and office management. All parents must work in the child care center at least one semester. Parents gain pre-vocational skills, such as learning to be on time and to be responsible for themselves and others in the workplace. This program has developed specific training for fathers, instigated when a male child care worker stated that he thought fathers were feeling left out. Now the teen fathers work in the classrooms, in other areas of the program, and in car detailing (restoring cars).

Professional services include nursing, counseling, early intervention, and speech therapy. Families are referred to other community support services if the services they need cannot be provided at the center. At the center, service providers and families meet together regularly to review the overall social service plans for the families.

"These meetings help families feel empowered," notes Susan Harding, co-director of the program with Cheryl Mitchell. In the beginning, family participation at these meetings was controversial, in that it took time for some of the professionals to feel comfortable openly discussing issues with the family present, but now it is highly valued. Integration of support for parents is the heart of the program, according to Mitchell. "The major goal is to help families with their children, to feel comfortable with themselves as parents and as human beings."

In effect, the center has become a community center. The staff is also involved in outreach programs, including a pregnancy prevention program in the public schools. The center also helped found the Addison County branch of the Community College. The Parent/Child Center was the college's first home, before it found its own space. Services include community classes and workshops and parent education on positive parenting issues. The center also operates two houses for teen parents where they can live for 18 months while learning to be independent.

The greatest obstacle to this endeavor is money, stated both Mitchell and Harding. Funds often come from short-term contracts and one-year foundation grants.

Parent Services Project

For more than a decade, Parent Services Project (PSP) has been providing a wide range of services and activities to families already enrolled in child care programs. These include parent education classes, adult outings, skill-building classes for parents, peer group discussions, mental health services, leadership training, respite care, multicultural experiences, mental health workshops, ESL (English as a second language) classes, cardiopulmonary resuscitation training, and recreational trips and activities for families. The program also offers referrals for counseling services, exercise classes, nutrition information, men's groups and activities, and single-parent support groups. PSP serves African-American, Chinese, Latino, Southeast Asian, and Caucasian families, many of whom do not speak English. Family income levels are low to modest.

The goal of PSP is to develop parent leadership teams that help design, budget, and implement the program. Family support programs are designed "to provide parents with choices, to promote parents' expertise and to assist them in becoming the decision-makers," according to Ethel

Seiderman, director of PSP. As logical as that mission sounds, it is far from standard practice in most programs serving poor families. In order to make a program like this work, there needs to be a core of committed believers who carry out the work and begin to spread the word.

The program originated in 1980. The Zellerbach Family Fund, a local foundation in the San Francisco Bay Area, created a Primary Prevention Advisory Committee composed of mental health leaders to advise the foundation on its prevention funding strategies. The group concluded that child care centers could serve as places to offset crises and promote the family. They chose to develop PSP programs in four publicly funded child care programs serving at-risk families. These programs provided the flexibility to adapt parent services in ways appropriate to the population they served. In just a year and a half, this project expanded to four other state-funded centers. Currently there are eleven PSP centers in the Bay Area, six in the California Central Valley, and six in Florida. Replication has begun with the Neighborhood Child Care Network of Save the Children in Atlanta, Georgia, and the Pacific Oaks College/Pasadena Unified School District partnership in California. The PSP staff provides three to four training sessions a year, with on-site follow-up training. "The trainees then become the trainers for their site and begin to train others in their area," states Seiderman.

Money for these programs comes from foundations. The Zellerbach Family Fund continues to be a supporter, as is the San Francisco Foundation, the Ford Foundation, the Marin Community Foundation, the Haigh Scatena Foundation, Mervyn's, and the Walter S. Johnson Foundation.

The PSP philosophy is:

> The child care agencies that comprise the Parent Services Project recognize that the well-being and sense of significance of the parent is of central importance to the development of the child. In a cooperative and supportive relationship, the agencies' staffs and the parents participate in activities, services and events that respond to parents' needs in order to give them greater opportunities for richer, more enjoyable lives. Parents who possess a sense of fulfillment will enrich their children's lives, take more active roles in their communities and strengthen their families, adding to the overall quality of life. (Parent Services Project brochure)

The goal of direct service is to raise the parents' sense of importance, diminish feelings of isolation, increase their parenting skills, and help them secure the resources they need for themselves and their families.

The greatest obstacle is the lack of public awareness of and support for programs of this nature. For this reason, PSP is working to build support for the concept of family-centered programming, training others to replicate the program, and assisting community, state, and national policymakers to understand how much they can achieve by making funding commitments that promote the health and well-being of the family.

CONCLUSION

These program examples make it clear that it takes a committed individual or group of individuals to develop comprehensive family-centered child care. Such individuals have one characteristic in common: a deep and genuine respect for the parents and children with whom they work. This respect entails listening to and observing family needs, then custom designing a program in response. The program is ever changing as family issues change. The parents are not recipients but active participants in the design and delivery of services. The champions are able to garner financial and public support to fashion their programs. They reach out into the community, building links. They persevere when there is opposition and, in doing so, they create collaborations.

Family-centered child care has economic as well as psychological benefits. The focus on prevention will undoubtedly save money. The provision of good quality care and early education is, likewise, a cost-effective investment. Furthermore, creating social service linkages prevents unnecessary duplication among service providers.

Although the examples we have chosen serve those families with the greatest needs, they represent our vision of what the child care system of the twenty-first century should look like for all families. Child care programs should be family centered, supported by an adequate community infrastructure of services and funding. But family centeredness begins with a different way of feeling about and interacting with families. It means making existing interactions between parents and teachers, such as parent-teacher conferences and parent education events, more family-friendly.

How quickly will this concept catch on? How widely will it spread? We cannot say, but it is clearly a trend that makes sense for programs and the families they serve.

Acknowledgment

The authors thank Mary Beth Ostendorf Harvey for her excellent work in locating, interviewing, and writing up the case studies of family-centered child care programs.

Program Addresses

Gail Nelson, Executive Director
Carole Robertson Center
2020 West Roosevelt
Chicago, IL 60608

Cheryl Mitchell and Susan Harding, Co-Directors
Addison County Parent/Child Center, Inc.
Box 646
11 Seminary Street
Middlebury, VT 05753

Ethel Seiderman, Director
Parent Services Project, Inc.
Fairfax-San Anselmo Children's Center
199 Porteous Avenue
Fairfax, CA 94930

REFERENCES

Andrews, S. R., Blumenthal, J. M., Bachs, W. L., & Weiner, G. (1975, May). *The New Orleans model: Parents as early childhood educators.* Paper presented at the biennial meeting of the Society for Pediatric Research. (ERIC Document Reproduction No. ED 104 522)

Barbrack, C. R., & Horton, D. M. (1970). *Educational intervention in the home and paraprofessional career development: A second-generation mother study with emphasis on costs and benefits.* Mimeographed. Nashville, TN: DARCEE, George Peabody College.

Benedek, T. (1970). Parenthood during the life cycle. In E. J. Antony & T. Benedek (Eds.), *Parenthood: Its psychology and psychopathology* (pp. 185–206). Boston: Little Brown.

Boukydis, C. F. Z. (1982). Support groups for parents with premature infants in NICU's. In R. E. Marshall, C. Kasman & L. S. Cape (Eds.), *Coping with and caring for sick newborns* (pp. 215–222). Philadelphia: Saunders.

Bronfenbrenner, U. (1979). *The ecology of human development: Experiments by nature and design.* Cambridge, MA: Harvard University Press.

Feeney, S., Christensen, D., & Moravcik, E. (1983). *Who am I in the lives of children?* Columbus, OH: Merrill.

Galinsky, E. (1987). *The six stages of parenthood.* Reading, MA: Addison-Wesley.

Galinsky, E. (1988). Parents and teacher-caregivers: Sources of tension, sources of support. *Young Children, 43*(3), 4–12.

Galinsky, E., & Friedman, D. E. (in press). *Education before school: Investing in quality child care.* New York: Committee for Economic Development.

Galinsky, E., Shinn, B., Phillips, D., Howes, C., & Whitebook, M. (1990). *The parent/teacher study.* New York: Families and Work Institute.

Garbarino, J., & Sherman, D. (1980). High-risk neighborhoods and high-risk families: The human ecology of child maltreatment. *Child Development, 51,* 188–198.

Gordon, T. J., & Guinagh, B. J. (1974). *A home learning center approach to early stimulation.* Final Report. (ERIC Document Reproduction No. ED 11S 388)

Gottlieb, B. H. (1983). *Social support strategies.* Beverly Hills, CA: Sage.

Kogan, K. L., & Gordon, B. N. (1975). A mother-instruction program: Documenting change in mother-child interactions. *Child Psychiatry and Human Development, 5,* 189–200.

Kontos, S. J. (1984). Congruence of parent and early childhood staff perceptions of parenting. *Parenting Studies, 1,* 5–10.

Kontos, S. J. (1987). The attitudinal context of family day care relationships. In D. Peters & S. J. Kontos (Eds.), *Continuity and discontinuity of experience in child care* (pp. 91–113). *Annual Advances in Applied Development Psychology,* vol. 2. Norwood, NJ: Ablex.

Kontos, S. J., Raikes, H., & Woods, A. (1983). Early childhood staff attitudes toward their parent clientele. *Child Care Quarterly, 12,* 45–58.

Kontos, S. J., & Wells, W. (1986). Attitudes of caregivers and the day care experiences of families. *Early Childhood Research Quarterly, 1*(1), 47–67.

Lally, J. R., Mangione P. L., & Honig, A. S. (1987). *The Syracuse University family development research program: Long range impact of early intervention on low-income children and their families.* San Francisco: Center for Child and Family Studies, Far West Laboratory for Educational Research and Development.

Leler, M., Johnson, D. L., Kahn, A. J., Hines, R. P., & Torres, M. (1975, April). *The Houston model for parent education.* Paper presented at the biennial meeting of the Society for Research in Child Development, Denver.

Levenstein, P. (1974). *A message from home: A home-based intervention method for low income preschoolers.* (ERIC Document Reproduction No. ED 095 992)

Lightfoot, S. L. (1975). Families and schools: Creative conflict or negative dissonance? *Journal of Research and Development in Education, 9,* 34–44.

Littel, J. H. (1985, November). *Research in family support programs.* Paper prepared for the National Association of Social Workers Conference, Chicago.

Mann, M. (1970). *The effects of a preschool language program on two-year-old children and their mothers.* Final Report. (ERIC Document Reproduction No. ED 045 224)

McCubbin, H. T., & Patterson, J. M. (1981). Broadening the scope of family strengths: An emphasis on family coping and social support. In N. Stinnett, J. DeFrain, K. Kind, P. Knaub & G. Rowe (Eds.), *Family strengths: 3 roots of well-being* (pp. 177–194). Lincoln, NE: University of Nebraska Press.

Parent Post. (1990). Publication of Parent Action, P.O. Box 1719, Washington, DC 20013-1719.

Parent Services Project (brochure). Fairfax-San Anselmo Children's Center, 199 Porteous Avenue, Fairfax, CA 94930.

Pizzo, P. (1987). Parent-to-parent support groups: Advocates for social change. In S. L. Kagan, D. R. Powell, B. Weissbourd & E. F. Zigler (Eds.), *America's family support programs* (pp. 228–242). New Haven, CT: Yale University Press.

Sandler, H. M., Dokecki, P. R., Stewart, L. T., Britton, V., & Horton, D. M. (1973). The evaluation of a home-based educational intervention for preschoolers and their mothers. *Journal of Community Psychology, 1,* 372–374.

Slaughter, D. T. (1983). Early intervention and its effects on maternal and child development. *Monographs of the Society for Research in Child Development, 48* (4, Serial No. 202).

Spiegel, J. (1982). An ecological model of ethnic families. In M. McGoldrick, J. K. Pearce & J. Giordano (Eds.), *Ethnicity and family therapy* (pp. 31–51). New York: Guilford.

Wandersman, L. P. (1987). New directions for parent education. In S. L. Kagan, D. R. Powell, B. Weissbourd & E. F. Zigler (Eds.), *America's family support programs* (pp. 207–227). New Haven, CT: Yale University Press.

Weiss, H. (1979). *Parent support and education: An analysis of the Brookline early education project.* Unpublished E.D. dissertation, Harvard University Graduate School of Education.

CHAPTER 5

Meeting the Needs of Special Populations in Child Care

K. Eileen Allen

A special population, as used here, is a term that refers to children who have similar developmental differences that distinguish them from what is considered the norm in the child population at large. Figures on how many children are part of special populations vary from 3% to 15% of the total child population. Fraas (1986) estimates the number to be 10.9% of all school-age children. Special populations include children who have physical or sensory impairments, such as limited vision or hearing, motor disabilities, chronic health or neurological conditions, or behavior disorders. A special child population also may be composed of children who are at risk for serious developmental problems incurred prenatally, at the time of birth, or during the early months or years of life. With many of these children, adverse biological and environmental events become intertwined and compounded to the extent that the original problem, whatever it may have been, is nearly impossible to identify. Such children could be viewed as members of several special populations. Gifted children, the unusually bright or talented, also may be regarded as a special population, though these children are not necessarily free of handicapping conditions.

DEMOGRAPHICS

The last decade has witnessed a marked increase in actual numbers of impaired infants and young children and an accompanying increase in the need for child care services for these children. In many cases, the cause of a child's problems is readily identified, often beginning with prematurity and low birth weight, either of which put an infant at risk for developmental problems. The greater incidence of these conditions can be correlated, in large part, with a disturbing increase in the number of children born into poverty. Poor nutrition, substandard housing or homelessness, and lack of medical care before, during, and after birth not only put infants at high risk for developmental problems, but add to the severity of the problems a child may be born with. These children experience far greater family stress, maternal depression, and lack of social support as well more serious consequences from biological risk conditions than do children from families who are not so severely burdened. In summing this up, Kaplan-Sanoff, Parker, and Zuckerman (1991) note that children living in poverty experience double jeopardy. As an example of double jeopardy, they cite lead poisoning: Children growing up in poor urban neighborhoods are far more likely to be exposed to toxic levels of lead from such things as old lead-based paint on walls and window sills and to be in greater peril because of the disorganized family environments that permit such exposure to occur.

Still another cause of the marked increase in developmental problems and the need for special child care services is increasing maternal alcohol consumption, either alone or in combination with other drugs. The developmental deviations associated with maternal substance abuse are compounded by the likelihood of infections (especially AIDS and HIV) and their long-term impact on a child before and after birth. To further complicate the developmental picture, the primary concern of addicted mothers is not caring for their infants or children but getting the drugs they have come to depend on. This preoccupation often leads to poor infant-mother attachment, neglect, and placement of the child in out-of-home caregiving facilities.

LEGISLATION

The sociopolitical demand for early identification and treatment of developmental irregularities in infants and young children is a major policy factor in the increased need for early childhood programs. Legislation passed in 1986, Public Law (P.L.) 99-457, contains important early childhood amendments to the precedent-setting P.L. 94-142, the Education for All Handicapped Children Act, enacted in 1975. P.L. 99-457 allows states to serve families and infants from birth to age three who have or are at risk for developmental problems. Even more decisively, the law requires that all three- to six-year-old children with developmental problems receive educational services geared to their special needs, and that they be served in the *least restrictive environ-*

ment (LRE). To the maximum extent possible, these children are to be integrated into early education and child care programs with children who are developing normally. That ruling is the crux of the *main-streaming* concept. A comprehensive review of recent research (Guralnick, 1990) documents the benefits of mainstreaming for all children, assuming the availability of quality programs where teachers and families are supported by the interdisciplinary child study team required by law. In any event, families with children with disabilities must be provided the same child care and early education options as all other families (McLean & Hanline, 1990).

Developmental disabilities (the preferred term to describe the problems of young, atypical children), as defined in Part H of P.L. 99-457, are problems in development as measured by appropriate diagnostic instruments and occurring in one or more of the following developmental areas: cognitive, physical, language and speech, psychosocial, or self-help skills. *Developmental delay* refers to a diagnosed physical or mental condition with a high probability of seriously interfering with a child's developmental progress. The law stipulates that the term *developmental delay* is to be defined specifically by each state. The term *at risk* is defined as referring to those children likely to experience substantial developmental delays if appropriate services are not provided.

Implications for Child Care Staff

With full implementation of P.L. 99-457, all early childhood teachers in all kinds of early education and child care programs will work with children with developmental delays and disabilities. This does not imply that teachers will need special education degrees or extensive retraining. Teachers will need thorough and up-to-date knowledge on the range and variations of normal growth and development. With that foundation, they can apply specific information about a given disability as each special child joins the group. The law mandates that programs for children with special needs have ongoing interdisciplinary support from the team members most relevant to each child's disabilities, be it a communications specialist, physical or occupational therapist, or health and nutrition practitioner, to name but a few. These professionals, skilled in working with children and families with developmental problems, can share intervention strategies and impart practical knowledge to teachers. Once involved in the process, teachers find that they seldom have trouble fitting therapeutic activities for special children into the basic developmental curriculum in ways that are compatible with everyday classroom practices.

Communicating effectively with parents is especially important when working with children with developmental disabilities. Parents need special understanding and special help as they cope, day after day, with ongoing stress, all-too-frequent emergencies, and the financial strains that often accompany a child's disability (Griffel, 1991). Teachers benefit too from good communication between home and school. Parents have much to share with teachers about what their children can do, what approaches are effective in working with their children, and what pleases their children.

Adapting physical space and curriculum activities to individual needs is a major aspect of working with special children. This, however, is what most early childhood teachers thrive on. They are trained to meet developmental diversity among children through individualized planning based on systematic observations of each child in the context of the program. An observant teacher, noting a child who cannot quite connect with a small ball when trying to kick it, provides a larger ball or a steadying hand, or both. Such responding is the essence of a sound early learning environment and the dominant theme in developmental and adaptive programming (Allen & Hart, 1984).

SPECIAL POPULATIONS

The special populations discussed in this chapter are grouped as follows:

- Children with health or orthopedic impairments
- Children with vision or hearing disorders
- Children with speech or language problems
- Children with behavior disorders
- Children with learning problems
- Children who are abused
- Children with AIDS or children born into substance-abusing families
- Children who are gifted and talented

Classification Issues

Before overviewing particular populations, a few general statements must be made about the terms *emotionally disturbed* and *mentally retarded*. Putting either of those labels on a young child is premature, nonfunctional, often fallacious, and likely to become a self-fulfilling prophecy. Early development is characterized by change;

classifying a young child in either of the above ways is developmentally inappropriate because it suggests a fixed condition. Experience plays an enormous, if not dominant, role in determining both emotional and cognitive outcomes in children. Therefore, the terms *behavior disorders* and *behavior problems* (with the implication that new experiences will allow new and better behaviors to be learned in their stead) will be used rather than emotionally disturbed. As for mental status, even though a child may be behind age-mates in cognitive skills, teachers design programs for that child in terms of his or her immediate abilities. Here an important teaching concept comes into play, the "problem of the match" (Hunt, 1961): providing activities familiar enough to attract a child's active engagement but having motivating or novel elements just a bit beyond the child's level of functioning.

Other special populations that will not be discussed separately are those associated with inborn errors of metabolism such as phenylketonuria (PKU) and galactosemia, or the various syndromes such as Down, Turner, or Prader-Willi. Children with these conditions are first of all children. Thus, if a child with Down syndrome has recurring ear infections with an intermittent hearing loss, speech problems, and a tendency toward obesity, it is these conditions that call for special intervention and individualized programming rather than the fact that the child has Down syndrome.

Health or Orthopedic Impairments

Children with health or orthopedic problems account for approximately 2% of all children with handicaps. P.L. 94-142 defines health impairments as conditions that contribute to a child's limited strength, vitality, or alertness due to chronic or acute health problems. Illnesses that early childhood teachers are most likely to encounter include leukemia, cystic fibrosis, diabetes, epilepsy, hemophilia, heart conditions, asthma, and sickle-cell anemia. Obesity and malnourishment may be considered health problems in that both interfere with a child's vitality. Autism, though typically viewed as a behavior disorder, is sometimes seen as a health problem. Orthopedic impairments involve muscles, joints, and skeletal structure; included are missing limbs, congenital hip dislocations or club feet, damage from diseases such as tuberculosis of the bone or polio, and neurological disorders such as cerebral palsy. Health and orthopedic problems often occur together and may be accompanied by neurological involvement. For example, a child with cerebral palsy often has ongoing health problems, limited mobility, and a nonprogressive neurological condition.

Health Problems.   Teachers, when first called upon to work with children with health problems, may feel anxious, inept, fearful of doing the wrong thing. The best way to gain confidence and a sense of control is to have adequate information about each child's condition. "When you know what to do — whether it is taking a temperature, performing CPR, or keeping a child relaxed during an asthma attack — both you and the child are going to profit from your knowledge" (Kendrick, Kaufmann & Messenger, 1988, p. 20). Information about managing a child's illness comes from parents, from members of the interdisciplinary team, and from each individual child's health records. The records need to be updated frequently and contain complete, current, and specific information about the child and his or her medication schedule.

Teachers are not required to give medication, though most are willing to do so if it enables a child to stay in a program. When a child with an unfamiliar medical problem is enrolled, teachers need advance briefing as well as ongoing consultation during and following the child's settling-in period. Children with health problems tend to be fairly reliable about monitoring their limitations, to know when "enough is enough." Nevertheless, parents, clinicians, and teachers need to exchange information regularly so as to match and rematch curriculum activities to a child's current health status.

Planning for emergencies is an essential part of early childhood programs. For children with health problems, special emergency measures are formulated with the child's parents and perhaps the physician or nurse. What to do during and following a crisis and when to call for aid are important issues, as is information about the frequency of and precipitating factors in a child's health crises. Teachers also need to learn to recognize the early signs of an impending crisis — how a child behaves *before* as well as during and after an episode. Every crisis must be reported to parents and entered, with the date and the teacher's initials, on the child's health record.

Orthopedic Problems.   Orthopedic disabilities take many forms, from misshapen fingers, to crippling cases of cerebral palsy, to spinal injuries that may or may not include lack of bowel and bladder control. In spite of their differences, children with orthopedic problems have common needs. It is especially important to have a developmental therapist on the interdisciplinary team whose pediatric training is a meld of occupational and physical therapy. This professional recommends (and often provides) adaptive equipment and materials such as mobility devices in the form of crutches, braces, walkers, or "tummy boards" that allow the child to move about; positioning equipment such as wedges, bolsters, and prone boards to help children achieve varying degrees of body control; and chairs designed to assist children in gaining enough trunk, head, and neck control to maintain a sitting position and allow them to reach, grasp, and learn by manipulating objects. (NOTE: *Teachers do not introduce positioning devices or initiate positioning activities except in collaboration with an accredited specialist.*)

Everyday preschool materials are easily adapted to the needs of children with motor problems by an observant teacher who is willing to exercise a touch of ingenuity. Play boards fitted with such things as bolts, locks, switches, and telephone dials can be mounted on the wall for easy access by a child in a wheelchair. For children with uncertain fine motor control, teachers can push pencils, crayons, and colored pens through a small rubber ball and tape the child's paper to the table to prevent slipping and rumpling. To facilitate self-feeding, suction devices can be put under the plate or bowl to keep it from slipping, and the spoon handle can be built up with foam rubber, enabling the child to hang on to it better. In every instance, major goals are to facilitate children's maximum, yet safe, participation in program activities and to help children learn to do as much as possible for themselves so the disability does not dominate their lives.

Vision or Hearing Disorders

Vision and hearing problems account for less than 2% of all developmental disabilities; vision impairments account for approximately .5%, hearing impairments for a little more than 1%. Infants and young children with severe vision or hearing problems need the services of specially trained professionals who will work with the family. During infancy, this often takes place in the home setting; later it can occur outside the home in a special program, in a regular preschool, or in a dual enrollment. The developmental needs of children who are blind or deaf are similar to those of other children. Beginning in the toddler years, most benefit from a dual enrollment — part time in a special class and part time in a mainstreamed setting.

Vision Impairments. For educational purposes, the American Foundation for the Blind describes visually disabled individuals as either *blind* or *partially sighted*. Children classified as blind have a vision loss so severe that they cannot be educated by reading print; instead, they must use braille and various electronic devices. Children who are partially sighted have limited vision but can read large print under special conditions and can use certain other visual materials.

Impaired vision affects every aspect of development. Substantial delays in localizing sounds and in exploring the environment through reaching, crawling, and walking deprive the child of essential early learning opportunities (Fraiberg, 1977). The inability to seek out and play with everything in visual range, as normally developing children do, is also a grave deterrent to development. Fewell (1983) points out that when sighted infants begin deliberately reaching for nearby objects, blind babies remain passive and continue to hold their hands in the shoulder-high position typical of very young infants. They also exercise fewer social options since they are not visually stimulated by the play going on around them. Facilitating exploration and play becomes a major program challenge for all who care for children with visual impairments (Fewell & Kaminski, 1989). By preschool age, assuming earlier participation in a sound infant-toddler-parent intervention program, most blind and partially sighted children function well in an adequately staffed mainstream program. Teachers need the help of a vision consultant or resource teacher in arranging curriculum activities that will engage whatever residual vision the child may have and will stimulate use of the other sensory modalities such as hearing, touch, taste, and smell. The consultant also can help teachers learn to be less protective of a child who cannot see, to understand that he or she must be allowed to explore the environment and learn to weather the occasional mishap. A safe environment is essential if a child with a vision loss is to develop confidence in moving about independently. To this end, the classroom must be kept free of clutter, obstacles, and "surprises" such as changes in room or yard arrangements for which the child is not prepared.

Teachers work, almost incidentally, throughout the program day on promoting basic developmental skills in children with impaired vision. Acquiring orientation and mobility skills is a top priority. Vision-impaired children learn these skills readily when teachers familiarize each child with the classroom layout and use identifying materials and sound makers in strategic spots: a wind chime near the draft from the play yard door, a circle of textured fabric pasted on the child's locker, a piece of ribbed matting in front of the main door. Teachers also talk about everything a child is engaged with, giving the names, over and over again, of common objects as each is encountered. Understanding is further increased by encouraging the child to manipulate objects while hearing the accompanying action words and labels: "You are *stirring* the *applesauce* with a *spoon*." As needed, teachers provide physical prompts and hand-over-hand demonstrations such as physically and verbally putting the child through the applesauce stirring.

Screening tests cannot be relied on to identify vision problems in young children. A child may have passed a vision screening test not because of intact vision but because of unintentional coaching by the screener, or because the child, unnoticed, peeked around the occluder supposedly covering one eye. Children's caregivers are often the first to suspect a vision problem. Various behaviors may indicate possible trouble: a child shutting or covering one eye, tilting or thrusting the head forward, squinting or squeezing eyelids together, or frowning excessively (Marotz, Rush & Cross, 1989).

Hearing Impairments. For educational purposes, children with hearing problems are classified in two ways: as *deaf*, meaning a loss so severe that the child cannot hear spoken language even with maximum amplification; or as *hard of hearing*, a less severe loss, but one that is likely to have a negative impact on development. Generally speaking, the greater the loss, the greater the interference with overall development; the earlier the loss, the more pervasive the interference. Infants born with little or no hearing (congenital deafness) are more severely affected than children whose loss occurs after they have learned to talk. However, most congenitally deaf children do learn to communicate. Many learn lipreading, more accurately called speechreading; later they learn fingerspelling or one of several signing systems. (Learning to sign is also a great learning experience and a fun activity for children and teachers with intact hearing). Whether signing and speechreading go forward in a regular preschool classroom is determined by the type of program prescribed for a given child. Decades of controversy surrounds the programming issue. The decision about signing, speaking, or a combination must be made by parents. Teachers accept the parents' decision and work with them and the deaf education specialist in providing suitable classroom activities (Cooke, Tessier & Armbruster, 1987).

Long-lasting problems in deaf children may be the result of restricted play opportunities after two years of age. Until then, their play seems much like other children's; differences show up when language begins to be an integral part of the activities. Increasingly, the hearing-impaired child is left out of play interactions; his or her play becomes progressively more solitary and less imaginative (Gregory, 1976). Cognitive, language, and social development suffer. The child may remain a passive and silent observer unless adults take specific responsibility for helping him or her understand and become involved in everyday activities (Peterson, 1987).

Children with hearing impairments are likely to benefit from mainstreamed group experiences if the staff receives support from an early childhood deaf education specialist who helps to tailor the program and the teaching strategies to the child's special needs. The specialist's recommendations tend to be simply good early childhood practices. They include such things as teachers sitting, kneeling, or bending down to the child's level while talking to the child; looking directly at the child; speaking the child's name or touching the child to direct his or her attention; and gesturing, when appropriate. Too much gesturing is to be avoided, however. Excessive hand and facial movements distract young children learning to speechread; they interfere, too, with hearing children's early efforts to process spoken language auditorily rather than visually. Demonstrations are an important teaching strategy with young deaf children, who tend to catch on more readily when the teacher points to what is being talked about, holds the object up, and demonstrates how it is to be used. Sewing cards, for example, are one of many preschool materials that children, hearing impaired or not, master with less frustration when teachers demonstrate the "how-to."

Amplification devices, hearing aids of various kinds, help when the problem is in the outer or middle ear (conductive loss). Wearing a hearing aid, however, does not guarantee that a young child is hearing. Parents and teachers must check several times a day to be sure that the child has not turned the device off, the earmold is still in place, and the battery has not died.

Speech or Language Problems

Approximately a quarter of all developmental problems involve speech and language disorders. Speech and language are two very different processes that combine to allow individuals a common communication system. Speech is the audible aspect, the ability to produce or articulate the sounds of the language. Language is a symbol system with arbitrary rules of grammar (syntax) and word meanings (semantics) that allow individuals to express ideas, feelings, and thoughts to others who use the same code. The meshing of speech and language involves the interplay of complex physiological and psychological behaviors: crying, babbling, and self-echoing that progresses to first words, then to abbreviated utterances that stand for entire thoughts (holophrastic and telegraphic speech). By six years of age, most children have a vocabulary of 14,000 or more words and are in control of the basic grammar of their language.

Speech Disorders. Young children, 80% or more, experience speech irregularities in one form or another. These include common articulation errors and dysfluencies: omission of sounds, substitutions, and additions (for example, horshie for horsie); excessive repetition of particular sounds or words; prolonged hesitations between words and long drawn-out sounds. It is as if the child's ability to formulate thoughts and express ideas were outrunning, temporarily, the ability to reliably pronounce words correctly or get them into conventional order. Common speech irregularities seldom turn into a major problem unless the child is pressured to change, to slow down, to "think before speaking." Teachers help most when they practice what Rieke, Lynch, and Soltman (1977) term "benevolent neglect," accepting common errors. If speech and language skills are to improve, children must keep talking; frequent criticism results in less talk. Rieke et al. suggest: "Never force a child to repeat anything that you have understood" (1977, p. 43). In those rare instances when a child's speech is truly incomprehensible, the help of a speech clinician who specializes in young children is essential.

Healthy newborns arrive with a potential for language; they begin to exercise it with their first cries. From there, language skills seem to develop almost spontaneously during everyday routines, play activities, and casual social exchanges. When language acquisition is sidetracked or seriously delayed, all aspects of a child's development are likely to suffer. Intervention procedures should be carried out within the context of play activities with other children in a normal language environment so as to foster both immediate and long-range developmental progress. Without early intervention, the consequences of speech and language deficits may persist for years (Warren & Kaiser, 1989).

Language Problems. Language skills develop rapidly between two and five years of age. During these years most children acquire a large expressive vocabulary and an even larger receptive vocabulary (children always understand much more than they can talk about). They learn to ask who, what, where, and why questions, to convert positives to negatives, and to engage in other syntactic complexities. Accompanying this amazing progression are several kinds of so-called errors, which actually are grammatical misconstructions representing children's accurate knowledge of grammatical rules. Children who say "runned" instead of "ran" are using a rule they learned earlier about applying "ed" to a verb to indicate a past event. Thus, they are not wrong; what they now need is a new learning: when not to apply the rule. In response to such misconstructions, the adult simply uses the correct form: "Yes, the kitten ran away." Under such unpressured conditions, the irregularities are usually self-correcting.

The mainstreamed early childhood classroom can be ideally suited to enhancing language skills in all children, including those with serious delays or disorders. The requirements are commonplace but essential: plenty of things for children to talk about such as interesting materials, varied indoor and outdoor experiences, occasional excursions, books, stories, and age-appropriate games of all kinds. There must be many opportunities for children to talk woven into all program activities; and most important, teachers must expect children to talk. With children who have severe language delays, teachers respond to noises, gestures, grimaces, even eye contact as the child's first efforts at communicating.

Language develops best in a relaxed environment in which less verbal children feel that they have ample time to say what they want to say, and talkative children are helped to not dominate. Highly verbal children need to learn the art of listening. Many teachers also need to practice this skill. Being a good listener does not imply that teachers are not good responders — just that they refrain from talking too much. In an effective early language learning environment, there is a great deal of talking going on, but the children are doing most of it. Child language research indicates that the more a child talks, the better the child talks: Quality is highly correlated with quantity (Hart & Risley, 1980). Teachers serve best as facilitators — prompting, asking questions, reflecting audibly on what a child says, and making an occasional comment indicating interested listening.

English as a Second Language (ESL). Discriminating between children with language delays or disorders and children whose primary language is nonstandard English is essential. The latter population is made up of young children for whom English is, or is becoming, their second language. These children do not constitute a special population in terms of a developmental disability. Yet many of the same principles that apply to children acquiring their native language apply to helping children acquire a second language (or alternative dialect). Teachers refrain from reprimanding, pressuring, or excessively correcting, and they expect children to talk, talk, talk in their native language and in the language they are learning.

Behavior Disorders

The term behavior disorder can refer to a variety of social and emotional behaviors labeled by one group or another as socially inappropriate or maladaptive. Spodek, Saracho, and Lee (1984) define behavior disorders as "deviations from age-appropriate behavior that significantly interfere with the child's own development or with the lives

of others" (p. 12). In young children, the concern may not be so much
the behavior itself as how much of it the child engages in. Every normally developing child engages in inappropriate behavior on occa-
sion—throwing food, having a tantrum, hitting playmates, or careen-
ing about heedless of consequences. Such actions are a firsthand way of
learning to discriminate between acceptable and unacceptable behavior. Rarely are they cause for concern unless they become excessive.
The definition of excessive varies and is influenced by the values of those
making the judgment. A rule of thumb is that an excessive behavior is
one that interferes markedly with a child's (or other children's) ability
to engage productively in classroom activities (Allen, 1991). Thus, a
four-year-old who occasionally whines and cries over minor frustrations
is not likely to worry teachers; another four-year-old who whines and
cries several times a day over minor frustrations may be of considerable
concern.

An often repeated quip is that there are as many ways of classifying
emotionally atypical behaviors as there are psychologists. Notwith-
standing, certain terms have become popular for classifying behavior
disorders: *attention-deficit hyperactive disorders*, *conduct disorders*,
and *pervasive developmental disorders*.

Attention-Deficit Hyperactivity Disorders (ADHDs).   The American Psychiatric Association (1980) suggests that there are two types of
attention-deficit disorders: ADHD, or hyperactivity expressed mainly
by excessive motor activity, and ADD, or hyperactivity characterized
primarily by difficulty in concentrating. A number of the behaviors in
each category tend to be similar, and many are overlapping. Few young
children (1% to 3%) are truly hyperactive in terms of neurological or
organic causes. This explains the failure of special diets or medications
to "cure" most cases of hyperactivity.

Teachers usually can help excessively active children by reassessing
and revitalizing the classroom program. The first issue is program activities. Are they interesting, lively, and varied in terms of activity level?
Are they attractively presented and fun? The next issue is the problem
of the match. Are activities geared to the child's skill level to the extent
that frustrations are reduced? Are both success and challenge inherent
in each activity? The final issue: Is the child getting the teacher's attention when focused on an activity (even briefly) rather than when flitting
about? A number of case studies demonstrate that hyperactivity decreases markedly when developmentally appropriate activities and an
individualized behavior management plan are blended with teachers'

systematic observations and caring concern for an overly active child (Allen & Goetz, 1982).

Conduct Disorders. In young children, conduct disorders (defined as undersocialization by the American Psychiatric Association, 1980) include aggressiveness, noncompliance, disruptive behaviors, and severe tantrums. These behaviors seem to be somewhat evenly distributed among normally developing children and children with developmental problems or delays (Drotar & Sturm, 1991). Any child in any early childhood program who is too frequently physically aggressive toward other children or adults must learn more acceptable ways of expressing anger and frustration. Should a child with frequent and seriously aggressive behaviors be maintained in a group situation? When a classroom situation gives rise to such a question, teachers and parents must confront ethical issues related to both inclusion and exclusion (Feeney, 1988). According to Caldwell (1988), it is probably a tactical error to take the child out of the group until his or her behavior improves, because many of the outbursts are likely to stem from events within the group itself. In any event, the hurtful behaviors must be stopped, even in children who are viewed as delayed either emotionally or cognitively. All children can learn to conform to basic social expectations. Teachers who fail to provide opportunities for such learning are being unfair to the disruptive child, who will be disliked and rejected by other children, which often leads to further outpourings of aggression.

Behavior problems, for the most part, can be managed through systematic rearrangement of the learning environment—space, routines, materials, grouping of children, and specific redirection of adult attention to all the good things that even a highly disruptive child engages in (Allen, 1991; Allen & Hart, 1984). In extreme instances, when nothing seems to work, brief time-out periods may be needed. Time-out is a temporary expedient that is planned among teachers and parents and described matter-of-factly, in advance, to the child. It is used only when absolutely necessary, and always in tandem with program rearrangements. The rearrangements must be backed up by teachers' acceptance and understanding of the child's stresses and their renewed focus on the child's approximations to more desirable behaviors.

Pervasive Developmental Disorders. Schizophrenia, autism, and phobias are developmental disorders that characterize only a small population of children. Because the onset is usually in later childhood, preschool teachers are not likely to encounter schizophrenia. On the other hand, children with phobic reactions and children with autism are being enrolled with increasing frequency in community programs (usually after a child has begun to respond to treatment). Anxiety problems, overdependency, separation problems, and withdrawing from social contacts are found routinely among children in early childhood programs. Less frequent, but not uncommon, are older children with chronic soiling and wetting problems. There also may be an occasional case of pica — the eating of nonfood substances (some of which, like lead-based paint flakes, may be toxic to the point of causing mental retardation or death). In all these instances, the early childhood staff must have the support of relevant members of the interdisciplinary team.

Learning Disabilities

Technically, young children do not have learning disabilities because the condition is specific to reading, writing, and math activities. Nevertheless, most early childhood teachers note behaviors in certain children — distractibility, short attention span, sensorimotor confusions, atypical visual and auditory responses — that are similar to worrisome behaviors in older children who have been classified as learning disabled. Though labeling a young child as learning disabled is premature and nonfunctional, it is important to deal with these nonacademic problems before they worsen, become cumulative, and interfere with current learning opportunities as well as later school performance. A range of effective, research-based strategies for teaching young children with potential learning problems has been developed in the last ten years. These are described in considerable detail elsewhere (Allen, 1991; Allen & Hart, 1984; Bailey & Wolery, 1984; Cooke et al., 1987; Peterson, 1987; Thurman & Widerstrom, 1990).

Child Abuse

Child abuse and neglect includes any situation in which a child is unsafe because family or caregivers intentionally inflict physical pain or injury, fail to protect the child from hazardous situations, exploit the child sexually, or abuse the child emotionally or verbally. Abusive adults are found in all segments of society. Sexual and psychological abuse may be more difficult to recognize than physical abuse; nevertheless, sensitive caregivers who are skilled in observing children can usually spot a troubled child. It becomes their responsibility to seek immediate help. Every state requires mandatory reporting of all cases of suspected child abuse.

Abuse among children with developmental problems is greater than in the child population at large; the cause and effect of such abuse are not clear. In many cases, it is almost certain that the abuse caused the developmental problems. In other situations, the child's problems may have triggered a point at which a parent or caregiver lost control. An adult, abuse-prone or not, having to cope with the unremitting stresses related to caring for a handicapped youngster may eventually snap. Some impaired infants, for example, have a weak, high-pitched, inconsolable cry that seems to go on night and day. Such crying can put an infant-parent relationship in serious jeopardy (Frodi & Senchak, 1990). A parent may appear to be bearing up, but at one critical moment the incessant crying apparently becomes unbearable, and injury to the infant is the result. Crittenden (1989) suggests that most early childhood programs will have at least one child who is maltreated. Mainstreamed programs may have more. Infant and early childhood teachers must be aware of this greater potential for child abuse among families with handicapped children. Although teachers are a first line of contact (and support) as parents come and go with their special children, they will need assistance from specific interdisciplinary team members.

AIDS or Substance Abuse

In reviewing 20 years of early childhood history, Hymes (1991) indicates that certain groups of young children have been making headlines in the last decade (saddening headlines, it might be added). In Hymes's words:

> An estimated 375,000 "crack babies" — children whose mothers had used drugs during pregnancy — were born, a three- to four-fold increase over 1985. The number of young children with AIDS in 1988 was double that in 1987, making that disease the ninth leading cause of death among one- to four-year-old children. (p. 392)

Hymes goes on to quote the Centers for Disease Control, reporting that each year, 3,000 infants will be born with the AIDS virus, in addition to those who get the disease postnatally. Fetal alcohol syndrome (FAS) was the third headliner — 50,000 babies are born each year to mothers who consume alcohol during their pregnancies; it is estimated that FAS is responsible for 20% of all mental retardation. These alarming figures were substantiated in 1989 during hearings before the congressional Select Committee on Children, Youth, and Families, which noted, for example, that 15 of the hospitals surveyed reported that as many as one in five or six babies was born "hooked."

Maternal Alcohol, Drugs, and Other Substance Abuses. Children who are exposed in utero to maternal drug and alcohol ingestion are likely to exhibit one or more physical, neurological, or behavioral problems. The range and severity of fetal damage depends on each mother's biochemical reactions. One maternal system may tolerate very little usage before the unborn infant is affected; another system may tolerate considerably more. When a woman uses crack, cocaine, alcohol, or other chemical substances while pregnant, the physical and behavioral impact on her infant may include extreme irritability, tremors, seizures, difficulty in feeding, abnormal sleep patterns, and complex medical problems. As toddlers and preschoolers, these children often exhibit speech and language deficits, delayed and inappropriate play skills, and increasingly poor judgment (Dorris, 1989). Many also show stigmatizing physical features such as eye and facial malformations.

Children growing up in families where there is ongoing drug and alcohol use are in special need of consistent and trustworthy caregivers. As Robinson (1990) points out, the classroom may be the only place where the child can get away from the unpredictability of his or her chaotic home life. The classroom may also be the only place where the child encounters adults who make promises and keep them. Many of these children have a variety of learning and behavior problems due to early physical and neurological insult. At the same time, they have all the basic needs common to all young children, only more so. Especially urgent is nurturance from caring adults. Early childhood staffs must accept the charge of meeting the needs of these troubled children. Weston, Ivins, Zuckerman, Jones, and Lopez (1989) ask that this charge be carried even further: "The challenge for researchers and practitioners becomes one of learning how better to help drug-exposed infants with compromised capacities reach out to the world, and to support their families in creating a world worth reaching for" (p. 7).

AIDS and HIV. AIDS (and the human immunodeficiency virus, HIV) is likely to be of great concern to child care staff because of the fear of spread of the infection. This concern is rarely warranted, because the virus is transmitted primarily through intimate sexual contact, blood-to-blood contact as in the use of shared hypodermic needles, or contaminated blood used in transfusions. According to the American

Academy of Pediatrics (as cited by the NAEYC Information Service in response to a personal telephone query), no evidence points to the casual transmission of AIDS by means of children playing together, sitting together, or being together in group situations. The revisions in progress (personal communication, 1991) on the health handbook by Kendrick et al. (1988) include the recommendation that children with AIDS or HIV infection be permitted to participate in programs as long as their own health and developmental status allow them to benefit from participating. However, no child or adult, with or without AIDS, should be present if they have open, uncovered sores, any kind of bloody discharge, or diarrhea. Many children with AIDS experience progressive neurological disorders affecting motor, social, and cognitive functioning that hinder their participation in school (Bale, 1990). New information about AIDS and HIV is being generated almost daily; everyone working with children and their families must keep abreast of these new findings as they relate to infant and child care policies.

Children Who Are Gifted and Talented

Children who have unusual talents or appear to be intellectually advanced are often considered a special population. However, gifted and talented children are found among all populations of children — normally developing, developmentally disabled, and children reared in dysfunctional families or economic and educational impoverishment. Though theoretical constructs of intellectual and artistic giftedness vary, certain behavioral characteristics that are commonly associated with giftedness in young children have been identified. These include advanced verbal skills, elevated levels of curiosity and question asking, higher-order problem solving, greater ability to concentrate, and good recall or memory skills. Many children also show keen orientation skills, respond immediately to whatever is novel in the environment, exhibit a sense of humor by making up jokes and riddles, and exhibit greater empathy. (For a further discussion of traits related to giftedness in young children, see Roedel, Jackson & Robinson, 1980.)

Gifted Minority Children. Many of the above characteristics are related in one way or another to higher-order language skills. Thus, gifted children from minority cultures and differing ethnic or economic backgrounds may not be identified because their language skills do not match middle-class language skills. These children have no less potential, only less recognized ways of expressing their talents as well as fewer opportunities for verbal, intellectual, and artistic enhancement.

As Karnes and Johnson (1989) point out, no one can excel at anything unless given the opportunity to try. These authors argue further that underserving the gifted among low-income populations is a critical issue: To allow them to go "unnoticed and unnurtured is a tremendous waste of potential resources" (p. 50).

Gifted Children with Handicaps. Seldom do we search out giftedness among children with handicaps (Gallagher, 1988). True, giftedness may be difficult to identify in a child with developmental problems. Standard assessment instruments tend to miss even the basic strengths in such children and fail completely in identifying whatever unique talents they may have. A child with a learning disability may have superior intelligence, remarkable artistic abilities, or outstanding mechanical abilities that go unrecognized because they take an unfamiliar form or are obscured by the child's overriding problems. The same is true of the superior creative and intellectual potential of children with hearing or vision impairments, cerebral palsy, or other disabilities. Early childhood teachers must be trained specifically to identify and nurture giftedness in children of every developmental and social and economic level (Karnes & Johnson, 1989). According to these authors, a major task of early education is to foster in all children curiosity and an eagerness to learn so that no child's potential is allowed to wither.

CONCLUSION

Young children from special populations are being enrolled in child care programs in increasing numbers. Teachers' major charge is to recognize that a child is a child; young children with disabilities are more like normally developing children than they are different. They too require a caring, trustworthy, and stimulating learning environment. As Klein (1977) noted, any teacher who really understands young children can work with the handicapped. The National Association for the Education of Young Children (NAEYC) formalized this concept in its *Teacher Education Guidelines*: "all teachers must be trained to create environments and plan for individual needs of children, including children with disabilities and special abilities" (Bredekamp, 1982, p. 4). What most teachers find, as they acquire skill and confidence in working with children with developmental differences, is that they become better teachers of all children. They enjoy teaching more because the developmental diversity among children offers greater challenges and greater rewards.

REFERENCES

Abbott, C. F., & Gold, S. (1991). Conferring with parents when you're concerned that their child needs special services. *Young Children, 46*(4), 10–14.

Allen, K. E. (1991). *Mainstreaming in early childhood education.* Albany, NY: Delmar.

Allen, K. E., & Goetz, E. M. (1982). *Early childhood education: Special problems special solutions.* Rockville, MD: Aspen Systems.

Allen, K. E., & Hart, B. (1984). *The early years: Arrangements for learning.* Englewood Cliffs, NJ: Prentice-Hall.

Allen, K. E., & Marotz, L. R. (1989). *Developmental profiles: Birth to six.* Albany, NY: Delmar.

American Psychiatric Association. (1980). *Diagnostic and statistical manual of mental disorders* (3d ed.). Washington, DC: Author.

Bailey, D. B., & Wolery, M. (1984). *Teaching infants and preschoolers with handicaps.* Columbus, OH: Merrill.

Bale, J. F. Jr. (1990). The neurological complications of AIDS in infants and young children. *Topics in Early Childhood Special Education, 3*(2), 15–23.

Bee, H. (1989). *The developing child.* New York: Harper & Row.

Bredekamp, S. (Ed.) (1982). *Early childhood teacher education guidelines.* Washington, DC: National Association for the Education of Young Children.

Caldwell, B. M. (1988). Ethics commission member comments. *Young Children, 43*(2), 50.

Children's Defense Fund. (1991). *The state of America's children.* Washington, DC: Author.

Cooke, R. E., Tessier, A., & Armbruster, V. B. (1987). *Adapting early childhood curricula for children with special needs.* Columbus, OH: Merrill.

Crittenden, P. M. (1989). Teaching maltreated children in the preschool. *Topics in Early Childhood Special Education, 9*(2), 16–32.

Dorris, M. (1989). *The broken cord.* New York: Harper & Row.

Drotar, D., & Sturm, L. (1991). Mental health intervention with infants and young children with behavioral and developmental problems. *Infants and Young Children, 3*(4), 1–11.

Feeney, S. (1988). Ethics case studies: The aggressive child. *Young Children, 43*(2), 50–54

Fewell, R. R. (1983). Working with sensorily impaired children. In S. G. Garwood (Ed.), *Educating young handicapped children* (pp. 323–388). Rockville, MD: Aspen Systems.

Fewell, R. R., & Kaminski, R. (1989). Play skills development and instruction for young children with handicaps. In S. L. Odom & M. B. Karnes (Eds.), *Early intervention for infants and children with handicaps* (pp. 145–158). Baltimore: Paul H. Brookes.

Fraas, C. I. (1986). *Preschool programs for education of handicapped children* (Report No. 86-55 EPW). Washington, DC: Library of Congress.

Fraiberg, S. (1977). *Insights from the blind*. New York: Basic Books.

Freeman, J. (1981). The intellectually gifted. *New Directions for Gifted Children, 7*, 75–86.

Frodi, A., & Senchak, M. (1990). Verbal and behavioral responsiveness to the cries of atypical infants. *Child Development, 61*(1), 76–84.

Gallagher, J. J. (1988). National agenda for educating gifted students: Statement of priorities. *Exceptional Children, 55*(2), 107–114.

Gregory, H. (1976). *The deaf child and his family*. London: Allen & Unwin.

Griffel, G. (1991). Walking on a tightrope: Parents shouldn't have to go it alone. *Young Children, 46*(3), 40–42.

Guralnick, M. J. (1990). Major accomplishments and future directions in early childhood mainstreaming. *Topics in Early Childhood Special Education, 10*(2), 1–18.

Hart, B., & Risley, T. R. (1980). In vivo language training: Unanticipated and general effects. *Journal of Applied Behavior Analysis, 8*, 411–420.

Hunt, J. M. (1961). *Intelligence and experience*. New York: Ronald Press.

Hymes, J. L. (1991). *Twenty years in review*. Washington, DC: National Association for the Education of Young Children.

Kaplan-Sanoff, M., Parker, S., & Zuckerman, B. (1991). Poverty and early childhood development: What do we know and what should we do? *Infants and Young Children, 4*(1), 68–76.

Karnes, M., & Johnson, L. (1989). An imperative: Programming for the young gifted and talented. *Journal for the Education of the Gifted, 10*(3), 195–214.

Kendrick, A. S., Kaufmann, R., & Messenger, K. P. (Eds.). (1988). *Healthy young children*. Washington, DC: National Association for the Education of Young Children.

Klein, J. (1977). Head Start services to the handicapped: Mainstreaming the preschooler. *Head Start Newsletter, 9*(8).

Marotz, L. R., Rush, J. M., & Cross, M. Z. (1989). *Health, safety, and nutrition for the young child*. Albany, NY: Delmar.

McLean, M., & Hanline, M. F. (1990). Providing early intervention services in integrated environments: Challenges and opportunities for the future. *Topics in Early Childhood Special Education, 10*(2), 62–77.

Peterson, N. L. (1987). *Early intervention for handicapped and at-risk children*. Denver: Love.

Rieke, J. A., Lynch, L. L., & Soltman, S. L. (1977). *Teaching strategies for language development*. New York: Grune & Stratton.

Robinson, B. E. (1990). The teacher's role in working with children of alcoholic parents. *Young Children, 45*(4), 68–73.

Roedel, W. C., Jackson, N. E., & Robinson, H. B. (1980). *Gifted young children*. New York: Teachers College Press.

Spodek, B., Saracho, O. N., & Lee, R. C. (1984). *Mainstreaming young children*. Belmont, CA: Wadsworth.

Thurman, R. A., & Widerstrom, A. H. (1990). *Infants and young children with special needs: A developmental and ecological approach*. Baltimore: Paul H. Brookes.

Warren, S. F., & Kaiser, A. P. (1988). Research in early language intervention. In L. S. Odom & M. B. Karnes (Eds.), *Early intervention for infants and children with handicaps* (pp. 89–108). Baltimore: Paul H. Brookes.

Weston, D. R., Ivins, B., Zuckerman, B., Jones, C., & Lopez, R. (1989). Drug exposed babies: Research and clinical issues. *Zero to Three, 9*(5), 1–23.

CHAPTER 6

Caring for Children in a Diverse World

Patricia G. Ramsey

I grew up here in this town, and I used to know all of the families. But now there are so many new people, a lot from places like Cambodia and El Salvador. Sometimes I feel awkward talking to the parents, not knowing if we understand each other and whether or not they are comfortable with what we do here. With the kids it's easier, but even then I feel that I don't always know how to connect with them.

Things in this neighborhood are just getting worse and worse. Nobody has money. People are getting themselves killed, and everyone is scared to go out at night. At our day care center, we have almost no equipment, and the parks aren't safe. We are the best thing going for these kids, and we can't do half of what we should be doing!

In our family day care group, we have two children from families who recently came to this country. It is so exciting to watch them learn English, and we are all learning some words in Japanese and Spanish. The other children love to speak these new languages and the parents have taught us some songs as well. Having these two children has been challenging, but it has stretched all of us and enriched all of our experiences here.

These quotations illustrate some of the challenges that child care providers are confronting as they respond to the increasing ethnic diversity and economic polarization in this country. These anecdotal accounts reflect several national trends. According to Hodgkinson (1985), by the mid 1990s, 30% to 40% of all children in school will be members of groups formerly considered "minorities." Moreover, during the 1980s the gap between the wealthy and the poor widened considerably, particularly along predictable racial lines (Edelman, 1985; McLoyd, 1990). The diversity of backgrounds and needs affects relationships between caregivers and families and challenges many of the givens in child care programs. All aspects of programs, including their organization, staffing, curriculum, and types of parent involvement, are potentially affected by changes in the cultural, economic, and social environments.

This chapter focuses on several dimensions of diversity, including race, culture, socioeconomic status, and family composition. It also illustrates how a multicultural perspective can help child care providers understand children and families and more effectively meet the needs of a changing population. Specific examples are used to show how the structure and content of programs might vary across communities.

DIMENSIONS OF DIVERSITY

Families differ along many dimensions, including race, culture, socioeconomic status (SES), and family composition. Within each of these major categories are many variations. For example, two Japanese-American families share a common national and cultural heritage, but their level of assimilation into American culture may depend on when they immigrated to this country and where they settled. These dimensions also interact with each other, creating still more variations. Middle-SES European Americans may belong to the same racial group as low-SES European Americans but may have more in common with middle-SES African Americans. At the same time, these two middle-SES groups may work together but not necessarily socialize together. The well-being of children of divorced parents (family composition) may depend on their community's values regarding divorce (culture) and the amount of resources that the parents have to support two households (SES). Each dimension makes a unique contribution to the diversity of our society, but, at the same time, each is inextricably bound to the others. For example, race often determines status in our society, which, in turn, affects SES. Both of these dimensions interact with culture to influence family composition and lifestyle and child-rearing practices. (For more details on the effects of racial, cultural, and SES differences on family life and child development, refer to Spencer,

Brookins & Allen, 1985; McAdoo & McAdoo, 1985; Gibbs & Huang, 1989.)

In addition to these social and economic changes, more children with disabilities are being integrated into child care programs. Many child care providers find themselves adapting their programs to address a wider range of individual skills and deficits. The impact of these individual differences are not addressed directly in this chapter (see Chapter 5), but the discrimination and exclusion that are related to race, culture, and SES are germane to children who are differently abled.

This section includes a brief review of some of the effects of racial, cultural, socioeconomic, and family differences on children's development and their implications for child care. The reader should bear in mind, however, that all families are unique and that intragroup variations may be more pronounced than intergroup ones (Gibbs & Huang, 1989).

Racial Differences

We are a racially divided society, and throughout the history of the United States, race has determined a person's status and the distribution of opportunities and privileges (Gibbs & Huang, 1989). Where and how people live, work, and go to school are largely dependent on their racial membership. Although explicit racial exclusion is no longer legal, covert discrimination is evident in residential patterns, locations of employers, and the standards by which we judge students and workers. Because of the differences in backgrounds and the racial divisions in our society, many groups have maintained and developed distinct cultures. Thus, particular racial groups have become associated with particular cultural mores and values that influence children's lives and their potential child care needs. The impact of these differences is discussed in the next section.

The major impact of race itself is that it determines one's rank in society. According to John Ogbu (1978, 1983), most nonwhite racial groups in this country are viewed and treated as caste-like minorities. Ogbu claims that members of groups that were conquered, enslaved, or dispossessed (in particular, Native Americans, Mexican Americans, Puerto Rican Americans, and African Americans) have occupied the place of lower caste groups and have been the targets of the most severe and intransigent discrimination. Although many members of these groups function successfully in the larger society, people of color are more vulnerable to being stigmatized and excluded from higher-status opportunities and roles and relegated to menial jobs and poor neighborhoods (Spencer, 1990). Recent economic trends illustrate this pattern. In the early 1980s black children living in poverty increased from 36% to 41%, whereas white children living poverty increased from 12% to 13% (McLoyd, 1990). The resulting economic hardships cause stresses on families that may adversely affect children's socioemotional functioning (McLoyd, 1990). Moreover, constant exposure to racism means that many families of color live in a state of mundane extreme environmental stress (Peters, 1985) created by the day-to-day tension of enduring racially related episodes (such as name-calling, threats, and being ignored by salespeople) that range from annoying to life threatening.

The economic and societal disparities among racial groups are also reflected in the media. Children of color grow up in a world dominated by positive images of European-American history, lifestyles, and heroes and heroines. Often their own groups are invisible in the media or portrayed in negative stereotypes (Spencer, 1990). Not surprisingly, many children become alienated by being constantly exposed to and excluded from more affluent and privileged lifestyles. Often they learn to distrust and resist mainstream institutions such as schools because they want to maintain a sense of identity and control and do not want to be forced to "act white" (Slaughter-Defoe, Nakagawa, Takanishi & Johnson, 1990). In contrast, many European-American children grow up in monoracial communities or attend segregated schools and have little awareness of other racial groups. In the absence of cross-race contact, they often develop erroneous and negative perceptions about unfamiliar groups (Ramsey, 1991).

Not all ethnic groups have suffered the same level of discrimination. According to Ogbu (1978), immigrants who came more or less voluntarily to this country expected hardships but were generally optimistic about the possibilities for future generations. They often created communities that provided support, a connection with their former lives, and a buffer from the discrimination they experienced in this country. As a result, their members were able to take advantage of the opportunities that they found and became successful.

Child care providers are often hampered in their efforts to provide services for children of color because their training is based on research about the development and home environments of white middle-class children. Researchers and practitioners know relatively little about the life experiences and perspectives of non-European-American children because most studies of racial differences have been done from a Eurocentric perspective (Spencer, 1990). Currently researchers are beginning to study different groups of children within their own context. It is hoped that during the next few years our knowledge base will expand. (For some examples of this new wave of research, refer to the April 1990 (vol. 61) issue of *Child Development*.)

Cultural Differences

Culture influences all human activity, including the history, attitudes, values, beliefs, traditions, roles, tools, and arts that are unique to specific groups. According to Garcia (1991), a group's culture operates on two levels of reality: (1) the explicit level, which consists of overt behaviors and reactions; and (2) the implicit level, which consists of the covert, unstated, and largely unconscious values, attitudes, and assumptions that underlie the overt actions of group members. For example, a caregiver's compliment to an individual child for making an impressive block structure is the overt expression of the underlying belief in the value of individual achievement. Another provider who believes that a sense of community is more important than individual accomplishments might respond to the same situation by trying to get the child to involve other children in the project. The effects of different cultural values on caregiver-child relationships are vividly portrayed in Sally Lubeck's book *Sandbox Society* (1985), an ethnography of two preschool programs that contrasts the individualistic approach of middle-class preschool teachers with the collective orientation of Head Start teachers.

A family's culture influences all aspects of the members' lives and must be understood not just in terms of overt behaviors, traditions, and artifacts but as a system of beliefs and values that underlie a worldview (Garcia, 1991). Cultural values influence parents' developmental goals and their interactions with their infants and children (Coll, 1990). Child care providers need to be sensitive to these cultural values and the possible stress caused in families when children begin to come home with behaviors and beliefs that conflict with those of their families.

Culture and language are inextricably bound, as culture is learned by observation and language (Garcia, 1991). Not only does language define membership in a group, but it also embodies the implicit beliefs and attitudes of a group. For example, in many languages there are different words for "you" that convey the relationship and status of the conversants. In English, as spoken in the United States, we have only "I" and "you," which are used universally and do not vary across different relationships (Chud & Fahlman, 1985). Thus, simply translating words does not ensure a meaningful dialogue between two people from different cultural backgrounds. This connection between language and culture must be considered in decisions about which languages to use and support in a child care program.

Many of the behaviors that distinguish groups from one another are quite subtle, yet they may jeopardize communication among members of different groups and affect children's school performance. Longstreet (1978) identified five aspects of ethnicity that potentially influence communications among members of different groups: (1) verbal communication, which includes language and conventions about when and how speech is used; (2) nonverbal communication, which includes body language and gestures; (3) orientation modes, which are behavior patterns (such as accustomed sitting positions) that are learned socially, but do not have any communicative intent; (4) social values, which are roles and priorities that are common to a particular group; and (5) intellectual modes, which refer to individuals' learning styles and preferred ways of learning. These differences can affect many facets of children's interactions with peers and caregivers. Children may express their ideas and feelings in different ways, use divergent rules for initiating and continuing conversations, enact domestic and occupational roles differently, and prefer particular kinds of activities.

Culture also influences how people perceive, classify, and remember information (Cole & Scribner, 1974). The classic example of this phenomenon is the highly differentiated vocabulary the Eskimo people have for snow. Thus, some educational materials and teaching may be more meaningful to some groups than to others.

From studies of elementary and secondary education, several researchers (e.g., Moll & Diaz, 1987; Tharp, 1989; Tharp & Gallimore, 1988) have suggested that education that is compatible with children's home cultures is more effective. One successful example is the Kamehameha Early Education Program (KEEP), a language arts program (K–3) designed for native Hawaiian children, who have traditionally been less successful in schools. In this program, teachers use more collaborative social structures and observe the conventions, courtesies, and rhythms of Hawaiian conversation. Concepts are presented in a holistic approach, which is more compatible with the style of learning in Hawaiian homes. The success of this program suggests that teachers can make their classrooms and teaching methods more accessible to children from different cultures (Tharp, 1989).

Many children grow up biculturally; they must learn how to negotiate between two cultures, which requires considerable skill and flexibility. Many are competent in both cultures and have high self-esteem and achievement motivation, but some find the stress of straddling two cultures debilitating (Gibbs & Huang, 1989). Caregivers must often help children bridge the gap and maintain a sense of self as they adapt their behaviors to the demands of the immediate situation.

Socioeconomic Status

Despite the idealized image of the United States as a classless society, our society is clearly divided by socioeconomic status. Usually the divisions are defined as upper, middle, and low, with some increments such as upper-middle. During the 1980s the income and lifestyle gap between the rich and the poor widened enormously. More and more, wealthy families are living in protected areas, sending their children to expensive and segregated centers and schools, and living in isolation from the rest of society. At the other end of the continuum, the number of poor families with young children continues to grow, and the level of poverty has become more extreme. Many children and their families number among the homeless population in our country (Edelman, 1985).

The gaps between groups in our society and between the American ideal of equality and the reality of people's lives are growing exponentially. Patterns of child care often contribute to this problem. Because of funding patterns, child care programs are often segregated by social class and ethnic group. Some centers are federally funded and admit only children with demonstrated economic need. Others are tuition-based and are accessible only to parents with fairly substantial incomes. Some programs are administered through community agencies, specific employers, or churches and draw children from these particular populations. For many working-class, poor, or rural families, no programs are available, and they have to rely on relatives and neighbors. Wealthy families, on the other hand, can hire highly trained nannies for their children or have their choice of well-run and beautifully equipped child care programs. Thus, not only are children being raised in segregated settings, but they are having qualitatively different child care experiences in their early years, which may contribute to the later educational gaps between groups.

Increasing numbers of families are living outside of the mainstream institutions of conventional jobs and schools. This group is often referred to by the unfortunate term "underclass." A better term is the "excluded class," as these people are most often from the caste-like minorities described by Ogbu. Despite affirmative-action legislation and other efforts to equalize resources, the strong relation between race and class persists. In absolute numbers, whites constitute the largest group of poor people, but in terms of percentages, African Americans,

Hispanic Americans, and Native Americans have the highest poverty rates (Garcia, 1991).

Children who live in poverty have higher school dropout rates, which appear to be related most closely to their accumulated discouragement about poor academic performance (Garcia, 1991). Children from poor families are often stigmatized and then internalize that negative self-perception. They become frustrated and give up easily because they have not had the experience of academic success. In addition, the practice of tracking often reflects socioeconomic divisions, with low-income children occupying the low-level classes and learning repetitive material by rote, while their middle- and upper-class peers are engaged in more intellectual and creative endeavors. The mismatch between the home and school environments may also make adjustment to school difficult, because many poor children encounter unfamiliar social and behavioral expectations. The quality of the schools is another potential factor. Poor children usually attend schools that are housed in dilapidated buildings with poorly functioning plumbing and electricity, staffed by teachers with low morale and poor attendance records, and inadequately equipped with out-of-date and decrepit books and equipment (Kozol, 1991). Aside from these accumulated in-school effects, children from low-income families may feel helpless about improving their success at school because they have watched their own families being buffeted by unpredictable and uncontrollable forces such as unemployment and changes in welfare and immigration rules (Gibbs & Huang, 1989).

Clearly, erasing the devastating effects of poverty and homelessness is beyond the purview of child care providers. However, we must create environments that provide maximum support for these children and develop activities to foster the development of positive self-esteem to help them survive and deflect the alienating experiences they will encounter when they go to school. One clear role of child care providers is to begin to prepare children for their initial school experiences by exposing them to some of the unfamiliar expectations in a safe environment.

Family Composition

Families come in all sizes and shapes. Child care providers need to learn how to identify the needs and strengths of individual families. The structure of the care, the kind of support provided for families, and the ways in which families are involved may vary depending on the strengths and needs of particular families.

Today many children are being raised by single parents. A common assumption is that these households are lacking in both material and psychological resources. Although they are often under great stress, many single parents create extensive networks of relatives or friends that provide support and camaraderie. By knowing about these networks, child care providers can dovetail their own efforts with these other support systems. Many divorced parents share custody or visitation rights. This situation can be a source of either stress or support. Providers need to be aware of the impact of specific custody arrangements on both the children and the families and support children's efforts to maintain positive relationships with both parents.

Remarriages often result in complex family structures and relationships with stepparents, stepsiblings, and half-siblings. Some children find these blended families to be a source of support because they have more adults and siblings in their lives. However, the potential for feeling rivalrous or rejected is also great. Parents and child care providers need to stay in close contact about how children are experiencing the different facets and vicissitudes of family life.

Many children have gay or lesbian parents. Given the social stigma that is often attached to homosexuality, some child care providers may assume that these parents are unfit to raise a child. They may also find it difficult to accept the fact that a child has two mothers or two fathers. It is important that providers work through their feelings and reach a point of being able to respect lesbian and gay people as effective parents. Because so many children's stories and materials are oriented toward heterosexual families, providers may need to make a concerted effort to include stories and pictures that show families with other compositions (Clay, 1990).

Child care providers also need to be aware of the role of family members other than parents. Extended families often provide a crucial buffer zone between the child and the stresses of poverty and discrimination (Gibbs & Huang, 1989). Moreover, grandparents, aunts, uncles, and older siblings often function as parents if the age or disability of the parents renders them unable to assume the responsibilities of parenthood. Child care providers need to identify the people who function as the parents of a child and establish relationships with them. Because parental responsibilities may be assumed by a number of different people, child care providers should involve appropriate members in decisions regarding the child and support them in their efforts to provide a positive home environment for the child.

An increasing number of families are homeless, meaning that many children do not have any permanent place to go to and call home.

Because this phenomenon is relatively new in our society, we do not know the long-term effects of this deprivation on children's development. However, the immediate needs of the children require that any child care arrangements provide a maximum amount of support and stability so that these children can have some continuity in their lives and develop a sense of trust in the future. Staffing patterns and organizational plans should be designed with these needs in mind. If possible, child care providers should work closely with parents to provide mutual support in creating a stable environment.

At the other end of the spectrum, the two-professional family is often rich in money and material goods, but poor in time and energy for children. Some parents are unrealistic in their goals to combine career and family life and may be tempted to displace children's needs by the demands of their jobs. Parents with high-pressure jobs may demand long day care hours and backup care for ill children. Often parents have to travel, which disrupts the household. Child care providers may find that they have to act as advocates for these children and as a counterbalance to work demands. For example, they may refuse to extend their hours and thereby help the parents resist the temptation to put in longer and longer hours at work. These parents often provide stimulating home lives with trips, books, and many activities. Their children may adapt easily to the demands of school but may worry about whether they are living up to their parents' expectations. These families may need help in learning how to simply relax and enjoy one another.

RESPONDING TO DIVERSITY

Staffing patterns are crucial to a program's ability to provide effective child care services. All child care providers should be well trained and particularly sensitive to the diverse and changing needs of families. As much as possible, members of the community should be represented on the staff. Sometimes community members are placed in secondary or menial positions such as teachers' aides or custodians. Hiring practices should be scrutinized and modified to ensure that efforts are made to have equal representation of all groups throughout the staff hierarchy.

To respond effectively to the particular needs, concerns, and interests of each group of children and families, child care providers need to systematically study the community and learn about children and their parents in that context (Ramsey, 1987; Williams & De Gaetano, 1985).

This analysis should include not only what racial, cultural, and socio-economic groups are represented in the community, but also whether those groups are over- or underrepresented in the media. Knowledge of current local controversies about or among different groups is another necessary context for understanding and interpreting children's comments and actions. Caregivers should also find out what community resources are available to enrich the educational experiences of the children in their care. Local newspapers and radio shows, community meetings, and conversations with store owners, community leaders, and parents are good sources of local news. (For specific questions and activities to guide such inquiries and staff discussions, see Ramsey, 1987; Williams & De Gaetano, 1985.) Child care providers who have lived in the community for a long time can use this inquiry to clarify and change some of their assumptions. New staff members, volunteers, and interns can use it to become oriented to the community and to begin to make some local contacts.

Many studies (e.g., Coates, 1972; Rist, 1973; Simpson & Erickson, 1983) have demonstrated the overt and covert ways in which teachers' responses vary according to race and gender of students (e.g., grouping patterns, supportive versus critical attention, eye contact and nonverbal gestures). Some teachers may not be aware of their differential reactions but are simply operating from their subconscious assumptions. Caregivers need to be aware of their own backgrounds and attitudes and consciously monitor their responses to children to ensure that they are not showing preferential treatment (Ramsey, 1987).

Multicultural Perspectives in Designing Programs

As our society becomes increasingly diverse, all children, including those that live in relatively homogeneous groups, need to learn about their own group within the larger social context. They also need to learn to respect and appreciate other ways of life and to gain skills in relating effectively with a wide range of people. Thus, child care providers should develop curricula and teaching practices that reflect a multicultural perspective. A multicultural perspective is a lens through which providers can examine all their decisions related to organizing programs, designing classrooms, choosing materials, selecting pictures and books, planning specific activities and events, and working with parents. The goals of multicultural education include the development of positive gender, racial, class, cultural, and individual identities; respect and appreciation for the ways in which other people live; willingness to include and cooperate with unfamiliar peers; commitment to play an active role in fighting discrimination and other social injustices; and the development of educational skills and social knowledge needed to become full participants in all aspects of society.

As can be seen from the preceding goals, multicultural education is a broad perspective that embraces a number of different approaches. Teachers are often uncertain about where to start and which goals to pursue most vigorously (Derman-Sparks, 1989). Five approaches have been articulated and critiqued by Sleeter and Grant (1988):

1. Some educators view multicultural education as primarily a way to help all children fit into the educational mainstream. Programs with this perspective may have special tutors and adapted curriculum to help children from different language and cultural backgrounds adapt to the demands of traditional schools. This orientation has been criticized because it supports the one-way adjustment of these individuals to the status quo as opposed to a mutual accommodation between schools and children.

2. The second approach identified by Sleeter and Grant (1988) is human-relations or intergroup education. Here educators help children develop interpersonal skills, identify and reduce their prejudices and stereotypes, and learn skills in getting along with a wider range of people. This approach has been incorporated into many multicultural programs because it enables teachers to work with children's skills at a concrete level. However, it has been criticized for not taking into account the structural inequalities of our society. It assumes that people can learn to get along regardless of the conflicts of interest and social injustices that make it almost impossible for some groups to bridge the communications gap between them.

3. The third approach grew out of the ethnic studies movement in the 1960s and 1970s and is called single-group studies. The curriculum includes units on specific groups of people focusing the curriculum for a period of a few months or a year on a particular cultural group. The goals are to promote more positive ethnic identities and to heighten awareness of ways of life and histories of underrepresented groups. In short, this approach is a way of making specific groups more visible to all children and to broaden the cultural base of the curriculum. However, it has been criticized because units of study are only added on to the existing curriculum, which basically remains unchanged.

4. The fourth approach is called multicultural education. It embodies the notion that we are a pluralistic nation and that all education should incorporate themes about similarities and differences, social equity, human rights, and respect for one's own group and other groups.

Underlying this approach is the expectation that the whole curriculum will be changed to reflect a broader worldview — a process that is often referred to as the "infusion" approach. In early childhood programs, many curricula with this orientation use themes to teach about human differences and similarities in a context of mutual respect (e.g., cultural differences in art, music, or holiday celebrations). This approach has been criticized because it is sometimes limited to superficial exposure to different groups (e.g., holidays, foods, and costumes) and does not pay enough attention to the basic social inequities.

5. The fifth approach focuses on social reconstructionist goals. It embodies an activist orientation aimed at developing children's skills to fight discrimination and to radically change the structures of our society that create and maintain unequal opportunities and distribution of wealth. This approach, sometimes referred to as anti-bias curriculum, is favored by Sleeter and Grant (1988). However, it has been criticized for being unrealistic and for potentially diverting energies toward the elusive goals of social change at the expense of providing more useful education for children.

Each model reflects a particular perspective on caring for children in a diverse world. Caregivers' decisions about which approaches to follow often reflect their own worldviews and the priorities of the communities in which they work. Ways to apply these approaches in a number of different child care situations are illustrated in the remainder of this section. These examples are by no means exhaustive, but they illustrate the relevance of a multicultural approach to diverse situations. The examples are drawn from the following groups: children from families who are relatively affluent and live in an all-white community, children who are recent immigrants to this country, and children in neighborhoods where tensions exist among different groups.

Children from Affluent Homogeneous Groups. The main goal of a multicultural perspective for these children is to help them see their own lives and lifestyles in a larger and more realistic perspective and to challenge their assumptions about the ways in which the rest of humanity lives. Children from affluent families may equate material advantage with personal value, and caregivers in these settings can provide children with books, pictures, and activities that portray a range of lifestyles and convey positive images of less affluent ways of life. These children can also benefit from enjoying activities that do not rely on expensive gadgets but can be done with recycled objects and natural materials. They also need to be exposed to some of the social realities of poverty and discrimination and learn how they can contribute to make our society more open and fair for all people, as indicated by the social reconstructionist approach. In their classrooms, children can develop their helping skills by caring for younger children and assisting with food preparation and cleanup. They can gain confidence in their abilities to effect change by identifying stereotypes in books and dictating letters to publishers registering their complaints (Derman-Sparks, 1989). Older children can assist in cleaning up a local park or collecting food for a nearby shelter. Although young children do not have a full understanding of what is fair, they can participate in role-plays and puppet shows in which they explore the effects of inequities and learn how to challenge them.

Children Who Are Recent Immigrants. Children who are recent immigrants confront many challenges. They often have to negotiate between two cultures and languages, learn new behavioral norms without the guidance of their parents, endure overt and covert acts of discrimination, and deal with their invisibility in mainstream institutions and media. Because these children need to be supported as they adjust to unfamiliar ways, some strategies reflective of the first approach, such as tutors and curriculum adaptations, might be applicable. However, the children must not experience the adjustment as a one-way assimilation. Child care providers should incorporate the children's cultures into a range of activities, such as those suggested by the single-group studies and multicultural education approaches, so that these children feel that their home cultures are respected and valued. Throughout the program, children need to learn that their ways of speaking, living, moving, singing, cooking, and celebrating are valued. Photographs of their former and current communities may help them feel more at home. Stories about their countries of origin and the immigration experience may validate their experiences and their cultures. Teachers should make efforts to make the classroom culture compatible with that of the children's homes (Tharp, 1989). At the same time, these new arrivals need to learn skills to function successfully in their new culture. Often child care providers serve as a bridge between the two worlds for both the children and their parents.

Children may speak a language other than English at home, and caregivers need to decide how intensively to encourage children to learn English. Some people argue that maintaining the home language interferes with the acquisition of English and isolates children from the mainstream (Porter, 1990). Others argue that maintenance of home languages fosters earlier development of academic skills and eventually more proficient English (Crawford, 1989). The stance most consistent with a multicultural approach is to respect and support children's home languages and, at the same time, provide a rich language environment where children can learn English as they play and work (Ramsey, 1987). Optimally, all children — including native English speakers — would be in bilingual classes so that children learning English would not be isolated from their English-speaking peers and all children would have the benefit of learning a second language (Ovando, 1990).

Because immigrant families often feel distant from and intimidated by traditional schools, child care providers can help parents see that they have something to contribute to the schools. In the more intimate and informal settings that typify most child care programs, teachers can make parent participation comfortable and create a sense of community among parents that can continue when their children enter the more formal environment of the public schools.

Many parents who are new to this country are isolated from social services and need support and assistance to deal with social services and jobs. Child care programs should collaborate with other agencies or have staff available to help parents with these aspects of their lives. Providers may also want to give workshops about child development and ways to support children's learning. However, such workshops should be conducted in ways that support and expand, not undermine, the parenting styles and techniques currently used in these families.

Children and parents in these communities often lack a feeling of control over their lives and may benefit from the social reconstructionist approach. At first they may resist experiences that involve decision making and other kinds of active participation. However, each person is an expert on his or her own life, and by starting with activities in which parents and children feel knowledgeable, teachers can help families develop a sense of efficacy and control. For example, parents might raise money by selling tickets to a dinner consisting of their traditional foods. Although this activity may seem far removed from reconstructing society, it can inspire people to begin to feel more powerful and to take more control of their world.

Children in Ethnically Mixed Communities. Children in multiethnic communities are at an advantage in that they directly experience the fact that they live in a diverse society. If the conditions are favorable, children learn from an early age how to relate to peers and families who may speak, dress, eat, and act in unfamiliar ways. Teachers in programs with this kind of mix can easily implement a multicultural approach by taking advantage of the richness of the local community and neighborhood. They can also work directly with children to foster their skills in interacting with people who are different from them.

Unfortunately, many heterogeneous communities are torn by intergroup conflict. Although young children are not fully conscious of the reasons for and the implications of these tensions, their behavior often reflects the early stages of own-group preference. Many studies have demonstrated that even at young ages, children, especially white children in our society, are more attracted to peers who are similar to them (Fox & Jordan, 1973; Katz, 1982; Newman, Liss & Sherman, 1983; Ramsey & Myers, 1990; Rosenfield & Stephan, 1981; Stabler, Zeig & Johnson, 1982). Thus, the segregation and friction that often characterize adult cross-group relations may be reflected and replicated in children's peer relationships.

Programs in these communities might emphasize the human-relations aspect of multicultural education. Child care providers need to be sure that they themselves are modeling positive intergroup relations with the children and their families. Staffing patterns should reflect fair and equal representation of members of different groups, and teachers should demonstrate how people who are different can communicate and cooperate effectively. Classrooms and activities should be structured in order to bring members of disparate groups together in positive and egalitarian ways. Family meetings can be organized to help parents overcome their resistance to communicating with other groups and to facilitate their children's cross-group contacts. A multicultural approach in which the contributions and lifestyles of the different groups are highlighted might also help break down cross-group antagonisms.

Often the tensions between groups are based on economics. By helping parents see their intergroup conflicts in the larger context of the uneven distribution of wealth, providers and parent advocates might help families recognize their common interests and foster collaboration in pressuring the local government or employers to make changes that will improve life for all residents of the community. For example, parents from several groups may collaborate to push for better funding for the local school or the neighborhood library.

CONCLUSION

We are becoming an increasingly diverse nation and, as we approach the twenty-first century, we have the opportunity to be a truly multicultural and egalitarian society. However, we also face many challenges because diversity often means divisiveness, and differences frequently evoke discrimination. Moreover, economic disparities are polarizing our country and creating large numbers of children and families who are excluded from mainstream educational and occupational opportunities. Within these broad social changes family compositions are also becoming more diverse, which introduces still more variability in family needs and children's experiences. Child care providers are often confronted with a dizzying array of family backgrounds and needs.

A multicultural perspective offers a framework for analyzing the needs and strengths of families and communities and designing appropriate child care services and educational programs. There are a number of different models of multicultural education. The ways in which they are implemented depend on the needs and the previous experiences of the children in that group. As illustrated in this chapter, all children, regardless of their backgrounds, need to see themselves as members of a diverse society. We need to prepare children to live and thrive in a multifaceted and complex world. The challenges are great, but so are the opportunities.

REFERENCES

Chud, G., & Fahlman, R. (1985). *Early childhood education for a multicultural education*. Vancouver, BC: Western Education Development Group.

Clay, J. W. (1990). Working with lesbian and gay parents and their children. *Young Children, 45*(3), 31–35.

Coates, B. (1972). White adult behavior toward black and white children. *Child Development, 43*, 143–154.

Cole, M., & Scribner, S. (1974). *Culture and thought: A psychological introduction*. New York: Wiley.

Coll, C. T. G. (1990). Developmental outcome of minority infants: A process-oriented look into our beginnings. *Child Development, 61*, 270–289.

Crawford, J. (1989). *Bilingual education: History, politics, theory, and practice*. Trenton, NJ: Crane.

Derman-Sparks, L. (1989). *Anti-bias curriculum: Tools for empowering young children*. Washington, DC: National Association for the Education of Young Children.

Edelman, M. W. (1985). The sea is so wide and my boat is so small: Problems facing black children today. In H. P. McAdoo & J. L. McAdoo (Eds.), *Black children: Social, educational, and parental environments* (pp. 72–82). Newbury Park, CA: Sage.

Fox, D. J., & Jordan, V. B. (1973). Racial preference and identification of black, American Chinese, and white children. *Genetic Psychology Monographs, 88*, 229–286.

Garcia, R. L. (1991). *Teaching in a pluralistic society*. New York: Harper-Collins.

Gibbs, J. T., & Huang, L. N. (1989). *Children of color: Psychological interventions with minority youth*. San Francisco: Jossey-Bass.

Hodgkinson, H. L. (1985). *All one system: Demographics of education, kindergarten through graduate school*. Paper presented at the Institute for Leadership, Washington, DC.

Katz, P. A. (1982). Development of children's racial awareness and intergroup attitudes. In L. G. Katz (Ed.), *Current topics in early childhood education*, vol. 4 (pp. 17–54). Norwood, NJ: Ablex.

Kozol, J. (1991). *Savage inequalities: Children in American schools*. New York: Crown.

Longstreet, W. S. (1978). *Aspects of ethnicity*. New York: Teachers College Press.

Lubeck, S. (1985). *Sandbox society*. Philadelphia: Falmer.

McAdoo, H. P., & McAdoo, J. L. (Eds.). (1985). *Black children: Social, educational, and parental environments*. Newbury Park, CA: Sage.

McLoyd, V. C. (1990). The impact of economic hardship on black families and children: Psychological distress, parenting, and socioemotional development. *Child Development, 61*, 311–346.

Moll, L., & Diaz, R. (1987). Teaching writing as communication: The use of ethnographic findings in classroom practice. In D. Bloome (Ed.), *Literacy and schooling* (pp. 193–221). Norwood, NJ: Ablex.

Newman, M. A., Liss, M. B., & Sherman, F. (1983). Ethnic awareness in children: Not a unitary concept. *Journal of Genetic Psychology, 143*, 103–112.

Ogbu, J. U. (1978). *Minority education and caste*. New York: Academic Press.

Ogbu, J. U. (1983). Socialization: A cultural ecological approach. In K. M. Borman (Ed.), *The social life of children in a changing society* (pp. 253–267). Norwood, NJ: Ablex.

Ovando, C. J. (1990). Politics and pedagogy: The case of bilingual education. *Harvard Educational Review, 60*, 341–355.

Peters, M. F. (1985). Racial socialization of young black children. In H. P. McAdoo & J. L. McAdoo (Eds.), *Black children: Social, educational, and parental environments* (pp. 159–173). Newbury Park, CA: Sage.

Porter, R. P. (1990). *Forked tongue: The politics of bilingual education*. New York: Basic Books.

Ramsey, P. G. (1987). *Teaching and learning in a diverse world: Multicultural education for young children*. New York: Teachers College Press.

Ramsey, P. G. (1991). Salience of race in young children growing up in an all-white community. *Journal of Educational Psychology, 83*, 28–34.

Ramsey, P. G., & Myers, L. C. (1990). Salience of race in young children's cognitive, affective, and behavioral responses to social environments. *Journal of Applied Developmental Psychology, 11*, 49–67.

Rist, R. C. (1973). *The urban school: A factor for failure*. Cambridge, MA: MIT Press.

Rosenfield, D., & Stephan, W. G. (1981). Intergroup relations among children. In S. S. Brehm, S. M. Kassin & F. X. Gibbons (Eds.), *Developmental social psychology* (pp. 271–297). New York: Oxford University Press.

Simpson, A. W., & Erickson, M. T. (1983). Teachers' verbal and nonverbal communication patterns as a function of teacher race, student gender, and student race. *American Educational Research Journal, 20,* 183–198.

Slaughter-Defoe, D. T., Nakagawa, K., Takanishi, R., & Johnson, D. J. (1990). Toward cultural/ecological perspectives on schooling and achievement in African- and Asian-American children. *Child Development, 61,* 363–383.

Sleeter, C. E., & Grant, C. A. (1988). *Making choices for multicultural education: Five approaches to race, class, and gender.* Columbus, OH: Merrill.

Spencer, M. B. (1990). Development of minority children: An introduction. *Child Development, 61,* 267–269.

Spencer, M. B., Brookins, G. K., & Allen, W. R. (1985). *Beginnings: The social and affective development of black children.* Hillsdale, NJ: Erlbaum.

Stabler, J. R., Zeig, J. A., & Johnson, E. E. (1982). Perceptions of racially related stimuli by young children. *Perceptual and Motor Skills, 54,* 71–77.

Tharp, R. G. (1989). Psychocultural variables and constants: Effects of teaching and learning in schools. *American Psychologist, 44,* 349–359.

Tharp, R. G., & Gallimore, R. (1988). *Rousing minds to life: Teaching, learning, and schooling in social context.* New York: Cambridge University Press.

Williams, L. R., & De Gaetano, Y. (1985). *Alerta: A multicultural, bilingual approach to teaching young children.* Menlo Park, CA: Addison-Wesley.

CHAPTER 7

Family Day Care

THE "OTHER" FORM OF CARE

Susan Kontos

Depending on the source, the image of family day care varies between two extremes. At one extreme is a house full of fussing infants and young children receiving little adult attention and staring mindlessly at daytime television. At the other extreme is an image of a grandmotherly type showering attention on two or three young children busily engaged in developmentally appropriate activities. Such images are frequently based on hearsay, stereotypes, wishful thinking, or misinformation and bear little or no relationship to reality. Compared to center-based care, family day care is more difficult to depict because it is home based and thus less visible, more informal, and more often unregulated. The purpose of this chapter is to use our growing knowledge to draw a data-based picture of family day care in the United States. First I examine the regulatory context of family day care and the characteristics of caregivers and parents involved with family day care. Then I review the literature that compares family day care with home- and center-based care to define some common and distinguishing characteristics among the three forms of child care. Finally, implications of the characteristics of family day care and its similarities to and differences from center-based care are drawn for the children enrolled in family day care.

WHAT IS FAMILY DAY CARE?

Family day care is usually defined as care of up to six children in the home of a nonrelative (Children's Foundation, 1990). Typically the caregivers' own preschool children are included in the total group size

and, in some states, the maximum group size allowed varies by the ages
of the children. There are some exceptions to the basic definition. For
instance, in 12 states the maximum number of children allowed per
caregiver is more than 6, varying from 7 to 12. In 36 states, family day
care homes with more than 6 (but less than 12) children are required to
have another adult present and are called "group homes" or "large
family day care homes." Although it is important to keep these exceptions in mind, the definition given by the Children's Foundation (1990)
is sound, based on Phillips, Lande, and Goldberg's (1990) findings that
the median allowable group size for regulated family day care homes is
6. Thus, as formally defined, family day care is home-based child care
for a relatively small, mixed-age group of children with one caregiver.

Regulation

Discussions of the nature of family day care seem inevitably to turn
to regulation. This is ironic, since only a minority of family day care
providers (10% to 40%) adhere to regulation (Kahn & Kamerman,
1987). The majority of caregivers who are unregulated are unaware of
the regulation requirements in their states, are legally unregulated due
to the number of children they care for, or choose not to comply. To
understand family day care in the United States and to interpret the
results of family day care research, one must understand the regulatory
context in which it functions.

Child care regulation, in general, is designed to protect the welfare
of children in the absence of their parents (Class, 1980; Phillips et al.,
1990). To accomplish this goal, states typically have taken a "facilities
licensure" approach for both center- and home-based care. Licensed
centers and family day care homes have the state's "guarantee" that
they meet the standards set forth in the regulations deemed necessary
to protect the welfare of children. In order to back up this guarantee,
states must inspect each center or home for compliance with the regulations. Best estimates suggest that there are currently one and one-half
to two million family day care providers in the United States (Hofferth
& Phillips, 1987; Kahn & Kamerman, 1987), 223,351 of whom are
regulated (Children's Foundation, 1990), compared to 67,000 regulated
child care centers (Phillips & Whitebook, 1986). Needless to say, family
day care licensing is an enormous task for which states are ill prepared.
The discrepancy between the intent of family day care regulation and
its actual impact provokes discussion.

Although no one questions the need to safeguard the health and
safety of children in child care, there are those who question whether

current regulatory approaches for family day care are appropriate (Children's Foundation, 1990; Class, 1980; Morgan, 1980; Phillips et al., 1990). More specifically, questions have been raised regarding the appropriateness of applying a regulatory approach designed for center-based programs to family day care. More innovative regulatory approaches that protect children but are sensitive to the uniqueness of family day care have been called for.

The most frequently advocated alternative regulatory approach for family day care is registration. Registration differs from licensing in several ways: States do not guarantee that registered family day care homes meet their standards, and routine monitoring is not done. This form of regulation is currently used in 16 states (in three states it is voluntary).

The arguments for registration are that universal compliance is a realistic goal (the need for exemptions is eliminated) and that simply identifying the family day care providers is a significant part of the role of regulation (Morgan, 1980). Morgan also takes the position that parents are better able to assess quality in family day care than in center care, so the protection of the state is needed less or not at all for family day care services. Although not everyone agrees with Morgan's position, there seems to be a growing consensus that the regulatory status quo is inadequate and that change is in order.

In spite of the growing consensus regarding the need for regulatory changes, actual change is slow in coming. The Children's Foundation's 1990 family day care licensing study found that there were few new regulatory approaches initiated between 1985 and 1990. Consequently, the regulatory context for family day care in the 1990s remains one in which states license the few caregivers who choose to be licensed, exempt many caregivers, and, for all practical purposes, neglect the job of enforcing regulations among caregivers who, by law, should be regulated but are not.

Characteristics of Caregivers

With the exception of the decade-old National Day Care Home Study (NDCHS) (Divine-Hawkins, 1981; Fosburg, 1982) and some recent studies on child care supply and demand, the vast majority of studies of family day care providers have been conducted with regulated caregivers — who are the minority. Thus, our descriptions of caregivers are limited in scope. Nonetheless, the research does provide a glimpse of a portion of the family day care provider population.

Research consistently shows that, on the personal side, the typical family day care provider is married, in her thirties (black caregivers are older, on average), and has several children of her own (Eheart & Leavitt, 1986; Fischer, 1989; Fosburg, 1982). These data suggest that caregivers do not invariably have preschool children of their own at home all day, since a significant proportion of caregivers' children are over the age of six. This same body of research indicates that caregivers typically have a high school education. Most family day care providers are members of lower- or middle-income families and earn one-fourth to one-third of their family's income (Divine-Hawkins, 1981; Fischer, 1989; Pence & Goelman, 1987).

It is possible to portray the professional characteristics of family day care providers as well. The majority of caregivers who have participated in research have more than three years of experience. When considering all caregivers, however, this number is likely to be inflated, since most of the data are based on regulated caregivers and evidence suggests that unregulated caregivers are less experienced than regulated caregivers (Fischer, 1989; Fosburg, 1982; Pence & Goelman, 1987). It is difficult to determine a typical group size for a family day care home. Research reveals that caregivers who are regulated or who belong to the Child Care Food Program tend to care for more children than unregulated caregivers (Fischer, 1989; Fosburg, 1982; Kisker, Maynard, Gordon & Strain, 1989; Pence & Goelman, 1987). The majority of studies including regulated caregivers report average group sizes varying from five to eight children; those that include unregulated caregivers report group sizes of three to four children.

The workday of a family day care provider is long. Studies consistently indicate that caregivers typically work 9 hours or more per day and average 43 to 51 hours per week (Bollin, 1990; Fischer, 1989; Goelman, Shapiro & Pense, 1990). There is some evidence that unregulated caregivers work fewer hours than regulated caregivers (Pence & Goelman, 1987). It is difficult to determine exactly how well paid caregivers are for the long hours they devote to their work. Based on several recent national or multisite studies, it appears that in the late 1980s, family day care providers charged between $35 and $65 per week for full-time care, depending on how "full-time" is defined (Kisker et al., 1989). The most recent evidence suggests that, holding geographic region constant, regulated family day care providers do not charge significantly less per hour than center-based programs. Unregulated family day care providers do charge lower hourly rates, but the differences are not dramatic (Hofferth & Kisker, 1991).

Estimates of turnover among family day care providers range from 37% to 59% annually (National Association for the Education of Young

Children, 1985; National Commission on Working Women, 1985; Nelson, 1990). Thus, turnover in family day care is comparable to turnover among center-based staff, if not higher. In spite of the high turnover, the research on job satisfaction among family day care providers shows that it is uniformly high (Bollin, 1990; Rosenthal, 1988). At first glance, these data seem counterintuitive: Why would people who like their work quit? Recent research suggests that turnover is more frequently associated with financial concerns associated with low enrollment or parents' nonpayment than with job dissatisfaction (Bollin, under review). As far as commitment to their work is concerned, studies show that from one-third to two-thirds of caregivers consider family day care to be a permanent occupation (Eheart & Leavitt, 1986; Fosburg, 1982; Pence & Goelman, 1987).

It is difficult to describe the typical training received by family day care providers, since studies may report whether caregivers have received training, what kind of training (source or content), or how much training. It is safe to say that informal training—workshops, conferences, and the like—is more common among caregivers than formal training—courses and degree programs (Abbot-Shim & Kaufman, 1986; Fischer, 1989). Levels of training among family day care providers are consistent with state child care regulations, which mandate little or none (Children's Foundation, 1990), and with the perceptions of caregivers (and probably the general public) that motherhood is adequate preparation for family day care work (Divine-Hawkins, 1981; Fischer, 1989; Nelson, 1990).

In sum, the research portrays family day care providers as lower- to middle-income married women in their thirties who work long hours but like their work even though they are not well paid. They typically care for three to eight children (other than their own) and are unlikely to have received formal training. This portrayal is more likely to reflect regulated than unregulated caregivers.

Characteristics of Family Day Care Users

Twenty-two percent of working mothers with children under the age of five use family day care, compared with 16% who rely on their husbands, 15% who use out-of-home care with a relative, and 23% who use centers (Bureau of the Census, 1987). In assessing trends in child care usage, Hofferth and Phillips (1987) detected slower growth rates for use of family day care than for center-based care. It is impossible to know whether the differential growth rates for usage of these two different forms of child care are related to parental preferences, child care availability, or both. The small increase in family day care usage between 1965 and 1982 can be accounted for by families with children under the age of three whose mothers work part time (Hofferth & Phillips, 1987). Younger children are less likely to be in center-based care than older children, reflecting the fact that more family day care homes than centers enroll infants and toddlers and that parents prefer more formal programs once their children near three years of age (Kahn & Kamerman, 1987).

In general, research shows that parents tend to prefer and be satisfied with whatever form of child care they are using (Kamerman & Kahn, 1981). However, when parents using family day care were asked if they would like to change the form of care they were using, many reported a desire to change to center-based or in-home care, whereas parents using center-based care were unlikely to desire a change to family day care (Kisker et al., 1989). Sixty-two to 74 percent (depending on the community) of family day care users in one study desired no change in the form of child care they used (Kisker et al., 1989).

The results of the NDCHS (Divine-Hawkins, 1981) revealed that parents using family day care earned less than the national median income, leading to the inference that family day care users have lower incomes than center care users. Other recent studies have found few or no differences in the socioeconomic status of families using family day care and those using center-based care (Clarke-Stewart, 1984; Pence & Goelman, 1987; Steinberg & Green, 1979; Rapp & Lloyd, 1989).

Although the research on parents who use family day care is not voluminous, available evidence gives us no reason to believe that users of family day care differ systematically from users of center care in any way besides the age of the children in care and the mothers' work schedules. Parents are generally satisfied with their family day care arrangements, but may increasingly prefer center-based care as their children get older.

Summary

So far, we have described family day care by defining it and putting it into its regulatory context, by describing the caregivers, and by describing the families who use it. But this description fails to help us understand the dynamics of family day care as a child-rearing context. One way to do that is to contrast family day care, a lesser known environment, with environments about which we are more familiar — homes and child care centers.

A HOME AWAY FROM HOME OR A SMALL CENTER?

Family day care is more difficult to classify than center-based care according to the niche it occupies. It takes place in a home, involves a relatively small group of children, and is informal. Thus, one might assume that it resembles a family more than a center. On the other hand, the number and age distribution of children in family day care as well as the "businesslike" origins of the caregiver-child relationship are unlike a family and similar, in some respects, to a center. To understand how family day care is similar to and different from families and centers, we must review the small body of research that compares family day care settings with homes and centers with respect to caregiver behaviors, children's behavior and/or development, and the environmental context.

Family Day Care versus Home

Surprisingly few studies have compared home and family day care settings. Those that have have examined some aspect of the adult-child relationship in each setting. The earliest comparison assessed mother-infant and caregiver-infant attachment in 15 infants enrolled in full-time family day care (Krentz, 1983). Results revealed that infants were much more likely to be securely attached to their mothers (80%) than their caregivers (46%) and were more likely to be unclassifiable with their caregivers (33%) than with their mothers (0%). There were no significant differences in the social interaction of infants with their mothers or their caregivers. Analysis of episode effects for the social interaction variables indicated that infants reacted to the stresses of the Strange Situation identically whether they were with their mothers or their caregivers. These results were interpreted as support for the notions that infants can become attached to nonparental adults and that the attachment relationship serves the same purpose for infants regardless of the attachment figure. However, the researcher also suggested that the results demonstrate that even though the rates of social interaction behaviors were the same, the pattern of infants' behaviors toward mothers and caregivers differed, and infants were less likely to have well-organized relationships with their caregivers. Thus, though infants can be attached to both mothers and caregivers, the nature of those attachment relationships is probably qualitatively different.

Stith and Davis (1984) studied 30 infant-adult dyads. Ten were employed mothers and their infants, 10 were nonemployed mothers and their infants, and 10 were family day care providers and the employed mothers' infants. Thirteen caregiving characteristics were coded during two-hour observations of each dyad (e.g., contingent vocalization, social play, encouragement of emerging gross-motor responses). The babies were also administered the Bayley Scales of Infant Development. Results revealed that infants received less stimulating and responsive care and environments in family day care than in their own homes whether or not their mothers were employed. Follow-up analyses of the family day care provider subsample suggested that the factor most likely responsible for these differences was the total number of children cared for during the observation, not the behavior of the infants. There were no significant differences in Bayley mental or psychomotor scale scores between the day care and home care infants. These data suggest that infants receive lower-quality care in family day care than they do at home due to "competing demands" on the caregiver by her other charges.

The subsample of children in family day care in the Chicago Study of Child Care and Development were observed with both their caregivers and their mothers (Clarke-Stewart, 1986). When comparing mother-child and caregiver-child interactions, Clarke-Stewart (1986) found that children had significantly fewer one-to-one interactions with their caregivers than with their mothers. Like Stith and Davis (1984), Clarke-Stewart (1986) attributed these differences to the greater number of children caregivers must supervise. Differences in the quality of interactions also were investigated. Mothers and caregivers were found to be similar in the educational quality of their interactions, the appropriateness of their responses, and how often they gave children choices, orders, or punishments. Caregivers were more directive and less responsive in the interactions they had with the children and were more likely to speak to the children as part of a group. Mothers expressed significantly more positive emotion than caregivers. These differences in the quality of interactions were also attributed to the larger number of children in family day care homes.

Long and Garduque (1987) observed 36 preschool children at home with their mothers and again with their family day care providers. The type and frequency of children's initiations with adults in each setting were observed, as well as the quality of the adults' responses to the children. Children were more likely to instrumentally seek or request initiations with mothers than with caregivers. Mothers engaged in more social and facilitative responses than caregivers and also restricted or redirected child behavior more.

A subsequent log-linear analysis indicated that, overall, children experienced more frequent facilitation responses from mothers than from caregivers across all types of initiations. However, family day care providers were more likely to facilitate and mothers more likely to ignore instrumental requests, and caregivers were more likely to ignore children's social initiations. When adult-initiated behavior sequences were analyzed, results revealed that the children were contributing to the differences between settings rather than vice versa (in contrast to Stith & Davis, 1984).

Long and Garduque (1987) inferred from these data that there were differences between adult-child interactions at home and in family day care, but these differences were complementary and, to a great extent, created by the children rather than the adults. The differences between these results and those of Stith and Davis (1984) may be partially due to the vast differences in ages of the samples and to the small sample employed by Stith and Davis (1984).

Results of these studies suggest that, as one might expect, there are differences between adult-child relationships in homes and in family day care. However, these differences do not necessarily reflect a deficit on the part of family day care homes. It is probably safe to conclude that the intensity of the caregiver-child relationship and the frequency of caregiver-child interaction are less than for mothers and children. The quality of the relationships appears to be comparable across settings, however.

Family Day Care versus Center

Caregiver Behavior.   One of the earliest studies of infant day care (Golden, Rosenbluth, Grossi, Policare, Freeman & Brownlee, 1979) compared caregiver behavior in centers and in family day care homes. There were no differences in the amount of cognitive-language or socioemotional stimulation between the two types of programs across a day's time, although the amount of socioemotional stimulation at the noon meal was greater in family day care. Family day care providers were observed to give more individual attention to the children than caregivers in centers. Overall, the differences between caregiver behavior in centers and family day care homes were few.

Cochran (1977) compared child-rearing techniques of caregivers in centers with those of caregivers in family day care homes and mothers in their own homes for a sample of Swedish toddlers. Of ten comparisons, four were significant. Caregivers in centers did less teaching and supervising and expressed fewer "do's" and "don'ts" than either family day care providers or mothers. Behaviors such as praise, ignoring, or helping were similar across settings. According to the researcher, these results suggest that children receive more restrictions and directions in home settings of either type than in centers, perhaps due to more "off-limits" areas in homes than in centers.

Twenty family day care providers and 20 center caregivers were observed in interactions with toddlers (Howes, 1983). Out of eleven comparisons of caregiver behavior between the two settings, Howes (1983) found only one significant difference. Family day care providers were more likely to ignore toddler requests than center caregivers. This difference was not of particular importance, since the frequency of ignoring requests for either group was so small.

Clarke-Stewart's (1986) comparisons of family day care homes and centers revealed no differences in caregiver behavior between the two settings. Both the quantity and quality of caregiver behaviors were similar in homes and centers.

There is little evidence of any important differences in the behavior of family day care providers and that of caregivers in centers. Rather, in most of the studies, the behavior of the two groups of caregivers was remarkably similar.

Environment/Context.   Several studies have compared contextual factors of family day care homes and centers. It is relevant to compare such things as facilities, equipment, and amount and type of program structure, since these are factors that are likely to affect the children in these settings.

Golden et al. (1979) reported that family day care in New York City had better adult-child ratios than center care but had poorer play materials, equipment, and play space and more safety hazards. Howes (1983) found adult-child ratios to be comparable for family day care and center care, but found smaller group sizes in family day care (3.5 versus 10.4). Centers had significantly more child-designed space than family day care homes, and caregivers in centers spent less time in housework activities than family day care providers.

Floody and Weiberg (1982) found that family day care homes were significantly less structured and had fewer children per adult than center-based programs (similar to Golden et al., 1979). Contrary to Golden et al. (1979), they found no differences between centers and family day care homes in the quality of the physical space, materials and activities, and health and safety. Floody and Weiberg (1982) attributed this relative lack of significant differences between settings to the fact that they compared only five centers to eight family day care homes.

Another study (Innes, Woodman, Banspach, Thompson & Inwald, 1982) took the unusual step of controlling for adult-child ratios and group size by comparing large or group family day care homes (12 children with 2 adults) to classrooms in day care centers that were matched on those variables. One difference between settings that remained was the mixed ages in the family day care homes and the homogeneous age groupings in the centers. Two centers and four family day care homes were compared. The biggest differences in context between the two types of settings were in the amount of indoor structured time (higher in family day care), transition time (higher in centers), and indoor unstructured time (higher in centers). Children in family day care homes were more likely to be assigned to an activity or to be involved in a structured group activity (e.g., singing, cutting and pasting) when playing indoors; children in centers were more likely to be allowed to engage in free play. The researchers explained their results in terms of space (enough space for free play in centers but not in homes) and the more "institutional" organizational climate of centers, resulting in greater regimentation (more transition time) and less flexibility in scheduling than in family day care. Since the sample is extremely small, it is difficult to know how representative these data are of typical family day care homes with fewer children and one caregiver.

Clarke-Stewart (1986, 1987) combined results for in-home care and family day care because there were few significant differences between them. These data revealed that home care in Chicago was more dirty, messy, and even potentially dangerous (e.g., sharp and/or broken objects) than center care. There were fewer toys and educational materials available to the children in family day care and more adult-oriented decorations (plants, televisions, stereos, vases). Centers were more likely than family day care homes to have a regular schedule, a curriculum, and to provide learning activities (e.g., stories). Children in family day care spent more time watching television than those in centers. Adult-child ratios were similar for family day care and center care in this study.

Taken together, these studies suggest that family day care homes have similar or better adult-child ratios to centers but poorer facilities and play equipment. Two large studies (Golden et al., 1979; Clarke-Stewart, 1986, 1987) found that family day care homes are more likely to have safety hazards than centers. Finally, it appears that family day care homes are, as one might surmise, more flexible in their schedules and less oriented toward "formal" learning experiences than centers.

Children's Behavior and Development. The majority of studies examining infants and toddlers in family day care versus center-based programs have found no differences. Howes and Rubenstein (1981) found no overall differences in toddlers' socially directed behavior or peer play as a function of child care setting. Likewise, the Bermuda Infant Care Study (Schwarz, Scarr, Caparulo, Furrow, McCartney, Billington, Phillips & Hindy, 1981) found few or no differences in 22 cognitive and personality variables among infants in three care settings (home, relative, or sitter), nor did the Stanford Day Care Project on measures of cooperation, compliance, and sharing (Everson, Ambron, Sarnat, Kermoian & Wenegrat, 1983). Melhuish, Lloyd, Martin, and Mooney (1990) reported no differences in the cognitive or language development of British 18-month-olds as a function of child care setting (home, relative, child-minder, or nursery).

Only two studies have found differences between infants and toddlers in family day care and those in centers. The New York Infant Day Care Study (Golden et al., 1979) reported that infants in family day care scored lower on the Stanford-Binet Intelligence Test than the infants in center care. However, for the most part, infants' cognitive-language behavior and social-emotional behavior did not differ as a function of care setting. Melhuish, Mooney, Martin, and Lloyd (1990) found that even though toddlers' cognitive and language development did not vary as a function of care setting, their interactional experiences did. In general, that study found that infants with "child-minders" experienced better interactions than did infants in nurseries. Even in the studies in which differences were found, however, there were a substantial number of nonsignificant differences. Overall, the balance of results shows few to no differences in infants' and toddlers' development or behavior as a function of care in family day care homes versus centers.

Similar to the research on infants and toddlers, the majority of studies comparing preschool children or school-aged children with family day care or center care experience find few or no differences between them. It is important to note where the studies were conducted, however, since results vary to some degree by country. Lamb and colleagues (Lamb, Hwang, Broberg & Bookstein, 1988; Lamb, Hwang, Bookstein, Broberg, Hult & Frodi, 1988) found no differences in the social competence of Swedish preschoolers who were enrolled in day care centers, day care homes, or cared for at home. Likewise, Floody and Weiberg (1982) reported no differences in the behavior of American preschoolers enrolled in family day care versus those enrolled in centers.

Three studies assessed children in the public schools to determine whether the child care setting to which they had been exposed as pre-schoolers had any carryover effects. One of these studies assessed the adaptive behavior of children in kindergarten and found no differences as a function of type of child care. Andersson (1989, 1990) conducted a longitudinal study of the effects of child care experiences on later cognitive and social development of Swedish children. He found that type of care was not a significant predictor of children's development at either age 8 (Andersson, 1989) or age 13 (Andersson, 1990).

Several studies have found differences in children's behavior or development as a function of child care setting. Cochran (1977) observed that children in day care homes in Sweden explored more and played more than children in center-based programs. On the other hand, he also reported no differences in children's developmental status as measured by the Griffiths Mental Development Scale. Innes et al. (1982) found that children had more positive group contact in group family day care homes and engaged in more associative and sociodramatic play than children in centers. The children in centers engaged in more onlooker play than children in family day care. In both of these studies, there were more similarities than differences between children as a function of child care setting.

The most striking differences in development between children in family day care versus those in centers were reported by Clarke-Stewart (1984, 1986). The Chicago Study of Child Care and Development found that these differences were consistently in favor of the children in center-based programs (child care or nursery school). Children in center-based programs performed better than children in home care (baby-sitter or family day care homes) on observations of cognitive development, social cognition, and social competence with adults. Clarke-Stewart attributes these differences to the greater educational orientation of center-based programs. It is not possible to judge the viability of that hypothesis, since the data were correlational and did not allow causal attributions to be drawn.

Overall, the research on preschool children's development in family day care versus center care suggests that there may be some differences for American, but not Swedish, children. Only in the Clarke-Stewart (1984, 1986) study, however, do these potential differences appear to be worthy of concern. Also, in several instances, differences favored the children in family day care (Innes et al., 1982). The stronger evidence for differential effects of care settings for preschoolers over infants may indicate the greater sensitivity of older children to the types of differences that characterize the two settings. Most of these differences were found to involve context as opposed to caregiver behavior. Evidence of differences in children's behavior or development as a function of care setting should not be overstated in light of the relatively few studies and the lack of comparability of measures across studies.

CONCLUSION

Descriptive and comparative research concerning family day care is relatively abundant. Family day care has been shown to be comparable to center care in terms of its "market share" of the children in need of care (Bureau of the Census, 1987) and the rates parents pay (Hofferth & Kisker, 1991). Parents who choose family day care are no different demographically from parents using center care (Clarke-Stewart, 1984; Rapp & Lloyd, 1989) except that the mothers are more likely to work part time and are more likely to have an infant or toddler in need of care (Hofferth & Phillips, 1987). Family day care homes are less likely to be regulated than centers, and caregivers are unlikely to be formally trained. Adult-child ratios in family day care are similar to or better than those in centers, and group sizes are usually smaller (Howes, 1983; Golden et al., 1979).

The research suggests that one area of significant difference between family day care homes and centers is the environmental context in which child care services are provided. Family day care homes typically have smaller spaces and are more poorly equipped than centers (Clarke-Stewart, 1986; Golden et al., 1979). There is even evidence that they may be more hazardous environments, since family day care homes are not arranged for children's exclusive use (Clarke-Stewart, 1986). On the other hand, there is little evidence of differences in caregiver behavior or caregiver-child interactions between centers and family day care homes. Caregivers in family day care homes appear to have high-quality relationships with the children but, compared with mother-child relationships, they are less intense and less frequent (Krentz, 1981; Stith & Davis, 1984).

How are these contextual differences reflected in the behavior and development of the children in family day care? Assessments of developmental status of infants and preschoolers find few differences as a function of form of child care (Cochran, 1977; Stith & Davis, 1984). Some differences in preschool children have been found using observational measures of cognitive and social competence. Some of these differences favor the family day care children (Cochran, 1977; Innes et al., 1982), and some favor children in center-based care (Clarke-Stewart, 1984,

1986). There is some evidence that differences in children's behavior as a function of setting can be attributed more to the child than to the setting (Long & Garduque, 1987). Thus the research does not make a strong case for family day care being either inferior or superior to centers as a rearing environment for children.

This body of descriptive and comparative research supports the notion that the developmental potential of family day care for children is probably no different than that of other child care settings, although it makes its impact in its own unique way. Given these conclusions, it is safe to say that the time for making blanket comparisons between child care settings is past. "Good" family day care ought not to be defined in terms of what are considered "good" homes or "good" centers.

To understand the ecology of family day care and its effects on children, we must form realistic conceptions of family day care as a unique child-rearing setting and interpret associations between the conditions of care and children's development independently from what we know about other settings. To do so will require a fresh agenda and a new wave of research on family day care in both regulated and unregulated homes and in states with varying types and levels of regulation. This will be no simple task, since family day care providers are notoriously reluctant to allow observers into their homes and unregulated caregivers are difficult to locate. Moving family day care research past its infancy will require looking beyond descriptions of caregivers and its resemblance to homes and centers, instead capturing its unique ecology as a child care setting. Based on a few relatively recent attempts at this "new wave" approach (Howes & Stewart, 1987; Kontos, 1990), it appears that research on family day care has a bright future before it.

REFERENCES

Abbot-Shim, M., & Kaufman, M. (1986). *Characteristics of family day care providers*. (ERIC Document Reproduction No. ED 287 585)

Andersson, B.-E. (1989). Effects of public day-care: A longitudinal study. *Child Development, 60*, 857–866.

Andersson, B.-E. (1990, April). *Effects of day care on cognitive and socio-emotional competence in 13-year-old Swedish schoolchildren*. Paper presented at the annual meeting of the American Education Research Association, Boston.

Bollin, G. (1990, April). *An investigation of turnover among family day care providers*. Paper presented at the annual meeting of the American Educational Research Association, Boston.

Bollin, G. (under review). An investigation of turnover among family day care providers.

Bureau of the Census. (1987). *Who's minding the kids: Child care arrangements: 1986–87* (Series P-70, No. 20). Washington, DC: U.S. Government Printing Office.

Children's Foundation. (1990). *1990 family day care licensing study.* Washington, DC: Author.

Clarke-Stewart, K. A. (1984). Day care: A new context for research and development. In M. Permutter (Ed.), *Minnesota Symposium on Child Psychology* (pp. 61–100). Minneapolis: University of Minnesota Press.

Clarke-Stewart, K. A. (1986). Family day care: A home away from home? *Children's Environments Quarterly, 3,* 34–46.

Clarke-Stewart, K. A. (1987). Predicting child development from child care forms and features: The Chicago study. In D. Phillips (Ed.), *Quality in child care: What does research tell us?* (pp. 21–41). Washington, DC: National Association for the Education of Young Children.

Class, N. (1980). Some reflections on the development of child care facility licensing. In S. Kilmer (Ed.), *Advances in early education and day care,* vol. 1 (pp. 3–18). Greenwich, CT: JAI Press.

Cochran, M. (1977). A comparison of group day and family childrearing patterns in Sweden. *Child Development, 48,* 702–707.

Divine-Hawkins, P. (1981). *Family day care in the United States: Executive Summary. Final Report of the National Day Care Home Study.* (ERIC Document Reproduction No. ED 211 244)

Eheart, B. K., & Leavitt, R. (1986). Training day care homes providers: Implications for policy and research. *Early Childhood Research Quarterly, 1,* 119–132.

Everson, M., Ambron, S., Sarnat, L., Kermoian, R., & Wenegrat, A. (1983, April). *Effects of day care on the socialization of toddlers.* Paper presented at the biennial meeting of the Society for Research in Child Development, Detroit.

Fischer, J. (1989). *Family day care: Factors influencing the quality of caregiver practices.* Unpublished doctoral dissertation, University of Illinois, Champaign-Urbana.

Floody, D., & Weiberg, J. (1982). *A comparison of group and family day care.* (ERIC Document Reproduction No. ED 242 425)

Fosburg, S. (1982). Family day care: The role of the surrogate mother. In L. Laosa & I. Sigel (Eds.), *Families as learning environments* (pp. 223–260). New York: Plenum Press.

Goelman, H., Shapiro, E., & Pence, A. (1990). Family environment and family day care. *Family Relations, 39,* 14–19.

Golden, M., Rosenbluth, M., Grossi, H., Policare, H., Freeman, H., & Brownlee, E. (1979). *The New York infant day care study.* New York: Medical and Health Research Association of New York City. (ERIC Document Reproduction No. ED 167 260)

Hofferth, S., & Kisker, E. (1991). *The changing demographics of family day care in the United States.* Unpublished paper.

Hofferth, S., & Phillips, D. (1987). Child care in the United States: 1970–1995. *Journal of Marriage and the Family, 47,* 93–116.

Howes, C. (1983). Caregiver behavior in center and family day care. *Journal of Applied Developmental Psychology, 4,* 99–107.

Howes, C., & Rubenstein, J. (1981). Toddler peer behavior in two types of day care. *Infant Behavior and Development, 4,* 387–393.

Howes, C., & Stewart, P. (1987). Child's play with adults, toys, and peers: An examination of family and child care influences. *Developmental Psychology, 23,* 423–430.

Innes, R., Woodman, J., Banspach, S., Thompson, L., & Inwald, C. (1982). A comparison of the environments of day care centers and group day care homes for 3-year-olds. *Journal of Applied Developmental Psychology, 3,* 41–56.

Kahn, A., & Kamerman, S. (1987). *Child care: Facing the hard choices.* Dover, MA: Auburn House.

Kamerman, S., & Kahn, A. (1981). *Child care, family benefits, and working parents.* New York: Columbia University Press.

Kisker, E., Maynard, R., Gordon, A., & Strain, M. (1989). *The child care challenge: What parents need and what is available in three metropolitan areas.* Princeton, NJ: Mathematica Policy Research, Inc.

Kontos, S. (1990, April). *Children, families, and child care: The search for connections.* Paper presented at the annual meeting of the American Educational Research Association, Boston.

Krentz, M. (1983, April). *Qualitative differences between mother-child and caregiver-child attachments of infants in day care.* Paper presented at the biennial meeting of the Society for Research in Child Development, Detroit.

Lamb, M., Hwang, C.-P., Bookstein, F., Broberg, A., Hult, G., & Frodi, M. (1988). Determinants of social competence in Swedish preschoolers. *Developmental Psychology, 24,* 58–70.

Lamb, M., Hwang, C.-P., Broberg, A., & Bookstein, F. (1988). The effects of out-of-home care on the development of social competence in Sweden: A longitudinal study. *Early Childhood Research Quarterly, 3,* 379–402.

Long, F., & Garduque, L. (1987). Continuity between home and family day care: Caregivers' and mothers' perceptions and children's social experiences. In D. Peters & S. Kontos (Eds.), *Continuity and discontinuity of experience in child care* (pp. 69–90). *Advances in Applied Developmental Psychology,* vol. 2. Norwood, NJ: Ablex.

Melhuish, E., Lloyd, E., Martin, S., & Mooney, A. (1990). Type of childcare at 18 months. II: Relations with cognitive and language development. *Journal of Child Psychology and Psychiatry, 31,* 861–870.

Melhuish, E., Mooney, A., Martin, S., & Lloyd, E. (1990). Type of childcare at 18 months. I: Differences in interactional experience. *Journal of Child Psychology and Psychiatry, 31,* 849–859.

Moore, B., Snow, C., & Poteat, M. (1988). Effects of variant types of child care experience on the adaptive behavior of kindergarten children. *American Journal of Orthopsychiatry, 58*, 297–303.

Morgan, G. (1980). Can quality family day care be achieved through regulation? In S. Kilmer (Ed.), *Advances in early education and day care*, vol. 1 (pp. 77–102). Greenwich, CT: JAI Press.

National Association for the Education of Young Children. (1985). *In whose hands?* Washington, DC: Author.

National Commission on Working Women. (1985). *Child care fact sheet: Working mothers and children.* Washington, DC: Author.

Nelson, M. (1990). Mothering others' children: The experiences of family day care providers. *Signs: The Journal of Women in Culture and Society, 15*, 586–605.

Pence, A., & Goelman, H. (1987). Who care for the children in day care? An examination of caregivers from three types of care. *Early Childhood Research Quarterly, 2*, 315–334.

Phillips, D., Lande, J., & Goldberg, M. (1990). The state of child care regulation: A comparative analysis. *Early Childhood Research Quarterly, 5*, 151–179.

Phillips, D., & Whitebook, M. (1986). Who are child care workers? *Young Children, 41*, 14–20.

Rapp, G., & Lloyd, S. (1989). The role of "home as haven" ideology in child care use. *Family Relations, 38*, 426–430.

Rosenthal, M. (1988). *Attitudes and behaviors of caregivers in family day care: The effects of personal background, professional support system and the immediate caregiving environment.* (ERIC Document Reproduction No. 306 040)

Schwarz, J. C., Scarr, S., Caparulo, B., Furrow, D., McCartney, K., Billington, R., Phillips, D., & Hindy, C. (1981, August). *Center, sitter, and home day care before age two: A report on the first Bermuda infant care study.* Paper presented at the annual convention of the American Psychological Association, Los Angeles.

Steinberg, L., & Green, C. (1979). *How parents may mediate the effect of day care.* (ERIC Document Reproduction No. ED 168 698)

Stith, S., & Davis, A. (1984). Employed mothers and family day care substitute caregivers: A comparative analysis of infant care. *Child Development, 55*, 1340–1348.

CHAPTER 8

Before- and After-School Child Care for Elementary School Children

Michelle Seligson
Ellen Gannett
with Lillian Cotlin

The term "school-age child care" is used to describe a wide range of programs for children aged 5 to 14 before and after school, during school holidays, and when schools are closed. Many programs consider their primary function to be recreational rather than academic. Most say they provide child care to assist working parents, although program hours and scope of service do not always conform to parents' needs. Some programs are designed only for students in kindergarten and the lower elementary grades. Others include or are specifically organized for older elementary-age children or those in middle school. Some programs focus on the arts, others on sports or field trips. Others emphasize intellectual enrichment. Many combine these and more. Program names include "extended day," "latchkey," "kids club," and "after-school" — names as varied as their locations and administrative auspices. School-age child care programs may be located in schools, recreation centers, day care centers, Y's, Boys and Girls Clubs, art centers, park and recreation facilities, a variety of other youth centers and camps, and family day care homes.

The provision of school-age child care is not identified with any single organization or profession. Many groups have been involved for decades, even generations. Others came forward in the 1980s in response to increased attention to this issue. The range of models for service delivery can be bewildering to newcomers to the field. Child care for school-age children in the United States, like care for younger children, has been accurately characterized as a "patchwork quilt."

Parent groups, public and private schools, churches, preschool day care centers, municipal recreation departments, and youth-oriented recreational institutions have all been part of the development of school-age child care in the United States.

Collaborative models provide many of the best examples of quality school-age child care. There are several reasons for this. First, it is logical for organizations and agencies with expertise in meeting the out-of-school recreational and social needs of children to continue to deliver these services. However, school-age child care may pose challenges to such agencies that they cannot meet without help from other groups. Second, the scarcity of resources within the field makes collaboration a sensible way to share costs. Third, the wide range of ages and developmental needs within the school-age child care population, from kindergarten through age 14, demands varying opportunities for the youngsters involved. Ultimately, the culture of a particular community determines where and by whom programs will be developed and to what extent collaboration will exist. In some places, there are no resources geared to school-age children other than the public schools. In such communities the school has become a key partner. In other places, there is a host of potential partners for collaborative program development.

During the last decade, mothers of young school-age children have entered or reentered the out-of-home labor force at an accelerating rate. Three-quarters of the mothers of school-age children work outside the home, most of them full time (70%). In response to this trend, school-age child care has been the fastest-growing segment of nonfamilial child care services.

However, school-age child care is not new to the United States. During the late 1800s, settlement houses, religious institutions, and schools offered services to this age group that were variously designed to protect, educate, and acculturate children of immigrant families. The history of school-age child care mirrors the multiple-service agenda of many contemporary programs as they attempt to respond to societal crisis and upheaval. Child care for working parents remains the most often cited rationale for school-age programs. But increasing concern about the physical and emotional safety of children now motivates many program planners, especially in deteriorating cities and economically depressed areas. As more children experience social anomie, school-age child care programs emerge as a unique source of continuity in children's lives.

This chapter surveys trends in school-age child care during the past decade; reviews existing research on latchkey children and outcomes from participation in programs, and discusses some of the issues and questions that must be addressed as society grapples with the need to create environments of care for children of all ages.

LATCHKEY PRACTICES

The majority of young school-age children remain regularly unsupervised or in a variety of patchwork arrangements of varying developmental appropriateness. Such latchkey practices are a de facto form of school-age child care, utilized by parents through choice or necessity.

Several attempts have been made to determine the total number of young school-age children without some form of regular care and supervision. In 1987 the U.S. Bureau of the Census released the most conservative estimate to date. The number of latchkey children (children in "self-care") nationwide was estimated at 7% of 5- to 13-year-olds, or 2.1 million children.

Many parents, educators, and policymakers have questioned the Census Bureau's figures for three reasons. First, there is no consensus about how many hours of self-care constitutes latchkey arrangements. Second, it is not always possible to disaggregate data on self-care by age of child. Third, underreporting may be a significant problem, since parents may be reluctant to admit on surveys that their children regularly care for themselves.

The findings of a Louis Harris poll, commissioned by the Metropolitan Life Study of American Teachers in 1987, confirmed these doubts. It found that 12% of parents of elementary school children acknowledged regular use of self-care. Localized studies of child care practices conducted during the 1980s show that although kindergartners are unlikely to be alone after school, by the time children reach age 10, as many as 70% are on their own. Many are beginning to be responsible for themselves and younger siblings at age 7 or 8.

How successful families are at managing these arrangements depends on availability of networks or support, discretionary income, and community resources. But mounting evidence points to school-age children's need for care, attention, and mentoring. Thousands of children return home from school each day or hit the city streets to care for themselves or each other without benefit of adult guidance or community responsiveness.

Thus far, published research on the impact of the latchkey situation is inconclusive. However, most studies suggest that children's loneliness, social isolation, lower academic performance, and exposure to negative peer influences, coupled with unrealistic parental expectations of their children's maturity, are possible results of self-care experiences.

Some of the most interesting data comes from children responding to questions about their experiences when alone (Grollman & Sweder, 1986; Long & Long, 1981; Steinberg, 1989; Zill, Gruvacus & Woyshner, 1977). In these studies, children expressed fear of accidents, assault by older siblings or strangers, and sexual victimization. Such fears appear less frequent in rural than in suburban settings (Galambos & Garbarino, 1982; Long & Long, 1983). In general, research projects conducted in urban areas have found that self-care and sibling care have negative effects (Entwistle, 1975; Long & Long, 1981; Woods, 1972). Similar surveys of rural and suburban children have tended to find no negative outcomes (Galambos & Garbarino, 1982; Vandell & Corasiniti, 1985). The perceived safety of the neighborhood may play a role in mitigating the effects of the latchkey experience.

Risks may also be mediated by the parent-child relationship, parenting style, and peer relationships. Steinberg (1989) concluded that it is not enough to categorize children as latchkey or nonlatchkey in order to predict their behavior. The family context and neighborhood environment have to be considered in order to determine the impact of self-care. Steinberg found that latchkey children who "hung out" and lacked parental structure faced greater risks than those going home to an environment with consistent parental rules. The further removed children are from adult supervision, the more susceptible they are to peer pressure. Steinberg also found that parenting style made a difference. Parents using an authoritative approach (neither authoritarian nor permissive) seemed to have children with internalized parental norms and values, who were more resistant to peer pressure. Steinberg concludes that a few hours of self-care are of less significance than the overall quality and the nature and degree of available adult supervision.

When asked to rank seven possible causes of students having difficulty in school, 51% of teachers interviewed for the 1987 Harris poll singled out children being left on their own after school as the number-one factor. *The Communicator*, published by the National Association of Elementary School Principals, reported in February 1988 that 37% of principals sampled believed that children would perform better in school if they were not left unsupervised for long periods.

In summary, latchkey children appear to experience more negative effects than their supervised peers. Children most at risk are younger, live in inner-city neighborhoods where they remain inside for many hours each afternoon, and are out of contact with their parents. But while the debate by researchers over the potential risks of self-care continues, the loss of opportunities for these children may be taking its toll on personality and skills development. Research is needed on the impact of self-care on the child, but researchers also need to look at the larger picture—what latchkey arrangements ultimately mean for parents, families, and the community as a whole.

Some Responses to Latchkey Practices

Books, pamphlets, films, videotapes, and other materials have been created to respond to concerns about children who are regularly unsupervised. The American Home Economics Association and the Whirlpool Foundation's Project Home Safe focus on developing resources for parents and for children who are on their own after school. Survival skills courses are taught in some schools, and a number of communities have instituted a telephone "warm-line" for children who are home alone. Experts agree that the key consideration in deciding on a child's readiness for self-care involves parental knowledge of the child's developmental level and readiness for new responsibilities and continual review of how self-care is working for both parent and child.

The American Library Association recognizes the urgent need to assist libraries in serving latchkey children. The topic is controversial, with librarians disagreeing about their appropriate role in serving this age group. Latchkey children present awkward choices and challenging opportunities; serving them seems to both coincide and conflict with the basic mission of public libraries. Traditionally, libraries' professional ethics assure free public access to all patrons. Thus latchkey children are welcome to utilize their resources and materials. Yet most public libraries are not staffed, equipped, or licensed to function as child care centers. Indeed, librarians generally agree that their role should not be that of disciplinarian or baby-sitter. Many believe that service to other patrons will be impaired if their attention and time are spent supervising or entertaining these children (Dowd, 1991).

However, many libraries are working with latchkey children in a positive way. At the Greenfield Public Library in Indiana, a "Junior Friends of the Library Club" meets monthly after school, sponsors programs such as the adopt-a-book campaign, elects officers, and writes letters to their favorite authors. In Augusta, Georgia, the Wallace Branch Library, which circulated few materials and was underutilized, has been designated a "homework center." Library staff are trained in tutoring in math and reading. Other libraries are scheduling after-school programs such as film showings, puppet shows, or crafts projects.

CONTENT AND QUALITY OF SCHOOL-AGE CHILD CARE

Several surveys of school-age child care programs have gathered descriptive information regarding such topics as physical facilities; hours and days of operation; parent fees; staffing patterns; and the number, age range, and demographics of the children served. These studies have provided important data on the overall picture of school-age child care in the United States (Hebard & Horowitz, 1986; Huling, 1985; Marx, 1989; Seligson & Marx, 1989; Weaver, 1988). Although they do not provide information on the developmental outcomes of school-age child care, they are an important first step in the research literature. They provide a picture of the state of the art, a sense of how programs vary and what they have in common. For example, a survey of school-age programs in New York City (Seligson & Marx, 1989) found that group size varied from 5 to 50 children. The number of children per staff member ranged from one caregiver for every 6 children to one for every 40.

Child care centers that in earlier years served mostly preschoolers have become increasingly involved in school-age child care. The state of Michigan, for instance, reported in 1988 that approximately 600 day care centers were licensed for both preschool and school-age services, and that another 50 centers were licensed exclusively for school-age (Seligson & Fink, 1989). National organizations do track program development: The National Association of Independent Schools estimated that approximately 300 of its 604 schools that serve elementary students have active extended-day programs. The YMCA reported that of the 1,869 branches responding to a 1990 statistical survey, 61% had school-age child care programs. Other youth-service agencies have increased their school-age services. The Boys Clubs of America found that as early as 1984, approximately 200 of its 1,100 clubs (81%) had switched from a traditional drop-in format to more formalized school-age child care for at least some children.

A 1988 study conducted by the School-Age Child Care (SACC) Project sought information from child care licensing agencies and departments of education in every state. It asked for the numbers of programs serving school-age children before and after school, the approximate number of children served, and the standards and regulations applied to the programs (Fink, 1990).

Research data on quality was derived from a second SACC Project study based on a national sample of 130 school-age child care providers in six geographic areas. The providers gave detailed information about nearly every aspect of their programs. Findings included information on physical facilities, program content, staffing patterns, staff qualifications, wages and benefits, evaluation procedures, parent fees, and scope of services (Marx, 1990).

Although school-age child care has been on the public policy agenda at all levels over the last decade, we found that most states have little information on the numbers of programs or children attending them:

• Only four state child care licensing agencies — Ohio, New Hampshire, Vermont, and South Dakota — were able to fully report the numbers of licensed, center-based school-age child care programs and their licensed capacity.

• The adult-child caregiving ratios mandated by states for six-year-olds ranged from 1 : 10 in Maine, Montana, and New York, to 1 : 26 in Texas. Seventeen states had ratio requirements of 1 : 20 or lower.

• All but 11 states exempted public school–run programs from licensing. A few also exempted other public entities (e.g., municipalities) and groups such as the Girl Scouts, the YMCA, and the YWCA. Many states exempted private and religious schools.

The response to our survey of state licensing agencies and education departments demonstrated that many were not yet closely monitoring and collecting data on the development of school-age child care. However, a few licensing agencies and a larger number of education departments had very accurate and up-to-date information.

The majority of programs sampled in the provider survey were affiliated with public schools, child care centers, and youth-serving agencies. Fewer programs were affiliated with churches, municipal park and recreation departments, or social service agencies, although in some communities, park and recreation departments and youth-serving agencies provide the bulk of services to school-age children. Nonetheless, the results of the survey do provide us with some insights into the programs:

• The majority of programs operate year round (81%), provide both before- and after-school care (75%), and provide services until 6 p.m. (76%). Thus in terms of access to services, the programs sampled appear to accommodate working parents.

• The majority of programs in the sample are licensed (69%), and five of the exempt programs reported that they voluntarily sought licensing. Public school programs are the most likely to be exempt from licensing.

- Ninety-three (71.5%) of the programs begin serving children at age five, clearly indicating that first grade is no longer the definition of when children are school age. (In many places three- and four-year-olds are in public school programs and also in need of after-school services.) The average maximum age served is 11.5 years.
- Salaries for caregivers in school-age child care are only slightly better than the low salaries of preschool staff reported by the National Day Care Staffing Study. Highest salaries were paid by public schools ($9.36/hour), the lowest by for-profit child care centers ($4.90/hour). On average, a teacher working an average 30-hour week for 46 weeks earns $9,431 a year.
- Eighty-five (65%) of the survey respondents reported that they had had staff turnover in the prior program year; 29% reported that they still had not filled the positions.
- On average, the staff-child ratio was 1 : 12.5. For five-year-olds, the ratio ranged from 1 : 1 to 1 : 20; for eight- and nine-year-olds, it ranged from 1 : 4 to 1 : 25.
- The survey listed 25 possible activities that programs might offer. The most frequently offered activity was arts and crafts, followed by free time, resting/quiet time, reading, field trips, athletics, and homework help. Formal tutoring and other school-like activities were far less frequent. The majority of programs encouraged children to select their own activities. By and large, 85% of the programs indicated that children were provided with opportunities to engage in individual self-directed activities.
- The average cost per child for Monday to Friday after-school care during the 1988 school year was $26.52 a week. The range was from $19.29 to $29.11; the most expensive was for-profit child care; the least expensive was municipal parks and recreation programs. Rural programs were the least expensive; urban programs the most expensive. For-profit programs were found to charge the highest fees, and their teachers were reported to earn the lowest salary ($4.90/hour).

The findings of the SACC in America study are somewhat reassuring. The programs appear to be offering a solid assortment of choices designed to help children relax and expand their horizons in a supervised environment. Staff turnover is a major concern, but openings appear to be filled within five to six weeks. Teaching staffs appear to be moderately well educated, and in-service training opportunities are frequent enough in most programs to help improve staff skills. Nevertheless, this study was only exploratory, and greater detail is needed.

By the fall of 1992, the U.S. Department of Education will have concluded a study of 1,300 nationally representative before- and after-school programs. This will be the first study of school-age child care undertaken by the federal government. RMC Research Corporation, Mathematica Policy Research, and the SACC Project are conducting the study, which will provide detailed data on the prevalence and quality of school-age child care programs in the United States.

RESEARCH ON PROGRAM OUTCOMES

As a relatively recent phenomenon, school-age child care has not yet received much attention from the education research community. Few studies have addressed the developmental outcomes of participation in school-age child care. A small number of outcome evaluations report academic and social gains for low-income, at-risk children (Entwistle, 1975; Howes et al., 1987; Mayesky, 1980a, 1980b).

In one of the few studies to compare children in a variety of supervised and unsupervised settings, Vandell and Corasiniti (1985) compared a group of third-graders from a middle-class suburb on sociometric, conduct, and academic variables. A total of 147 children were divided according to four possible arrangements: returning home after school to a parent or relative; attending a day care center; returning home to be cared for by a sitter; and returning home alone or with siblings. The day care children were rated more poorly by teachers on work and study skills than the comparison group of non-day care children. These third-graders, however, were enrolled in day care centers with no special provisions for older school-age children. The authors have speculated that these lower grades may have been the result of the poor quality of the day care centers, which "typically had a large number of children, a small staff with minimal training, and limited age-appropriate activities" (p. 18).

Data from a recent evaluation of a language development after-school program, funded through a grant from the U.S. Department of Education's School Dropout Demonstration Assistance Program, found that 79% of the participants showed a gain of one or more months in reading achievement per month of instruction (Springer & Long, 1989).

POLICY DEVELOPMENTS

Despite the lack of conclusive outcome studies, legislators and program planners at the federal, state, and local levels are moving ahead with large-scale funding and development projects, basing those initiatives on assumed benefits to children. In the mid 1980s Congress appropriated funds for new and improved school-age child care programs across the country. The Child Care and Development Block Grant passed by Congress in 1990 authorized $750 million for fiscal year 1991.

At this writing, at least 15 states have targeted school-age child care for special legislation, with and without funding allocations. Examples include California's $30 million latchkey initiative tied to the GAIN welfare/work program originally enacted in 1985; New York's statewide grants program; and Indiana's latchkey legislation, which pioneered earmarking funds for programs serving low-income children.

City and Local Initiatives

A handful of cities have mounted funding and coordination projects that focus on school-age child care. The projects have included documenting need, convening citizen advisory groups, designing community solutions, and coordinating services and information among the public and private parties involved. These cities have recognized that school-age child care and municipal governments have shared interests:

1. The city is the appropriate level of government to develop a program for school-age child care. It can easily facilitate a productive relationship between the public schools and community-based providers, family day care providers, and parents.
2. Effective city policies and programs in child care are critical to economic growth of the city and economic independence for its residents.
3. Some cities have recognized that high-quality school-age child care may prevent vandalism, juvenile crime, and other antisocial and destructive behavior.

Gannett (1990) profiles six models of citywide funding and coordination projects for school-age child care. These cities have seen the benefits of collaboration, and their models have potential for replication in both large and small cities across the country.

Public School Involvement

Perhaps the greatest expansion of school-age child care has been generated by the question: Why not have before- and after-school programs right in the public schools? Children are already there, classrooms are vacant after school, and parents can pick up their children after work. However, school-based programs do not yet provide the majority of school-age child care. Currently, far more school-age children attend community child care centers licensed for both preschool and school-age children that operate outside the schools (Fink, 1990). Nevertheless, public schools are a critical part of an expanded delivery system for school-age child care. Partnerships between schools, other public agencies, and community groups have been a cornerstone of the basic approach to supply building, and school-based programs may be the only viable alternative for expansion of services in some communities. In Boston, for example, all appropriate community-based facilities in churches, recreation centers, and municipal buildings are fully occupied.

Thus schools are emerging as major providers of school-age child care. According to a 1988 survey by the National Association of Elementary School Principals, 22% of 1,400 American elementary and middle schools have some form of after-school program. Most of these programs are supported by parent fees, which average $25 a week. Funding for school-based or school-administered programs rarely derives from education budgets, although there are exceptions.

A small but important group of studies, mainly unpublished dissertations and papers, discuss constructive administrative practices in public school school-age child care programs (Gehring, 1990; Riley, 1990). These reveal the disadvantages of centralized and overstandardized administration of school-age child care and the advantages of community-based assessment and planning.

During 1991–92, the SACC Project and the National Association of Elementary School Principals have collaborated in a two-year training program on public school involvement in before- and after-school programs aimed at elementary and middle school principals. Upwards of 1,000 principals and community representatives from 20 states with large concentrations of disadvantaged, low-income children and families will receive training on program administration, partnerships and collaborative models, legal issues, finances, staffing, serving children with special needs, quality, and curriculum.

THE ISSUES FACING SCHOOL-AGE CHILD CARE

Since 1979, the SACC Project has tracked policies and programs that have developed in response to the growing demand for alternatives. From our research and consultation with parents, policymakers, citizen groups, and educators, we have learned that the demand for alternatives far exceeds the supply. Many more parents would use after-school programs if they were available. Cost is an obstacle for low- and moderate-income families. Although quality is improving, it is uneven: Staff-child ratios and other elements that constitute good programs vary widely from state to state. Too few cities provide the kind of recreational opportunities that are necessary for children. The corporate sector has only just begun to invest in school-age child care. Training programs for staff are limited and should be made available at community colleges and other undergraduate and graduate institutions.

Financing

Most school-age child care programs depend on parent fees for most of their revenue. Most successful programs diversify their funding base by searching for both public and private sources or enticing new funders where they exist. For program start-up and expansion, some groups have been able to utilize Community Development Block Grant funds, especially for renovations. Other programs have benefited from federal Dependent Care Grant funds. At this writing, several major U.S. corporations (including IBM) are investing in school-age child care development and improvement on behalf of employees.

To help parents defray the increased costs, some corporations are starting to provide a new benefit to working parents: summer care for their school-age children. According to a new report by the Bureau of National Affairs (1990) entitled "Summer Child Care Programs: Employers' Options for Working Parents," about two dozen companies offer care that ranges from summer camps for employees' children to flexible summer schedules for working parents.

Quality

Repeated reference to the issue of program quality (or lack of it) has become an unavoidable theme for planners and practitioners involved in school-age care. As communities begin to offer more services for school-age children, some worry that these programs will not be carefully planned. Too many existing programs stock their facilities with little more than a few balls, board games, and a stack of mimeographed ditto papers to color. The environment is cold, institutional, and unfurnished. Unfortunately the staff provide little more than organized baby-sitting. The present situation pervades almost every city and town in the United States, even in the face of increasing agreement among practitioners on the core elements of high-quality programming. Quality programs promote opportunities for industry, autonomy, and peer relations that are recognized as critical to optimal human development in the middle years of childhood.

An increasingly important issue for good programming is space. Although many high-quality public school–based school-age child care programs have been allocated space, more often than not, shared space is the current reality. Adapting shared spaces such as multipurpose rooms, cafeterias, auditoriums, or gymnasiums has become a daily prerequisite to opening the doors of most school-age child care programs. Providers have learned to develop activity centers that are easily set up and dismantled and choose furniture and storage units that make the best of a difficult situation. Shared space is perceived by many as a necessary evil if children are to be served at all, but programs suffering from second- or third-class status do not easily achieve program objectives or developmentally appropriate goals for children.

The Process of Program Improvement

A review of research literature on quality, evaluation and assessment instruments, program standards, day care regulations, and other materials directed at program improvement demonstrates that the school-age child care field is committed to self-improvement in the absence of rigorous and consistent state licensing or program standards. Youth-serving organizations such as the YMCA, 4-H, and Campfire Inc. have set about determining quality criteria for affiliated programs throughout the country. The National Association for the Education of Young Children (NAEYC) recently revised accreditation standards to include more comprehensive criteria for school-age programs. New self-assessment instruments have been developed that offer participants a specific model designed to assess program quality, help develop a program improvement plan, and guide the development of new programs. Features of this approach include providing programs with the capacity to involve parents, children, and staff in evaluation as a program activity; a tested observation instrument that covers all program features; and a manual that provides resources and guides the users in developing a program improvement plan that will increase quality (Assessing Program Quality (ASQ), O'Connor, 1991).

Professional Development

A small number of universities and community colleges are beginning to generate courses to train practitioners of school-age child care. A consensus has developed among those operating many of the best programs that staff for these programs should have diverse educational backgrounds, life experience, and professional skills. Practitioners must adapt to the needs of the out-of-school child care setting: more child-centered activities, greater choice, more involvement in the community, and an emphasis on whole child development (physical, social, cultural, emotional, and intellectual).

Many providers have found that teachers with a background in child development can transfer their skills to the school-age child care setting because they are already familiar with child-centered concepts. They know how to create an environment containing multiple learning centers where children move freely between arts-and-crafts areas, nature and science, block building and manipulatives, sand or water play, housekeeping and dramatic play, and other areas. Other valuable backgrounds for school-age child care staff are recreation and therapeutic recreation, work in summer camps, scouting organizations, outdoor education, and cultural areas such as the performing arts, music, and theater. School-agers need teachers who will guide them toward artistic expression or sensory exploration. They have much longer attention spans than preschoolers and are ready for intensive and prolonged involvement in activities that interest them.

In 1986, NAEYC awarded a membership action grant to key school-age child care leaders to determine interest in establishing a national school-age child care professional association. One year later the National School Age Child Care Alliance (NSACCA) was created. NSACCA hopes to build a coordinated national school-age child care network of information and training.

Serving Children with Special Needs

Many programs have hesitated to mainstream children with severe disabilities. In the case of children who are mentally or physically challenged, some providers are worried about the extensive staff time that might be required. In the case of children with chronic illnesses or medically fragile conditions, they are worried about their own liability and about proper training for staff. With children who have emotional and behavioral disorders, they fear the potential for injury or psychological harm to other program participants (Fink, 1988). Two organizations have tackled these problems successfully for several years—the United Cerebral Palsy Extended Day Care Program of Madison, Wisconsin, and the Fairfax-San Anselmo Children's Center of Marin County, California. Both report that the presence of special-needs children has enriched the experience for everyone.

Fink (1988) reports on three recent legal cases initiated by parents of school-age children with disabilities. The cases involve the children's enrollment in school-administered after-school programs in Alabama, Florida, and Connecticut. These cases resulted in findings in favor of the parents and against local school departments. The state of Tennessee recently undertook a review of all federally and state-funded child care programs with the aim of discontinuing funds to those programs found to be discriminating on the basis of handicap.

Serving Homeless Children

According to the U.S. Department of Education, there are in excess of 220,000 homeless school-age children in this country. There may be twice that many. Whatever the precise number, homeless families and children have become a national concern. The lack of a fixed residence has become a reason for delay, disruption, and even outright denial of education to this most vulnerable population. In 1987, the Stewart B. McKiney Homeless Assistance Act, P.L. 100-77, was signed into law to protect and ensure the right of each homeless child and youth to a free and appropriate public education. Each state was offered the opportunity and resources to develop a plan intended to design and carry out activities equivalent to those provided to children of housed families.

Homeless children, like all children, need the opportunity to "just be kids." Schools and shelters are highly structured environments with schedules and procedures that demand compliance. School-age child care/latchkey models are uniquely suited to serving these children because they stress flexibility and are parent and child driven. In September 1990, the Georgia Department of Education initiated six pilot projects to provide after-school activities for school-age homeless children in sheltered environments. These projects provide tutorial and homework assistance, recreational and cultural enrichment activities, snacks, educational materials and supplies, parental involvement, transportation assistance, self-esteem and confidence building, noninstructional support, and assistance with health care services.

CONCLUSION

At the threshold of the 1990s, school-age child care finally achieved recognition as a neglected public service. For example, the Child Care and Development Block Grants target before- and after-school programs for attention and allocate funding specifically for program improvement. Evidence that the field has begun to mature is provided by the development of a national association, a growing body of knowledge about developmentally appropriate practice, and new partners engaged in financing expansion of services to enhance availability and affordability. But a caveat is in order. Wholesale program development to meet educational agendas may well result — after-school programs as remediation stations to pick up the slack from inadequate school experiences or faltering families — unless careful attention is paid to the inherent purpose of informal learning environments such as those provided by school-age child care programs. "Real development takes place slowly and wastes a lot of time." This phrase is borrowed from the Danish Fritidshem (free-time home) movement and emphasizes the conceptual framework that must inform all school-age child care program development and improvement. Creativity, spontaneity, nurturance, mentoring, and role modeling are qualities that all good school-age child care programs should strive to achieve. Program development, research, and policy should reflect these qualities as priorities for the future.

Acknowledgment

The authors would like to acknowledge the work of Fern Marx, SACC Project Research Director, whose evaluation research has informed and enriched this chapter.

REFERENCES

Baden, R., Genser, A., Levine, J., & Seligson, M. (1982). *School-age child care: An action manual.* Boston: Auburn.

Bureau of National Affairs, Inc. (1990, June). *Summer child care programs: Employers' options for working parents* (Special Report No. 30). Washington, DC: BNA PLUS Research and Special Projects Unit.

Dart, B. (1990, July 13). Firms' summer camps for kids offer workers a new benefit: Peace of mind. *The Atlanta Constitution.*

Dowd, F. S. (1991). *Latchkey children in the library and community.* Phoenix: Oryx Press.

Entwistle, B. (1975). *Evaluating Baltimore city's school-age day care program: Results of a pilot study.* Unpublished paper, Brown University, Providence, RI.

Fink, D. B. (1988). *School-age children with special needs: What do they do when school is out?* Boston: Exceptional Parent Press.

Fink, D. B. (1990). *School-age child care in America: Findings of a 1988 study* (Action Research Paper No. 3). Wellesley, MA: School-Age Child Care Project.

Galambos, D. L., & Garbarino, J. (1982). *Identifying the missing links in the study of latchkey children.* Paper presented to American Psychological Association, Washington, DC.

Gannett, E. (1988). *Boston school-age child care coordination project progress report.* Wellesley, MA: School-Age Child Care Project.

Gannett, E. (1990). *City initiatives in school-age child care* (Action Research Paper No. 1). Wellesley, MA: School-Age Child Care Project.

Garbarino, J. *Can American families afford the luxury of childhood?* Unpublished paper, Erickson Institute, Chicago.

Gehring, E. (1990). *School-age child care programs in public schools: A description and analysis.* Unpublished dissertation, University of Kentucky, Louisville.

Grollman, E., & Sweder, G. (1986). *The working parent dilemma: How to balance the responsibility of children and careers.* Boston: Beacon Press.

Hebard, A., & Horowitz, S. (1986). *Final evaluation of the 1985–86 after-school program.* New York: New York City Public Schools, Office of Educational Assessment.

Howes, C., Olenick, M., & Der-Kiureghian, T. (1987). After-school child care in an elementary school: Social development and continuity and complementarity of programs. *The Elementary School Journal, 88*(1), 93–103.

Huling, T. (1985). *School age child care: What next?* New York: Neighborhood Family Services Coalition.

Long, L., & Long, T. (1983). *Latchkey children.* Washington, DC: Catholic University. (ERIC Document Reproduction No. ED 226 836)

Long, T., & Long, L. (1981). *Latchkey children: The child's view of self care.* Washington, DC: Catholic University. (ERIC Document Reproduction No. ED 211 229)

Marx, F. (1989). *After school programs for low-income young adolescents: Overview and program profiles* (Working Paper No. 194). Wellesley, MA: Wellesley College Center for Research on Women.

Marx, F. (1990). *School-age child care in America: Final report of a national provider survey* (Working Paper No. 204). Wellesley, MA: Wellesley College Center for Research on Women.

Mayesky, M. E. (1980a, February). *Differences in academic growth as measured in an extended day program in a public elementary school.* Paper presented at the annual conference of the American Association of School Administrators, Anaheim, CA. (ERIC Document Reproduction No. ED 184 675)

Mayesky, M. E. (1980b, December). A study of academic effectiveness in public school day care program. *Phi Delta Kappan, 62,* 284–285.

Miller, B. M., & Marx, F. (1990). *Afterschool arrangements in middle childhood: A review of the literature* (Action Research Paper No. 2). Wellesley, MA: School-Age Child Care Project.

National Academy of Early Childhood Programs. (1991). *Accreditation criteria and procedures: A position statement of the National Academy of Early Childhood Programs*. Washington, DC: National Association for the Education of Young Children.

National Association of Elementary School Principals. (1988, February). *The Communicator, 11*(6), 1.

O'Connor, S. (1991). *Assessing school-age child care quality*. Unpublished manuscript, School-Age Child Care Project, Wellesley, MA.

Powell, D. (1987). After-school child care. *Young Children, 42*, 62–66.

Richardson, J., Dwyer, K., McGuigan, K., Hansen, W., Dent, C., Johnson, C. A., Sussman, S., & Brannon, B. (1989). Substance use among eighth graders who take care of themselves after school. *Pediatrics, 84*(3), 556–566.

Riley, D. (1990, May). *Grassroots research on latchkey children leads to local action*. Paper presented at the Extension National Invitational Conference on SACC, St. Louis, MO.

Scofield, R. (Ed.). (1985). Plan now for summer. *School Age Notes, 5*(4), 1–2.

Seligson, M. (1989). School-age child care and the public schools: A response to families' needs. *Family Resource Coalition, 8*(2), 11–27.

Seligson, M., Fersh, E., Marshall, N. L., Marx F., & Baden, R. K. (1990). School-age child care: The challenge facing families. *Journal of Contemporary Human Services, 71*(6), 324–331.

Seligson, M., & Fink, D. B. (1989). *No time to waste*. Wellesley, MA: School-Age Child Care Project.

Seligson, M., & Marx, F. (1989). *When school is out in New York City: A study of available resources for school-age children when school is not in session*. New York: Community Service Society.

Springer, T., & Long, S. (1989). *Youth enrichment programs/visions project evaluation report*. Shreveport, LA: Louisiana Tech University.

Steinberg, L. (1989). Latchkey children and susceptibility to peer pressure: An ecological analysis. *Developmental Psychology, 22*, 433–439.

Stirling, D. (1988). Why we stopped summer care. *School Age Notes, 8*(5), 1–2.

Todd, C. M., Albrecht, K. M., & Coleman, M. (1990). School-age child care: A continuum of options. *Journal of Home Economics, 82*(1), 46–52.

Vandell, D., & Corasiniti, M. A. (1985, May). *The relation between third graders' after school care and social, academic, and emotional functioning*. Paper presented at the annual meeting of the American Association for the Advancement of Science, Los Angeles.

Weaver, M. (1988). Personal communication regarding the evaluation of the Prince George's County Public School Extended Day Program, Prince George's County, MD.

Woods, M. B. (1972). The unsupervised child of the working mother. *Developmental Psychology, 6*(1), 14–25.

Zill, N., Gruvacus, G., & Woyshner, K. (1977). *Kids, parents and interviewers: Three points of view on a national sample of children*. New York: Foundation for Child Development.

CHAPTER 9

Staffing Issues in Child Care

Paula Jorde Bloom

Over the past decade, concern about the quality and stability of the child care work force has surfaced as the most emotionally charged issue related to program functioning. In some communities, the situation has reached crisis proportions. Survey data from across the country have documented staff turnover rates of 20% to 70% (Buck, 1989; Hartmann & Pearce, 1989; Russell, Clifford & Warlick, 1990; Whitebook, Howes & Phillips, 1989). These are sobering statistics given current projections that the need for caregivers will continue to increase during the 1990s. This chapter attempts to untangle the complex web of factors affecting the staffing of child care centers.

THE EDUCATION AND TRAINING
OF CHILD CARE STAFF

In the world of educational research, where multiple perspectives, diverse methodologies, and conflicting and contradictory results are the norm, it is rare for researchers to be in unanimous agreement. However, the important role that teachers play in children's growth and development is one area in which researchers are unequivocal. Studies conducted in a variety of settings consistently document that *competent* staff is a key determinant in the quality of the care and education provided to young children (see, e.g., Arnett, 1989; Berk, 1985; Howes, 1983). Educators generally also agree on the competencies needed for effective child care teachers or program directors (British Columbia Department of Education, 1979; Council for Early Childhood Professional Recognition, 1990; National Association for the Education of Young Children, 1984). But when one tries to translate these competencies into a formula for well-trained teachers or directors, the issue gets a bit more muddled.

The Importance of a Well-Trained Work Force

In order to discern what *competence* means in practical terms, we need to look at staff qualifications as they relate to attracting competent caregivers. Staff qualifications are generally divided into four categories: (1) age and other general background characteristics; (2) years of formal education (regardless of subject matter or specialization); (3) specialized preparation in child development, early childhood education, or program administration; and (4) experience working in a child care setting.

Teaching Staff. A debate exists about what combination of formal education, specialized training, and work experience constitutes optimum qualifications for teaching. Moreover, controversy remains over which is a more potent predictor of teaching competence — content or amount of education. Phillips (1988) states that the interplay between these factors is as subtle as the human variations that contribute to caregiver competence. Of course, all these indicators are influenced by the context in which the individual works. Katz and Raths (1986) also stress the importance of teacher "disposition" as an element in determining effectiveness. Although dispositional qualities are difficult to measure, they may well serve as potent predictors of teacher competence.

In the 1977 National Day Care Study (NDCS), Ruopp and his colleagues found that caregivers with specialized education or training relevant to young children delivered better care with somewhat superior development effects for children (Ruopp, Travers, Glantz & Coelen, 1979). Somewhat contrary findings surfaced in the National Child Care Staffing Study (NCCSS) (Whitebook et al., 1989), in which teachers' formal education (in contrast to specialized education) was the strongest predictor of appropriate caregiving. Both the NDCS and the NCCSS agree, however, that teaching experience is not a reliable predictor of teacher behavior. The NCCSS concludes that "hiring practices which give equal weight to experience, education, and training may be over-estimating the role of experience in producing good teaching behavior" (Whitebook et al., 1989, p. 42).

The conclusions of these two major studies regarding caregiver experience supports other research on the topic. Powell and Stremmel (1989) state that experience is not a substitute for formal child-related training in developing a professional orientation to career development.

Berk (1985) believes that practical experiences may be effective only in the context of a broad-based formal education program that serves as the necessary foundation for programmatic endeavors. Snider and Fu (1990) agree. They state, "Experience without a knowledge base does not provide a teacher with a framework for understanding what constitutes developmentally appropriate practice" (p. 76).

Administrative Staff.   The repertoire of competencies needed to effectively carry out the administrative role varies by the ages and backgrounds of the children enrolled, the range of services provided, the philosophical orientation of the program, and the legal sponsorship of the center. The size of the program also affects the scope and complexity of the administrative role.

Unfortunately, little systematic inquiry has been conducted on the role of directors in influencing the contextual factors that support or inhibit quality experiences for young children. In a study of 103 programs (Jorde-Bloom, 1989a), directors' levels of formal education proved to be the strongest predictor of overall program quality as measured by the accreditation criteria of the National Association for the Education of Young Children (NAEYC). The second most significant predictor was specialized training in early childhood education and program administration. Years of experience teaching or directing a child care center were not significant predictors of overall program quality.

A more recent study (Bloom & Sheerer, 1991) assessed the effects of leadership training on directors' perceived and demonstrated levels of competence. The results provide compelling evidence that the director is the "gatekeeper to quality," setting the standards and expectations for others to follow. These findings are consistent with previous research documenting the critical role that directors play in guiding the professional development of their staffs, particularly those with limited training in early childhood education (Bredekamp, 1989; Powell & Stremmel, 1989).

State Regulations Governing Staff Qualifications

Currently no federal regulations govern the qualifications of child care staff. The Federal Interagency Day Care Requirements (FIDCR), which were revised and upgraded in 1980 (and then rescinded almost immediately), did note staff qualifications for different child care positions. These FIDCR standards are still used by many child advocates as a guideline for minimum staff qualifications.

Qualifications for child care personnel are determined by state regulation. In most states, the regulation of child care center personnel is tied to center licensing and falls under the auspices of the Department of Public Welfare or the state's equivalent of the Department of Child and Family Social Services. However, regulations differ from state to state on almost every requirement. There is neither consistency nor a great deal of specificity in minimum qualifications (Morgan, in press). In many states, programs sponsored by churches, universities, and public school districts are not subject to licensing at all.

Some states spell out different qualifications for staff assuming different roles (e.g., assistant teacher, teacher, director). Others provide guidelines only for "teachers" or "caregivers." Each state has its own terminology for these different roles. Morgan (in press), Adams (1990), and Phillips, Lande, and Goldberg (1990) provide the most current summaries of the educational requirements for child care staff. Only 19 states require specified levels of preservice training for teachers; another 17 require some type of orientation or prior experience. Some states require training for all classroom teachers; others require that only the head teacher or teacher-director possess a requisite level of training. Only a handful of states differentiate roles and corresponding levels of training.

Approximately half the states require ongoing training for caregivers, but the requirements for in-service training vary considerably. Twelve states have no in-service requirement. Only 14 states have *both* a preservice and an in-service training requirement for teachers. Some states have neither educational qualifications nor requirements for ongoing training once a caregiver has been employed. A few states allow experience to substitute for preservice education. Very few states require specialized training in the administration of early childhood programs for directors of centers.

Despite the minimal qualifications for personnel working in child care centers, states are beginning to strengthen their requirements. Eleven states have implemented new requirements for staff qualifications since 1988. Perhaps the most innovative effort has been in Massachusetts, which now issues a "certificate of qualifications" specifying desired levels of training for staff in different positions.

The regulation of caregiver qualifications is complicated by the fact that a number of states have promulgated separate standards for early childhood personnel working in preprimary programs under the auspices of the public schools. The requirements for personnel working with preschool-aged children in these settings are typically tied to the state's teacher certification requirements. Training and qualifications under these standards are far more stringent than those required for personnel working in programs licensed under the state's department of social services.

In sum, the regulations concerning the qualifications and training of child care workers reflect the prevailing assumption that child care is unskilled work. Despite considerable evidence about the crucial impact of teachers on children's development, requirements for child care personnel are not specifically and uniformly regulated in the same manner as professional requirements for employment in the public schools (Peters & Kostelnik, 1981).

Current Approaches to Staff Education and Training

In response to the tremendous expansion of early childhood programs during the last two decades, the number and variety of training programs for child care staff have grown. The following provides a brief survey of the landscape using the classification categories proposed by Peters and Kostelnik (1981).

Sponsorship. The best-known early childhood training programs are the formal degree and certificate programs offered by four-year colleges and universities, community colleges, and vocational-technical schools. Programs are offered in home economics, family and child studies, child development, family and consumer education, human ecology, psychology, and, of course, early childhood and elementary education.

There is also a wide variety of informal training programs sponsored by local, state, or national nonprofit human service agencies, professional associations, and private entrepreneurial training organizations. In addition, many state licensing agencies conduct child care training at the local and state levels. Some of these are certificate programs offering specialized training in Montessori education, infant studies, or program management and administration. Informal approaches can range from intensive year-long institutes focusing on indepth investigation of an issue to one-time workshops, "how-to" guides, or videotape training packages on specific topics. As would be suspected, the quality and price of these training options vary widely.

Preservice vs. In-service. Preservice programs are those programs designed to prepare personnel at different levels for entry into a career in child care. In-service training is designed for personnel already employed in the field. Austin (1981) emphasizes that in-service training should never be viewed as the vehicle for achieving initial requisite competencies. He states, "Far from being helpful, it serves to maintain the child care worker in her lowly status by providing those in power with the useful argument that child care workers do not need to have degrees to be effective" (p. 251).

Many parents who are consumers of child care services assume that in-service training is both plentiful and well supported. This assumption may be erroneous. The NCCSS (Whitebook et al., 1989) found that only 25% of teaching staff in their sample had received 15 hours or more of in-service training within the previous year. A 1988 study of approximately 1,000 centers (Jorde-Bloom, 1989a) showed that less than two-thirds provided on-site staff development of any kind, and only 41% provided some form of tuition reimbursement for employees taking college courses. These statistics do not provide a glowing picture of the support provided for in-service professional development.

Academic or Professional Level. There are essentially five levels of academic preparation that correspond with the professional hierarchy of current child care career options: (1) nondegree and certificate programs for classroom aides, assistant teachers, and ancillary personnel; (2) two-year associate degree programs for assistant teachers, teachers, and specialty teachers; (3) bachelor's degree programs for the preparation of teachers and specialists; (4) master's degree programs for specialists, trainers, supervisors, and program directors; and (5) doctoral degree programs for trainers and program administrators.

Perhaps the most well-known certificate/credential program for the training of child care personnel at the nondegree level is the child development associate (CDA). The CDA grew out of efforts by Head Start to increase recognition for competent performance resulting from on-the-job training and experience with children. Since 1975, the CDA program has issued over 35,000 credentials. Individuals seeking a credential are assessed by a team and must demonstrate competent performance in six areas. In response to the need for additional training, the Council for Early Childhood Professional Recognition, which oversees the administration of the CDA program, has launched an expanded network of support services and materials for individuals seeking a CDA credential.

Content. There are two ways to look at the distinctions in program content. One is the general versus specialized nature of the content. Some programs seek to provide a broad-based foundation in liberal education and the theoretical, social, and cultural foundations of educational practice. Other programs focus on professional specialization in child development, early childhood education, program administration, or parent and community relations. The guidelines established by NAEYC for early childhood degree-granting institutions (1985, 1990b) provide the most definitive statement of the content of the specialized professional preparation component of programs for classroom teachers.

A second way to distinguish content is to think in terms of education versus skill training. VanderVen (1985) states that training refers to specific information and skill development that enable an individual to do a specific job in a specific setting. It focuses primarily on the "how-to" of an immediate situation rather than the "why." Education, on the other hand, is concerned with providing an individual with a broad perspective, a conceptual base for framing information and solving problems. It encourages the long-term transferability of knowledge and skills. VanderVen believes that academic programs at all levels should offer a blend of both orientations. That has not always been the case, however. University programs have tended to emphasize the education mode, and technical-vocational colleges and service agencies providing in-service staff development have tended to focus on training.

Issues relating to content extend beyond the general/specialized or practical/theoretical nature of programs to broader policy considerations regarding balance and sequence. Debate still exists, for example, regarding what combination of course work and field experiences should be required, how professional course content can best be integrated with liberal arts and sciences, and when courses in pedagogy should be taken in the general education sequence (Spodek & Saracho, 1990). Given the multidisciplinary roots of early childhood education, consensus on these issues will not be easily achieved.

A PROFILE OF CHILD CARE WORKERS

As a group, child care workers are overwhelmingly female (96%–98%) and fairly young (80% are 40 years old or younger). Unfortunately, much of the research focusing on caregiver characteristics has referred to child care workers as though they were a homogeneous occupational group. But research that relies on measures of central tendency to report background characteristics and outcome variables of the group as a whole masks the enormous variation that exists among workers in this field. Recent research suggests that the occupation may be more stratified than previously assumed. Significant differences have been found in background characteristics, professional orientation, job satisfaction, and commitment to the field. For the most part, these differences correspond to the hierarchical nature of the individual's role in the organization. Directors have more formal education, more experience, and exhibit a stronger professional orientation and greater commitment to the field than do teachers or assistant teachers.

Current Levels of Education and Experience

When compared to the civilian labor force, child care teachers are quite well educated. Survey data (e.g., Hartmann & Pearce, 1989; Jorde-Bloom, 1989a; U. S. General Accounting Office, 1990; White-book et al., 1989) show that over half the assistant teachers and three-quarters of the teachers have taken some college course work. Approximately half the teachers and three-quarters of the directors hold bachelor's degrees. More than a fifth of directors have obtained master's degrees.

With respect to experience, assistant teachers average almost four years in the field of early childhood and two and one-half years in their present positions. The typical teacher has worked in the field for six years and has been at her current position about three and one-half years. Directors average ten years in the field of early childhood and almost five years in their present positions.

Most teaching staff employed in programs take the minimum number of courses required by their state's regulatory policy. Once hired, they may then pursue a CDA credential or complete an associate or bachelor's degree. Most directors have been promoted to their positions from the ranks of teachers. Interest and experience appear to be the primary criteria for promotion rather than formal training in program administration. Few have had concentrated course work in child care administration. Those that have this specialized training received it after they had assumed their administrative positions.

Commitment and Professional Orientation

Early childhood educators perceive themselves as professionals, take their work seriously, and are committed to careers in child care. In the NCCSS (Whitebook et al., 1989), teachers reported that they spent approximately three and one-half hours a week in unpaid work. In another study (Jorde-Bloom, 1988b), 83% of teachers responded yes when asked if they would select a career in early childhood education if they had to make a career decision again. In a Pennsylvania study, Kontos and Stremmel (1988) report that 65% of their sample planned to stay in child care indefinitely. Head teachers were most likely to leave, planning to seek higher salaries by entering public school teaching.

There may be a discrepancy between self-reports of professional commitment and actual behavior. The NCCSS found no link between commitment to child care as a career and membership in professional associations; only 14 % of teaching staff belonged to a professional group. In another study (Jorde-Bloom, 1989b), less than a third of the teachers subscribed to a single professional journal or magazine; only a third of the assistants were working toward a degree; and barely a fifth of the assistants and teachers had attended two workshops or conferences during the previous year.

As individuals move into positions with more responsibility, they engage in more activities that are characteristic of professionals. They attend more conferences, subscribe to more journals, and engage in more advocacy activities on behalf of young children and their families. Still, the results of studies of directors' self-reported professional orientation do not portray a very positive picture. Powell and Stremmel (1989) found that 41 % of the directors in their study were not members of a professional organization. The Illinois Directors' Study (Jorde-Bloom, 1989a) found that a third of the directors did not subscribe to any professional magazines or journals.

Job Satisfaction

Research conducted in the area of job satisfaction underscores the importance of looking at different facets of a worker's job rather than using a global overall assessment of satisfaction (Jorde-Bloom, 1988b; Kontos & Stremmel, 1988; Whitebook, Howes, Darrah & Friedman, 1982). Child care workers typically express satisfaction with certain aspects of their work, but not with others. The nature of the work itself, particularly interactions with children, consistently surfaces as the leading source of satisfaction for child care assistant teachers and teachers. Salaries and benefits consistently surface as the greatest source of frustration and dissatisfaction. Some facets of a person's job are bipolar, contributing to both satisfaction and dissatisfaction. For example, coworker relations often surface as a source of both satisfaction and frustration.

Research also underscores the importance of differentiating job satisfaction by role. Some studies show that the level of job satisfaction increases as occupational responsibility increases. Individuals in higher occupational levels have greater autonomy and control over the pace and quality of their work. This, in turn, may provide increased opportunities for fulfillment. Other studies have found an inverse relationship. Assistant teachers are generally more satisfied with working conditions, salaries, and opportunities for advancement than their colleagues. In most professions, as level of education increases, individuals move into positions with greater control, status, and financial remuneration. In early childhood education, however, as level of education increases, there is often greater disparity between perceived expectations of job rewards and actual rewards. Thus job satisfaction may actually decrease. More educated workers may also perceive that they have better opportunities elsewhere and are making a sacrifice to remain in child care.

Will Supply Meet Future Demands?

Current demographic projections provide strong evidence that the demand for center-based child care will continue to increase during the next decade (Hill-Scott, 1989). Many believe that the supply of caregivers in the labor force cannot keep pace with the demand. Although the average rate of growth across all occupations is projected to be 25%, employment in preschool education is expected to increase by more than 40%. Acute shortages are likely to be found in certain geographic areas and for infant and toddler caregivers.

Because there are more opportunities for women in other fields, the pool of qualified personnel is becoming increasingly competitive. Anecdotal evidence by directors confirms that individuals who apply for jobs are not as committed to the field, nor as well trained, as they once were. This, coupled with the low wages that most teacher positions command, almost guarantees both higher numbers of untrained staff applying for positions and a continued high turnover rate among staff. In testimony before the Early Childhood Task Force of the National Association of State Boards of Education, Costley (1988) summarized the magnitude of the staffing crisis:

> There are about 650 4-year colleges in the United States offering degrees in early childhood education. By pooling all their graduates this year, we will have barely enough people to staff the currently existing early childhood programs of the state of Massachusetts. With the graduates of perhaps an additional 1,000 2-year community colleges also offering early childhood preparation, we might manage enough staff for the state of New York. (p. 4)

Phillips (1988) believes that the situation reflects the realities of the economic and demographic context of child care. There is a growing employment market for individuals with entry-level skills, but shrinking relative compensation for college graduates. As such, child care represents a more realistic job alternative for individuals with some college background, but not for those with four-year degrees.

CHILD CARE CENTERS AS WORKPLACES

The results of recent research highlight the importance of addressing the work environment for adults as it relates to the developmental consequences of the quality of child care (Cummings, 1980; Howes 1988). Caregiver stability and continuity are crucial in children's development.

The Importance of a Stable Work Force

Child care work has one of the highest turnover rates of all occupations. Turnover rates of 20% to 70% contrast sharply with turnover rates for public school teachers of 6% to 8%. And the turnover issue has clearly worsened in recent years (Willer & Johnson, 1989). The NCCSS average turnover rate of 41% across participating centers was close to three times the turnover rate reported in 1977. Granger and Marx (1990) report that 22% of the day care and Head Start teachers in their sample held their present positions less than a year. Other data confirm that the length of time teachers work at each center appears to be decreasing. Clearly, current conditions are encouraging not only an exodus from the field but greater mobility within the field.

Turnover does not necessarily represent a loss of an individual's talent to the field. In the NCCSS, 33% of individuals who left their jobs remained in child care. When one analyzes the impact of turnover from the perspective of the children in a child care center, however, the fact that some workers remain in child care is secondary. The damaging consequences to the children and to the center come from the disruption in the caregiver-child relationship and in the stress placed on remaining staff, who must deal with the constant influx of new teachers to orient.

Salaries, Benefits, and Opportunities for Promotion

Although the importance of salaries and benefits as a source of motivation is often downplayed in workers' self-reports of job satisfaction, the extrinsic rewards workers receive are important for their symbolic value. Pay is a means of communicating esteem, and for many, it is a symbol of the value placed on teaching by society. Wages also constitute a means of comparison, both within and outside the immediate center.

Based on 1988 data, the NCCSS reports that the average hourly wage of participating staff was $5.35 ($9,363 year), below the poverty threshold for a family of three. The study concludes that despite gains in overall education and experience, teachers' earnings fell by over 20% between 1977 and 1988 when adjusted for inflation. In most occupations the value of a benefits package adds worth to an employee's base income. Benefits such as paid vacation time, sick leave, health insurance, retirement plans, and paid breaks certainly contribute to the qualify of life for workers. In child care, however, these benefits are received by only a small fraction of caregivers.

Salaries and benefits have been the focus of several studies of child care workers (see, e.g., Goodman, Brady & Desch, 1987; Stremmel, 1990; Whitebook et al., 1982). Studies consistently underscore the strong role that workers' pay and benefits play in influencing employee job satisfaction and commitment to the field. Because the structure of the pay and promotion system in most centers is relatively flat, providing few opportunities for salary increases tied to professional advancement, the incentives associated with making a long-term commitment to the center are undermined.

The link between salaries and turnover has been firmly established. Many staff simply cannot afford to remain in teaching despite enjoying their work and being committed to the field of early childhood education. In addition, it has been found that turnover rates are higher in centers paying lower wages. In their study assessing correlates of program quality, Howes, Pettygrove, and Whitebook (1987) found that programs committed to better funding for teaching and administrative staff reported fewer problems in recruitment and retention. This same pattern has been documented by Olenick (1986), who found that programs offering better compensation attracted and retained more qualified staff. This, in turn, reduced staff turnover and the negative consequences of program disruption. Similar conclusions can be drawn by comparing data from the NCCSS and a U. S. General Accounting Office study (1990). Such an analysis shows that high-quality programs (those meeting NAEYC's accreditation standards) attract better qualified staff, pay high salaries, have better benefits, and report lower turnover rates for teachers and aides.

Goodman, Brady, and Desch (1987) report the impact of salary increases on staff turnover in Massachusetts Head Start programs. As a result of salary increases over a two-year period, the proportion of staff leaving programs for better pay went from 65% to 35%. Similar anecdotal evidence is reported from New York's salary-enhancement legislation (Marx & Zinsser, 1990). In general, it can be concluded that improved salaries increase a program's ability to compete for qualified staff in the child care labor market. The NCCSS highlights the disturbing consequences of ignoring the compensation issue. Across participating centers in the study, salaries and benefits surfaced as the most significant predictor of quality of care among all the independent variables examined. Centers that offered staff higher wages provided higher-quality care.

Although a wealth of empirical and anecdotal data clearly suggests a causal connection between salaries and turnover, Russell, Clifford, and Warlick (1990) remind us that the equation is more complicated than it may appear at first blush. They provide a useful model for understanding the multiple variables that work to determine whether a teacher will remain in the field (Figure 9.1). Their model underscores that the turnover equation is a complex one in which many influences at the community, center, and teacher level combine to predict overall staff stability.

Working Conditions

Salaries, benefits, and opportunities for advancement may serve as preconditions for making a long-term commitment to a center, but they are not alone in predicting job satisfaction or performance on the job. It has been found that the adequacy of a supportive work environment can temper some of the effects of low salaries and benefits. Working in child care is not easy; caregivers are subjected to occupational health hazards daily. These include strain from lifting children and moving furniture, exposure to poisons and pesticides, risk of infectious disease, injuries from children (e.g., biting), and injury from faulty equipment. Working conditions vary considerably from center to center and from state to state, depending on program sponsorship, stability of funding, state regulatory standards, and, of course, center leadership.

The conditions of teaching, including teacher-child ratios, hours, work schedules, physical environment, opportunities for professional growth, and opportunities for involvement in decision making, have been the focus of several studies (see, e.g., Kontos & Stremmel, 1988; Townley, Thornburg & Crompton, 1991; Whitebook et al., 1982). Consistent with Herzberg's (1966) theory of motivation, working conditions seldom serve as a source of satisfaction motivating individuals to higher levels of performance, but they are often a potent source of

Figure 9.1. Predictors of Teacher Intent to Remain in the Field

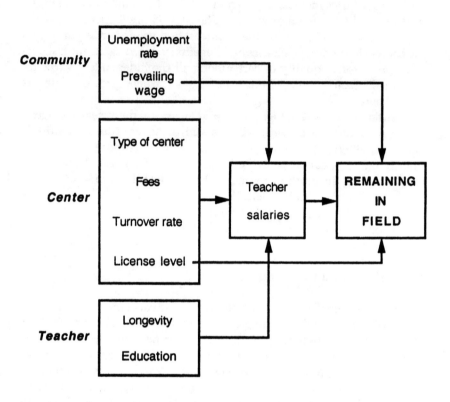

Source: Russell, Clifford & Warlick, 1990, p. 7. Reprinted with permission.

dissatisfaction that prevents workers from performing at optimal levels. It has been found that centers that provided for adult needs, such as offering opportunities for professional development and separate adult space, also offered higher-quality care (Whitebook et al., 1989).

Research has also found that the teaching and administrative staffs of programs often have vastly different perceptions of working conditions. Directors view the organizational climate of their centers in far rosier terms than their staffs do. There are significant differences in perceptions between teachers and administrators in a wide range of organizational practices, including the degree of decision-making influence of teachers, the perceived clarity of center policies and procedures, equity of the reward structure, and the adequacy of the physical environment (Jorde-Bloom, 1988a).

A VISION FOR THE FUTURE

A number of problems exist that limit centers' ability to assure stable and high-quality programs. Low salaries and limited benefits have decreased the supply of personnel, accentuated inequities, focused greater attention on working conditions, and, for many staff, made child care an untenable long-term career option. The forecast for the future is grim. But although we cannot dismiss the economic problems that plague the field, we can make a concerted effort on several levels to remedy the situation. Implementing the following strategies may create a more hopeful scenario for the future.

What Professional Organizations Can Do

Promote the Development and Implementation of a Comprehensive Career Ladder.   The lack of a uniformly accepted nomenclature to denote personnel in early childhood center-based programs plagues the field. An agreed-upon nomenclature can define (and standardize) the scope of responsibilities associated with different roles and serve as the springboard for the development of a professional career ladder for the field.

A career ladder can promote equity within the field of early childhood education as well as equity between child care and other occupations. Differentiated staffing models with salary scales that reflect different levels of qualifications and work experience have helped improve the status of workers in other occupations. Creating a career ladder may well serve as the first step in professionalizing early childhood education.

The National Association for the Education of Young Children has taken the lead in developing a comprehensive model of professional development that delineates specific child care roles, corresponding responsibilities, and requisite qualifications (NAEYC, 1990a). NAEYC's efforts mark a bold and important step in upgrading the professional status of the field. The work of the Center for Career Development in Early Care and Education at Wheelock College (Morgan, 1991) will also be important in achieving this goal. The Center's mission is to monitor state policies regarding staffing issues, work with state and community-based groups to develop innovative projects, and network with other national organizations to influence policy, program, and funding strategies in the area of early childhood career development.

Promote Standards That Improve the Quality of Work Life for Child Care Personnel. Teacher-child ratios, group size, administrative policies, and workplace safety and health standards directly affect the quality of life for child care workers and have a strong impact on the quality of services provided for children. NAEYC's center accreditation project provides powerful evidence of how profession-driven standards can upgrade staffing practices at the center level (Bredekamp, 1989).

Promote Interstate Consistency in the Adoption of Standards. Perhaps the most vital role that professional organizations can play is to promote interstate consistency in the adoption of standards. The Children's Defense Fund, the Child Welfare League of America, and the Child Care Action Campaign have played a vital role in this regard. Focusing national attention on standards through conferences, dissemination of current data, and the issuance of policy papers can provide the forum and the substance for collaboration.

Continue to Document Inequities in Compensation through the Use of Comparable-Worth Studies. The Child Care Employee Project stands as the vanguard in disseminating information to help local programs conduct salary surveys. The organization also serves as a clearinghouse for current statistics on regional differences in compensation and can assist local efforts to document inequities.

What States Can Do

Because the responsibility for establishing and enforcing child care standards will remain with the states, state regulatory agencies as well as state legislatures overseeing funding must play a central role in ensuring the provision of a highly trained and competent work force. There are several important strategies they can adopt.

Implement Initiatives to Improve Caregiver Compensation and Benefits. The NCCSS provides compelling evidence of the value of increasing child care salaries as an avenue for improving the quality of center-based care. But increasing salaries exacerbates the economic dilemma associated with providing affordable care for families with modest incomes. Nevertheless, salary-enhancement strategies do work, and efforts should be made to broaden the sources and amounts of funds available to pay the cost of improving salaries and benefits (Whitebook, Pemberton, Lombardi & Galinsky, 1990; Child Care Employee Project, 1991). Salary-enhancement strategies will attract a wider pool of qualified candidates. Such initiatives are also crucial for attracting and retaining minority caregivers.

With the passage of the Child Care and Development Block Grant and the Head Start Reauthorization Bill, additional funding will be available for implementing salary-enhancement strategies. The Military Child Care Act provides a good model of how salary-enhancement initiatives can be linked to incentives for staff to pursue additional training. Such links are essential for professionalizing the field.

Russell, Clifford, and Warlick (1990) suggest that states can create child care insurance pools to reduce costs for health insurance coverage and increase the likelihood that health insurance would be available to child care staff. Improvements in workers' benefits will enable well-trained staff to make long-term commitments to the profession.

Increase Education and Training Requirements for Child Care Workers. High standards for staff qualifications are important both to protect against poor practices and to convey a strong message to the public about the importance of the teaching and administrative roles in child care. Licensing requirements regarding staff qualifications need to be more comprehensive. Current standards often foster workers' participation in an unlinked collection of isolated training experiences. This occurs because most states have adopted a static model of child care personnel requirements in which preservice credentialing, education, and experience serve as primary indicators of competence to work in the field (Morgan, 1991). Personnel qualifications that are tied to a professional career ladder model, in contrast, represent a more dynamic approach in which different roles and requirements are assigned to different staff positions. Upward mobility is built into the staffing structure as individuals obtain additional training and skills. Such a career ladder can serve as a bridge between certified teachers in the public schools and specialized teachers in child care who could be required to have comparable educational backgrounds. At present the FIDCR standards and NAEYC's accreditation guidelines represent the most widely respected expert judgments about staff training requirements.

The link between salaries and educational qualifications is obvious. The short-term impact of raising educational qualifications would be to exacerbate labor pool shortages. Indeed, because of the difficulty of finding qualified staff at current salaries, there has been a push from some in the field to lower or eliminate existing child care standards for personnel. It is important that changes in state standards be accompanied by sufficient scholarship money targeted for low-income caregivers pursuing degrees and improved access to training. These steps will help ease the financial burden associated with pursuing additional training and education. The CDA Scholarship Act provides one model of how such support can be structured. Increasing requisite qualifications at the state level is a cost-effective way to affect the quality of program services and the quality of work life for child care staff.

Expand Opportunities for Training for Child Care Workers. The current crisis in recruiting staff has resulted in many programs employing staff who are underqualified for their roles and responsibilities. The provision of in-service training becomes a critical imperative under these circumstances. Because child care staff are overworked and underpaid, many have little incentive to find, pay for, and attend such training.

Both the Child Care and Development Block Grant and the Head Start Reauthorization Bill include provisions for funding staff training and technical assistance. However, training opportunities must be planned to take into consideration the constraints of time and mobility faced by many child care staff. Multiple training models such as on-site training, mobile training centers, and innovative media efforts should be employed. One ancillary benefit from expanded support and funding for staff training is that it may help change the image of the state licensing agency from a punitive, regulatory one to a supportive, technical-assistance one.

Reduce Disparities in Standards. The current regulatory system in states promotes inequities that exacerbate staffing problems. Disparities in the application of standards need to be eliminated. The current system of exemptions, for example, has created a situation in which thousands of children are served in programs that are essentially unlicensed. Disparities between standards for teachers working under the auspices of the public schools and those for teachers in child care centers must also be eliminated. Early childhood educators applaud having highly trained individuals work with prekindergarten children in the school system, but why do children who attend prekindergarten programs outside the public school system deserve less? We are at risk of developing a two-tiered system of early childhood educators in many states. Motivated by higher salaries, more attractive benefits, and better working conditions, the best and the brightest early childhood teachers enter the public school system. These significant differences in salary and status exacerbate the problem of staff turnover and compromise program quality in nonpublic child care.

What Center Directors Can Do

Barring a sudden infusion of federal dollars that would allow programs to double salaries, directors are left to implement some changes at the programmatic level to attract and retain staff. The following are some strategies to consider.

Implement a Differentiated Staffing Model Tied to a Career Ladder. In many centers there is little differentiation in the tasks performed and salaries earned by staff with different titles. A career ladder that delineates required levels of education and experience for specific center roles will help provide the framework for fairness and equity in job assignments and promotions. Table 9.1 provides an example of a career ladder that is consistent with NAEYC's proposed model of professional development. When a career ladder is tied to a salary index, it can work to promote both internal and external equity in a center's pay, benefits, and promotion system.

Implement Recruitment and Hiring Practices That Maximize a Good Fit. When hiring a new teacher, the prevailing practice in many centers is to hire the individual with the most impressive resume. But research on job satisfaction indicates that the best person for the job may not necessarily be the most qualified on paper. Ensuring a good fit between the needs, values, and expectations of the individual and the requirements of the job necessitates a holistic perspective in recruiting and hiring. Not only does the individual's philosophical orientation need to be considered, but also his or her need for intellectual challenge, variety, autonomy, creativity, and career advancement. Because the expectations of new teachers are often unrealistic, greater attention in assessing employee needs can reduce the incidence of mismatch in perceptions of what the work environment can offer. This in itself may promote greater professional fulfillment.

Expand Training Opportunities for Staff. Ample anecdotal evidence suggests that directors who have outmaneuvered the staffing crisis have consciously adopted an ethos of professional development at

Table 9.1. Career Ladder for Center-Based Program

Level	Step	Index	Education	Experience	Roles*
V	1	3.75	Ph.D or Ed.D. in ece or related discipline	3 or more years	Program administrator Education coordinator
IV	3	3.50	Step 2 plus an additional 15 s.h.	2 or more years	Program administrator Education coordinator Master teacher
	2	3.25	Step 1 plus 15 s.h.	1 or more years	Program administrator Education coordinator Teacher, master teacher
	1	3.00	MA in ece or related discipline**		Program administrator Education coordinator Teacher, master teacher
III	3	2.75	Step 2 plus an additional 15 s.h.	2 or more years	Program administrator Education coordinator Teacher, master teacher
	2	2.50	Step 1 plus 15 s.h.	1 or more years	Program administrator Education coordinator Teacher, master teacher
	1	2.25	BA in ece or related field with 45 s.h. in cd or ece**		Teacher

162

Table 9.1. Continued

II				
3	2.00	Step 2 plus an additional 15 s.h.	2 or more years	Teacher*** Assistant teacher
2	1.75	Step 1 plus 15 s.h.	1 or more years	Teacher*** Assistant teacher
1	1.50	AA in ece or general AA and 30 s.h. in cd or ece		Teacher*** Assistant teacher
I				
2	1.25	CDA plus 30 s.h. in cd or ece	1 or more years	Teacher*** Assistant teacher
1	1.00	CDA		Assistant teacher
PREPROFESSIONAL				
	.75	High school diploma or GED		Teacher aide

Source: Bloom, Sheerer & Britz, 1991, p. 144. Reprinted with permission.

Note: ece = early childhood education; cd = child development; s.h. = semester hours of credit.

* Education coordinator and program administrator require three years of successful teaching experience and specialized course work.

** Including supervised field experience (150 hours at primary level and 150 hours at preschool or infant/toddler level).

*** Teacher at this level is under the supervision of a master teacher.

their centers (Sheerer & Jorde-Bloom, 1990). Whenever possible, they provide incentives for career development including on-site training, reimbursement for college course work, and released time for staff to visit other programs and attend workshops and conferences. Many programs have also instituted an informal mentoring system under which seasoned staff orient and train less experienced staff.

Improve Working Conditions. Early childhood work environments need to nurture adults as well as children. Practices that promote quality of work life include providing flexible staffing schedules, ensuring breaks and sufficient substitutes for classroom coverage, rearranging the physical space to accommodate adult needs, organizing social functions that foster greater collegiality, and providing expanded opportunities for teacher involvement in decision making. These efforts can reduce employee job stress and make centers a more enjoyable place to work.

Educate Parents about the Components (and Costs) of Good Quality. Many parents still have outdated notions about the nature of child care work with regard to training and adequacy of compensation. They remain consumers of a product with limited inclination to pay the full cost of care. In addition to keeping parents current about staffing and quality issues through handouts and reprints from journal articles, directors can present parents with financial information reflecting the true costs of the center. The difference between true costs and actual tuition charged will show parents how their fees are being subsidized by the low wages of staff (Willer, 1990).

CONCLUSION

Phillips (1988) states that "unless our child care system can assure a supply of personnel that meets the demand, creates working conditions that attract and retain staff, and provides training and certification strategies which produce qualified personnel, quality experiences for young children will remain a mere wish rather than a reality" (p. i). Clearly there is no quick fix to the staffing crisis experienced by child care programs across the country. Though the issues are complex, they can be solved. Through the concerted efforts of professional organizations, state regulatory bodies, and the leadership of centers themselves, it is possible to ensure a more stable and effective child care system that meets the personal and professional needs of child care staff.

REFERENCES

Adams, G. (1990). *Who knows how safe? The status of state efforts to ensure quality child care.* Washington, DC: Children's Defense Fund.

Arnett, J. (1989). Caregivers in day-care centers: Does training matter? *Journal of Applied Developmental Psychology, 10,* 541–552.

Austin, D. (1981, Fall). Formal educational preparation: The structural prerequisite to the professional status of the child care worker. *Child Care Quarterly, 10*(3), 250–260.

Berk, L. (1985, Summer). Relationship of caregiver education to child-oriented attitudes, job satisfaction, and behaviors toward children. *Child Care Quarterly, 14,* 103–109.

Bloom, P. J., & Sheerer, M. (1991, June). *The effect of Head Start leadership training on program quality.* Paper presented at the Society for Research in Child Development National Working Conference on Child and Family Research, Arlington, VA.

Bloom, P. J., Sheerer, M., & Britz, J. (1991). *Blueprint for action: Achieving center-based change through staff development.* Mt. Rainier, MD: Gryphon House.

Bredekamp, S. (1989). *Regulating child care quality: Evidence from NAEYC's accreditation system.* Washington, DC: National Association for the Education of Young Children.

British Columbia Department of Education. (1979). *Competencies in early childhood education.* Victoria, BC: Ministry of Education.

Buck, L. (1989). *An assessment of the child care system.* Honolulu, HI: Office of Children and Youth.

Child Care Employee Project. (1991). *What states can do to secure a skilled and stable child care work force.* Oakland, CA: Author.

Costley, J. (1988). Testimony before the Early Childhood Task Force of the National Association of State Boards of Education.

Council for Early Childhood Professional Recognition. (1990). *Child development associate: Assessment system and competency standards.* Washington, DC: Author.

Cummings, E. M. (1980). Caregiver stability and day care. *Developmental Psychology, 16,* 31–37.

Goodman, I., Brady, J., & Desch, B. (1987). *A commitment to quality: The impact of state supplemental funds on Massachusetts Head Start.* Newton, MA: Education Development Center.

Granger, R., & Marx, E. (1990). Policy implications of compensation and working conditions in three publicly funded early childhood systems. *Early Childhood Research Quarterly, 5,* 181–198.

Hartmann, H., & Pearce, D. (1989). *High skill and low pay: The economics of child care work.* Washington, DC: Institute for Women's Policy Research.

Herzberg, F. (1966). *Work and the nature of man.* New York: World Publishing.

Hill-Scott, K. (1989). No room at the inn: The crisis in child care supply. In J.

Lande & S. Scarr (Eds.), *Caring for children* (pp. 197–216). Hillsdale, NJ: Erlbaum.

Howes, C. (1983). Caregiver behavior in center and family day care. *Journal of Applied Developmental Psychology, 4,* 99–107.

Howes, C. (1988). Relations between early child care and schooling. *Developmental Psychology, 24,* 53–57.

Howes, C., Pettygrove, W., & Whitebook, M. (1987, November). Cost and quality in child care: Reality and myth. *Child Care Information Exchange,* 40–42.

Jorde-Bloom, P. (1988a). Closing the gap: An analysis of teacher and administrator perceptions of organizational climate in the early childhood setting. *Teaching & Teacher Education: An International Journal of Research and Studies, 4,* 111–120.

Jorde-Bloom, P. (1988b). Factors influencing overall job commitment and facet satisfaction in early childhood work environments. *Journal of Research in Childhood Education, 3*(2), 107–122.

Jorde-Bloom, P. (1989a). *The Illinois Directors' Study: A report to the Illinois Department of Children and Family Services.* Evanston, IL: National College of Education, Early Childhood Professional Development Project.

Jorde-Bloom, P. (1989b, Winter). Professional orientation: Individual and organizational perspectives. *Child and Youth Care Quarterly, 18*(4), 227–240.

Katz, L., & Raths, J. (1986, July). Dispositions as goals for teacher education. *Teaching and Teacher Education, 1*(4), 301–307.

Kontos, S., & Stremmel, A. (1988). Caregivers' perceptions of working conditions in a child care environment. *Early Childhood Research Quarterly, 3*(1), 77–91.

Marx, E., & Zinsser, C. (1990). *Raising child care salaries and benefits: An evaluation of the New York State salary enhancement legislation.* New York: Bank Street College of Education and the Center for Public Advocacy Research.

Morgan, G. (1991). *Career development systems in early care and education: A concept paper.* Boston, MA: Wheelock College.

Morgan, G. (in press). *The national state of child care regulation.* Watertown, MA: Work/Family Directions, Inc.

National Association for the Education of Young Children. (1984). *Accreditation criteria and procedures of the National Academy of Early Childhood Programs.* Washington, DC: Author.

National Association for the Education of Young Children. (1985). *Guidelines for early childhood education programs in associate degree granting institutions.* Washington, DC: Author.

National Association for the Education of Young Children. (1990a). *Draft model of early childhood professional development.* Washington, DC: Author.

National Association for the Education of Young Children. (1990b). *Early childhood teacher education guidelines: Basic and advanced.* Washington, DC: Author.

Olenick, N. (1986). *The relationship between day care quality and selected social policy variables.* Doctoral dissertation, UCLA School of Education, Los Angeles.

Peters, D. L., & Kostelnik, M. (1981). Current research in day care personnel preparation. In S. Kilmer (Ed.), *Advances in early education and day care,* vol. 2 (pp. 29–60). Greenwich, CT: JAI Press.

Phillips, C. (1988, June). *Staffing for high quality early education.* Briefing paper for the National Association of State Boards of Education.

Phillips, D., Lande, J., & Goldberg, M. (1990). The state of child care regulation: A comparative analysis. *Early Childhood Research Quarterly, 5,* 151–179.

Powell, D., & Stremmel, A. (1989). The relation of early childhood training and experience to the professional development of child care workers. *Early Childhood Research Quarterly, 4*(3), 339–356.

Ruopp, R., Travers, J., Glantz, F., & Coelen, C. (1979). *Children at the center: Final report of the national day care study.* Cambridge, MA: Abt Associates.

Russell, S., Clifford, R., & Warlick, M. (1990). *Working in child care in North Carolina.* Carrboro, NC: Day Care Services Association, Inc.

Sheerer, M., & Jorde-Bloom, P. (1990, April). The ongoing challenge: Attracting and retaining quality staff. *Child Care Information Exchange,* 11–16.

Snider, M. H., & Fu, V. R. (1990). The effects of specialized education and job experience on early childhood teachers' knowledge of developmentally appropriate practice. *Early Childhood Research Quarterly, 5*(1), 69–78.

Spodek, B., & Saracho, O. N. (1990). *Yearbook in early childhood education. Vol. 1: Early childhood teacher preparation.* New York: Teachers College Press.

Stremmel, A. (1990, April). *Predictors of intention to leave child care work.* Paper presented at the annual meeting of the American Educational Research Association, Boston.

Townley, K., Thornburg, K., & Crompton, D. (1991). Burnout in teachers of young children. *Early Education and Development, 2,* 198–204.

U. S. General Accounting Office. (1990). *Early childhood education: What are the costs of high-quality programs?* Washington, DC: GAO/HRD-90-43BR.

VanderVen, K. (1985). Training and education for child care practice. *Journal of Children in Contemporary Society, 17*(3), 1–34.

Whitebook, M., Howes, C., Darrah, R., & Friedman, J. (1982). Caring for the caregivers: Staff burnout in child care. In L. Katz (Ed.), *Current topics in early childhood education,* vol. 4 (pp. 212–235). Norwood, NJ: Ablex.

Whitebook, M., Howes, C., & Phillips, D. (1989). *Who cares? Child care teachers and the quality of care in America: Final report of the National Child Care Staffing Study*. Oakland, CA: Child Care Employee Project.

Whitebook, M., Pemberton, C., Lombardi, J., Galinsky, E. (1990). *From the floor: Raising child care salaries*. Berkeley, CA: Child Care Employee Project.

Willer, B. (1990). *Reaching the full cost of quality*. Washington, DC: National Association for the Education of Young Children.

Willer, B., & Johnson, L. (1989). *The crisis is real: Demographics and problems of recruiting and retaining early childhood staff*. Washington, DC: National Association for the Education of Young Children.

CHAPTER 10

Designing Settings to Support High-Quality Care

Thelma Harms

Child care settings project vastly different personalities. We have all seen settings that are sterile and antiseptic like a hospital room, colorful and startling like a three-ring circus, cluttered with randomly placed objects like a used furniture shop, or cute enough to be a store window at Christmas. These settings are differentiated by more than style. Each is the reflection of a different set of values, and each setting affects the functioning of the children and adults that share the facility for many hours every day.

When we enter an ongoing child care program we immediately become aware of both the physical environment and the interactions that are occurring within it. Children and adults are interacting with one another and with the furnishings and materials in the setting. The setting as a whole conveys a definite ambience. What may not be so obvious at first is that the components of the setting are affecting the interactions and, beyond that, the very development of the children. Yet "there has been little empirical research on the links between the quality of the physical setting and human development" (Moore, 1987, p. 42), despite the fact that appropriate early childhood practice stresses active involvement with the environment.

This chapter deals with a number of issues relating to the design of settings to support the delivery of high-quality child care in center-based and home-based programs. The main focus is on exploring the relationship of the physical aspects of the setting to desired child outcomes in the areas of safety, health, and development. Recommendations for the design of settings are supported, when possible, by research as well as indications from widely accepted best practice.

Child care is delivered in two major settings, the family child care home and the child care center. What do we know about how these settings differ? Prescott (1987), reporting on a study comparing child care centers with family child care homes as child-rearing settings, described many contrasts between home and center child care settings. She characterized home care settings as having a greater variety of furnishings and objects for play, more provision for privacy, and fewer interruptions; as being cozier, softer, and more relaxing; and as allowing for more personalized play. In contrast, she characterized child care centers as more institutionalized settings with standardized furnishings that are "woefully simple compared to naturally occurring environments such as homes and neighborhoods" (p. 86). Centers, she found, also imposed more time constraints, were more schedule conscious, and offered less softness and privacy. The effects of these two contrasting settings were reflected in the children's expressive behavior. Prescott reported richer play and longer, more involved conversations in home care settings. Her observations led Prescott to admonish child care professionals to "hominize" centers.

A contrasting picture of family child care settings emerges in a study by Johnson and Dineen (1981), conducted with 300 informal family child care providers in Canada. Here the finding was that the family child care providers seriously restricted children's activity because they were concerned with "protecting their home from the children and with protecting the children from potential hazards in the home" (Johnson, 1987, p. 142). Johnson points out that homes are traditionally adult oriented in design, and unless that orientation can be changed to include children's needs, children are going to be restricted. In a further study of 25 homes that had achieved a good balance of use by both adults and children—roughly half family residences and the rest family day care homes—Johnson, Shack, and Oster (1980) found that 80% of these homes had been renovated to make the settings more suitable for children. These child-friendly homes allowed children considerably more freedom to use various parts of the home, family furnishings, and equipment for play. The authors point out that incorporation of children's activities to this degree in a home setting requires not only physical renovations but also an attitude that values children's activities and flexibility about the use of the home itself.

We must conclude, then, that neither the home nor the center setting is inherently superior, for each has potential strengths and weaknesses. The adult-oriented home requires adaptation to make it suitable for the group care of children. The child care center, although principally focused on caring for groups of children, needs to counteract the tendency of all institutions toward efficiency and routinization and must expand its focus to include adequate provision for adults — namely staff and parents. If we define quality child care as care that ensures children's safety, promotes their health, and provides many age-appropriate play opportunities to enhance their development, while including support for the adults involved, then we can examine the setting requirements of both homes and centers. This inclusive definition of quality child care is consistent with the accreditation criteria for centers and homes used by the two major national child care professional organizations, the National Association for the Education of Young Children (NAEYC) and the National Association for Family Day Care (NAEYC, 1984; Abbott-Shim & Sibley, 1987). Although the primary focus of this chapter is on the physical setting, necessary indications for supervision and interaction are also given from time to time.

DESIGN SUGGESTIONS THAT SUPPORT QUALITY CARE

Following each of the key child care components listed below is a review of the pertinent research and best practice, as well as practical suggestions based on these two sources.

Safety

Safety is an important component in all three major voluntary credentialing/accreditation programs — the Child Development Associate (CDA) credential for caregivers, the National Family Day Care Association accreditation for family child care providers, and the National Academy of Early Childhood Program accreditation for centers. Safety is also covered in varying degrees by most state child care regulations. A recent study of U.S. child care safety regulations examined the adequacy of state safety regulations against 36 model criteria based on three sets of national safety guidelines (Runyan, Gray, Kotch & Kreuter, 1991). From a combined list of 130 injury-related criteria, these 36 model criteria focusing on the environmental features of the facilities were chosen by four experts. The day care center regulations of 45 states were then reviewed and rated on these 36 criteria.

There was wide diversity among the states in regulation of safety, with only five of the criteria being met by at least half of the states and 15 not even mentioned by half or more of the states. More troubling than the diversity was the prevalent omission of regulations to prevent the most frequent cause of injury to preschoolers — falls on the playground. In a study of injuries in 68 day care centers (Sacks, Smith, Kaplan, Lambert, Sattin & Sikes, 1989), 58% of the 143 injuries reported by center staff over a one-year period were related to falls, and 82.8% of the severe injuries were the result of falls, most of them on the playground. These findings are substantiated by a study of children under two years of age in day care centers conducted through biweekly parent telephone interviews and day care staff reports (Kotch, Loda, McMurray, Harms & Clifford, 1991). Falls accounted for the major number of injuries both in the children's homes and in the child care centers, with human bites being the second highest cause of injury in the child care centers. It would seem, then, that state safety regulations should cover playground features that could prevent injury from falls. Yet the review of state regulations found that no state specified maximum heights for playground equipment, 96% neglected to mention playground surfacing, and 91% failed to specify an eight-foot clearance surrounding playground equipment.

In order to prevent injury to young children, especially from falls, there is a demonstrated need to design safety features into family day care homes and child care centers. In a study comparing rates and types of injuries in day care homes and centers, falls accounted for the highest number in both settings; burns and poisonings occurred more in homes, and injuries from other children occurred more in centers (Revara, DiGuiseppi, Thompson & Calonge, 1989). The authors concluded that children in centers are at no greater risk, and perhaps at less risk, than those in day care homes.

Further light was shed on the types of risks present in family day care homes by a study of injury hazards in 109 homes that enrolled a median of five children, many of them infants and toddlers (Wasserman, Dameron, Brozicevic & Aronson, 1989). A hazard checklist was devised containing 25 indoor items and 22 playground items based on the Massachusetts Statewide Comprehensive Injury Prevention Program. The categories included hazards in the kitchen, bathroom, child area, general hazards, safety supplies, and outdoors or playground. All the family day care homes visited were registered homes, yet the following safety hazards were observed: 69% had knives and other sharp objects within children's reach; 35% had cleaning supplies within reach; in 64% the water temperature was more than 120° F, and in 46% it was more than 130° F; 51% had ungated accessible stairways; 65% had no covers for unused electrical outlets; 33% had no enclosures around the outdoor playground; and 87% had no energy-absorbing cushioning material under climbing equipment. Analyses using housing information revealed that dwellings other than single-family homes (e.g., apartments, mobile homes) had significantly more outdoor playground hazards and higher hazard scores in general. Rented homes had significantly more kitchen hazards and higher hazard scores than owned homes.

Increasing concern about the safety and health of children in out-of-home care has prompted a cooperative three-year study by the American Public Health Association and the American Academy of Pediatrics. This study has resulted in the development of national health and safety performance standards for child care programs in home and center settings. The comprehensive guidelines cover environmental quality, prevention and control of infectious diseases, injury prevention and control, general health promotion and medical care, nutrition, prevention and management of child abuse, staff health, children with disabilities and chronic illnesses, environmental and cultural issues, and health and safety organization and administration. These guidelines will be helpful in the design of facilities as well as in the formulation of public policy, regulation, and practice (American Public Health Association, 1991).

In light of the research reviewed above, the following safety precautions for child care settings are suggested:

TO PREVENT INJURY FROM FALLS

For infants and children under three

- Put safety railings or safety belts on diaper changing tables.
- Use steady gates to close off open stairwells.
- Use safety belts when children are in high chairs, strollers, etc.
- Limit the height of climbing equipment to the height of the children.
- Provide protective cushioning under climbing equipment.
- Provide visual openness for easy scanning indoors and outdoors so the caregiver can see children from all parts of the room and yard.

For preschoolers 3–5

- Limit the height of climbing equipment to four or five feet.
- Use wooden rather than metal climbing equipment.
- Anchor climbing equipment.
- Keep equipment in good repair.

- Provide protective cushioning material under equipment.
- Provide visual openness for easy scanning and vigilant supervision, especially outdoors.

TO PREVENT BURNS

- Enforce no-smoking rules for staff; provide separate smoking areas.
- Provide protective covering for exposed heating equipment.
- Prevent access to kitchens or cooking ranges, except as a supervised cooking experience for older preschoolers.
- Cover unused electrical outlets.
- Develop an emergency exit plan and practice fire drills monthly.

TO PREVENT CHOKING AND ASPHYXIATION

- Make sure that the spaces in furniture and in the environment are either too small for children to get their heads through or too large for children's heads to get stuck in (check cribs, playpens, high chairs).
- Make sure crib mattresses fit properly.
- Have at least one staff member present at all times who can administer child-appropriate CPR (different from adult CPR).
- Be aware that hot dogs, peanuts, and grapes are the most common causes of choking and avoid these foods for young children.
- Do not allow children to eat while running or playing.
- Supervise children closely, especially those under three.

When designing facilities, keep in mind that planning for clear traffic pathways, ample access space around equipment, resilient surfacing under playground equipment, and equipment that is the right scale for the children's height and suited to the children's ability will reduce safety hazards. If there are rules that prohibit smoking and require poisonous materials to be secured, separate but convenient places for smoking and for storing hazardous materials must be provided.

Health

Health concerns are greatest for infants and toddlers in group care, especially increased incidences of respiratory illness and diarrhea. Very young children who are still in diapers have two times the incidence of diarrhea if they are in group care.

In a project aimed at reducing the transmission of infectious disease in day care centers serving infants and toddlers under three years of age, an educational program for staff involving both personal hygiene and environmental sanitation was offered (Kotch, 1990). In addition to group training, staff received site visits for assistance in implementing the procedures and for periodic performance monitoring. Illness reports were obtained from the parents of 371 children in biweekly telephone interviews over an eight-month period. A total of 23 centers were involved, approximately half randomly assigned to the intervention group and the rest to the control group. The study collected data in 66 rooms with a variety of questionnaires and observation forms that tapped information on the physical aspects of the facility as well as the daily health and hygiene practices of the staff. In addition, environmental samples for fecal coliform were collected. The intervention centers showed significant gains in hand washing (for both adults and children), sanitary food handling, general hygiene, and better performance in disinfecting the diapering area.

Environmental modifications such as the use of step cans for diaper disposal, relocation of the diapering area closer to the sinks, separation of diapering and food-preparation areas, and use of bleach solution to disinfect the diapering table were also significantly better in the intervention centers. The effect on the illness level was harder to determine, but cases of diarrhea were reduced by about 12 cases per year per child for children under 24 months of age. There was also a decrease in the fecal coliform colony-forming units on children's hands, the most contaminated surface in the centers, and on classroom faucet handles, the next most contaminated surface.

With the great increase in the number of infants and toddlers in group care, centers and family child care homes need to make modifications in their existing environments, and new facilities need to design infant and toddler areas that make it easier to practice sanitary diapering and food-preparation procedures. Following are some suggestions for design support to facilitate good health procedures.

FOR SAFE AND SANITARY DIAPER CHANGING

- Set up a special place for diapering as near to warm running water as possible.
- For easy supervision of the other children while one is being changed, place the changing table so it juts out into the room, not up against a wall, which puts the caregiver's back to all the other children.

- Put a lined step can nearby, but out of the reach of cruising children, to dispose of soiled diapers.
- Put up a shelf, within easy reach of the caregiver but out of the children's reach, on which to keep diapering supplies such as a spray bottle of sanitizing bleach solution, baby wipes, clean washcloths, and hand lotion.
- Keep paper handy to use under the baby when changing a diaper.
- In new facilities, install foot-pedal sinks to do away with faucet handle contamination. Where this is impossible, teach caregivers to turn water faucets off using a paper towel.
- Provide a washer and dryer for washcloths, cloth diapers, and pads so they can be washed after each use.
- Provide liquid soap and paper towels near the sink used for washing hands after changing diapers.

FOR SANITARY FOOD PREPARATION AND SERVING

- Provide sufficient counter space near a sink that is used only for food service; use this sink to wash hands before and after food handling only — not if hands are contaminated after diapering.
- Use paper towels rather than cloth ones; use liquid soap rather than bar soap.
- Make sure that hot foods are kept hot and cold foods are refrigerated until served.
- In infant and toddler rooms where supervision must be continuous, place food-related appliances for easy access, such as a small refrigerator for storing bottles and baby food in the feeding area.

FOR GENERAL HYGIENE

- To cut down on respiratory disease, place cots and cribs at least two feet apart to reduce airborne contamination.
- Use floor covering that is easy to wash frequently in infant and toddler rooms. Avoid carpeting, which can harbor germs for a long time and is hard to wash. Use smaller machine-washable rugs for softness.
- Protect cushions and mattresses in the soft area with plastic liners covered by cloth pillowcases and mattress covers that can be washed frequently.

Development

One of the more important developmental inputs is children's active engagement with the physical environment. In order for child care settings to enhance socioemotional, physical, and cognitive development, the skills and knowledge of the developmental psychologist, the early childhood educator, and the architect or designer must converge. The developmental psychologist can provide insight into the desired processes and outcomes, the early childhood educator can contribute the means to achieve the desired outcomes, and the architect or designer can operationalize a setting that facilitates development. Design elements and environmental changes can be linked to desired behavior processes and outcomes (Bailey, Harms & Clifford, 1983; Weinstein, 1987), but this seldom happens. One barrier is the relative isolation of these three fields from one another. Many architects manipulate design elements that, innovative and attractive as they may be, are not functional and practical in a child care center. Such showcase buildings are what might be termed "overdesigned," with a wide range of distracting and overly complex elements. If these elements are of a permanent structural nature, they are hard to remove if it is later discovered that they are not useful. It is therefore wise to produce child care buildings that are flexible and responsive to the changing needs of different groups of children and staff.

Getting architects and educators to work together as equal partners, each learning something about the other's concerns and approaches, is one solution. Through such active partnerships, teachers can become sensitive to the spatial messages their rooms are giving to the children. They can learn to identify problems in their settings and suggest solutions in functional, concrete design terms (Enseki & Ostroff, 1983). This cross-fertilization has resulted in a relatively new discipline, environmental psychology, which combines the skills and knowledge of three disciplines: design, psychology, and education.

If we want a setting to support development, it must first facilitate engagement — it must invite and guide the children's appropriate interaction with space, materials, and people. Engagement is promoted by making materials accessible — on low, open, uncluttered shelves for preschoolers, and on the floor, a low shelf, or any other reachable place for infants. There is greater possibility for prolonged engagement when there is little competition for materials, space for children to be protected from intrusion, and a choice of many attractive, age-appropriate materials and activities (Bailey, Harms & Clifford, 1983). Having a wide range of materials so that each child can find something of interest also helps engagement.

Moore (1987), an architect and educator attempting to relate spatial organization to children's behavior in settings, identifies ten critical dimensions of spatial organization in child care centers that influence program and behavior: (1) visual connection between spaces, (2) closure of spaces, (3) distance between different activity areas, (4) mixture of larger open areas and smaller enclosed areas, (5) separation of staff areas from children's areas, (6) separation of functional areas from activity areas, (7) separation of age groups, (8) separation of circulation pathways from activity spaces, (9) visibility of activity areas from entry, and (10) connection between outdoors and indoors. Using this framework in a study of children's engagement in cognitively oriented behavior in three spatial organizations—the totally open plan, the modified open plan, and the closed plan—Moore found that children in the modified open plan used significantly more activity centers, worked in small groupings, and engaged in more cognitively oriented behavior. In the totally open plan, children engaged in more random or unsustained activity; in the closed plan, there was more moving between activities and more staring into space. Both the totally open plan and modified open plan designs afford easy access to a variety of different activity centers, but the modified open plan provides acoustic separation and a greater feeling of containment and privacy for each area. This combination of privacy and access stimulates engagement. It seems that the level of engagement was influenced in this study by the spatial factors of visual connection, closure of spaces, and noise conduction. For example, in an open setting where there is little enclosure of activity spaces, play is frequently interrupted by noise from other areas and disrupted by circulation pathways. In such a setting, engagement is often sporadic, with a lot of random activity and wandering. On the other hand, in a modified open setting where areas are more protected from the interruptions of noise and traffic, engagement for a longer time permits more involved play.

The rules for access to materials also influence the level of engagement (Weinstein, 1987). Access can be completely open, guided open, or closed. In the completely open condition, toys and materials are always available to children. In guided open access, materials are available with explicit rules that structure their use but that the children can manage themselves—for example, using color-coded clothespins to limit the number of children allowed in a particular activity area at one time, or being able to reserve a turn in a particular area by putting one's name on a waiting list. The closed condition permits access only through a supervisor—for example, having to request art materials, which are then taken out of a closed cupboard by the supervisor. Each of these access condition affects the possibilities for engagement and independence.

Another basic environmental design consideration is deciding which activities to include in the indoor and outdoor areas. The goal is to provide a wide variety of experiences, taking the physical constraints of the setting into consideration. In cases in which the indoor area is relatively small, crowding must be avoided. Crowding causes conflicts and interrupts engagement. One way to minimize crowding is to organize activity spaces through which different activities are rotated during the day, rather than to organize activity centers that contain particular activities (Cryer, Harms & Bourland, 1987a, 1987b, 1988a, 1988b). These activity spaces might include a messy activity space for art, science, or cooking that has a washable floor covering and is near water; a quiet activity space for reading, listening to story records, or using puzzles and manipulative games; and a more active indoor area for blocks, dramatic play, or dance. The materials for the various activities that will be rotated through the indoor activity spaces can be kept in activity boxes that are stored elsewhere until they are needed. Thus the rotation of toys and activities at different times can compensate, to some degree, for a small physical space. Moving the noisier or messier activities into the outdoor space—preferably in a contained area that is separated from tricycle pathways, climbing equipment, and the open area—also helps make a small physical space calmer and less busy. The outdoors can include partially enclosed areas for noisy activities such as carpentry and very messy activities such as fingerpainting and sand and water play. A periodic assessment of how the outdoor area is being used can help staff create an outdoor classroom alongside the more traditional physical uses of the playground (Lovell & Harms, 1985).

Family child care settings must also deal with the issues of spatial organization and rules for access to materials. Johnson (1987) suggests the use of small "activity pockets" (Moore, Lane, Hill, Cohen & McGinty, 1979, recommendations 908 and 921). An activity pocket consists of a small unit of furniture and materials to support a specific activity for an individual child or small group of children, which can be located in various rooms of the home. A variety of activity pockets for different activities can be made available to children in a home setting, including a space for messy art activities in the kitchen, a low table for manipulative toys in the dining room, or books and puzzles on a rug in the living room. Consistent visual supervision of children is important in both center and home settings, so the number and placement of activity pockets will be limited by the availability of space that is within visual supervision.

Following are some specific design suggestions to enhance the development of a number of desirable socioemotional and cognitive outcomes.

FOR SECURITY AND COMFORT

- Create an inviting entryway that has warm colors and pleasant lighting, is neither chaotic nor cluttered, has an appropriate place out of traffic for parents and children to pause to remove outdoor clothing, and has individual storage cubbies with each child's name and picture to keep personal things.
- Provide a view of part of the activity room from the entryway so that children realize when they enter that they are returning to play with familiar toys and friends.
- Make sure that each child is greeted warmly by a familiar adult upon arrival.
- Provide softness throughout the setting in several ways: an area with cushions on a rug near bookshelves to be used for reading or for puzzles; small rugs that children can use to denote their own personal areas to work; upholstered furniture for children and adults; a sandbox outdoors.
- Separate active and quiet play areas for infants and toddlers so that the less mobile babies are not run over or fallen on by the more active ones.
- Make sure that very young children are held frequently for feeding, socialization, and cuddling.

FOR SELF-ESTEEM AND POSITIVE IDENTITY

- Provide display boards at the children's eye level for pictures of the children, their families, and their pets; change these pictures often to retain the children's interest.
- Make sure that the books and pictures around the room show children and adults of various races and ethnic groups doing interesting things. There should be a picture that every child can identify with as well as some unfamiliar people.
- Make sure that the children's books and the pictures in the room show girls and boys and men and women in nonstereotypic roles.

FOR PROSOCIAL BEHAVIOR

- Avoid conflicts over materials by providing duplicates of popular toys, and make sure there are enough toys available.
- For children three and over, provide clear systems for sharing and taking turns, such as a waiting list at the children's eye level where each child's name can be put on the list and checked off when his or her turn is finished.
- Provide activity pockets or small, cozy activity areas where an individual or a small group can play protected from intrusion by others.
- Have several alternatives for play available at all times and allow children to follow their interests. Permitting children choices and keeping them engaged cuts down on quarreling and competition.
- Provide spaces for several types of groupings: large groups, several small self-selected or teacher-selected groups, one-to-one adult-child interaction, and play-alone spaces.

FOR INDEPENDENCE

- Use child-sized chairs, tables, toilets, and sinks or adapt the equipment for self-help with the use of cushions, steps, and so on where necessary.
- Provide open access and guided open access to safe, age-appropriate toys at all times for all children, including infants, toddlers, and preschoolers.
- Use picture/word labels on open shelves so that preschoolers can put things back where they belong.
- Organize shelves so that they are not cluttered or crowded and things are placed together in a functional way that children can remember.

FOR VARIETY OF EXPERIENCES

- Provide activity pockets (small activity areas) indoors or outdoors for open-ended materials such as arts and crafts, mini-world dramatic play, dress-up clothes, puppets, carpentry, cooking, and sand or water play.
- Offer equipment and activities for fine muscle and eye-hand coordination such as scissors, drawing, pegboards, and manipulative toys.

- Offer some structured materials for individual and small-group use that require searching for the one right answer and following rules, such as puzzles, games, and lotto boards.
- Provide rules for guided access so that preschoolers can use materials constructively with minimal adult supervision.
- Design larger open areas for music and dance, block building, group meetings, and story time.
- Use the walls as activity easels and for displays related to the children; keep things at their level and involve them in putting things up and changing the materials frequently.
- Enhance language learning by controlling noise with acoustical ceiling treatments and wall and floor coverings and by partially enclosing activity areas.
- Use the outdoor area for some fine motor activities in well-defined, separated, semienclosed areas.
- Use the outdoor area for very noisy or messy activities, such as carpentry or fingerpainting, if there is no suitable indoor accommodation.

Adult Provisions

A setting that supports quality child care must provide appropriate space and equipment to meet both parents' and teachers' concerns. Parents and teachers need to be able to sit down privately for a conference at the intake visit and periodically thereafter, as long as the child is enrolled. An area that is separated from the children's program and supplied with adult furniture should be set aside solely for private conferences. Since sound as well as visual screening is important, a room divider does not offer enough separation. A larger adult meeting area is also needed for staff and parent meetings. If these meetings can be held while one of the children's rooms is free, adult-sized chairs can be brought in to adapt the room for its dual function as an adult meeting room.

Teaching staff need a place to keep personal belongings that is accessible while they are with the children, a lounge with soft furniture and a table and chairs for their breaks or lunchtime, a resource library with professional books and materials, and a preparation area where materials can be made for use in the classroom. Since records must be kept, accounts settled, and telephone access maintained, an office area is a necessity for the administrator. Also, since most child care centers are responsible for providing meals and snacks, equipment for food storage, preparation, service, and cleanup is another basic requirement. An observation area adjoining the children's playroom, where parents and staff can observe children but not be seen by them, permits these key adults to gain information of a more objective nature about how children are functioning in the program. All of the foregoing parent and teacher provisions can be considered basic requirements if parents are to be included in the program and teachers are to be treated as professionals.

Some centers have expanded the concept to include even more parent support functions, so that they have become "family care centers" rather than child care centers. A special parent room is needed in such centers, where parents can meet informally over refreshments, parent meetings can be held while the children's program is in session, and helpful adult-oriented equipment can be made available, such as a computer or sewing machine. A parent resource library containing books or toys that circulate can also help parents in their child-rearing role. This augmented parent support component is particularly helpful in centers serving economically deprived areas and transient groups. Following are suggestions for meeting the needs of staff and parents.

DESIGNING FOR STAFF NEEDS

- Provide adequate space for teachers to store personal belongings, including coats, a change of clothes, and a purse; make provision for security, such as a locked place, if necessary.
- Arrange for a sufficiently large conference area that can be used for parent meetings and staff development activities.
- Provide on-site space for a resource library for independent use in staff development, including books, audiotapes, and videocassettes.
- The resource library should include materials that can be checked out for use in the classroom with the children.
- Provide a lounge with upholstered adult furniture, a table and chairs, refrigerator, and stove for staff lunchtime and breaks. Smoking should not be permitted in this area; a separate smoking area should be designated that need not be used by nonsmokers.
- A materials preparation area should be provided, outfitted with a large, sturdy work table and adult-sized chairs; access to a laminating machine is helpful.

DESIGNING FOR PARENT NEEDS

- Provide an entry seating area that is comfortable for removing children's boots in rainy weather and helping children get ready to participate in the program.
- Designate a comfortable parent meeting room that can operate independently of the children's program and therefore can be open at the same time.
- Provide a parent resource library containing parenting books and articles, children's books, and games for circulation.
- Provide space for additional equipment helpful to parents for on-site use. The room should be capable of being secured when it is not being used. Include equipment such as a computer and a sewing machine. This is of particular value for low-income or transient parents who do not have access to such equipment at home.

CONCLUSION

Children are active learners who use the physical setting in a direct, hands-on mode. Careful planning is needed in a child care setting to create a physical environment that will help children reach desired developmental goals in the socioemotional, physical, and cognitive domains. Such informed design requires a convergence of knowledge and skills from three fields: psychology, education, and architectural design.

Early childhood settings in family child care homes and centers need to provide for children's safety, health, and developmentally appropriate activities, as well as make provision for the parents and staff. Here we have used some of the clear indications from both research and best practice to suggest ways of handling the spatial configuration, safety and health precautions, play opportunities, and adult provisions in child care settings to reach desired developmental goals for children.

A flexible, pleasant, and functional setting gives children and staff the opportunity to express their own personalities and philosophy through the program. In contrast, buildings that are overdesigned are expensive showcases that can become obsolete and confining as successive child care groups make different demands on the setting.

The physical setting conveys powerful messages to children about their personal worth, how they are to interact with the people and materials in the setting, and how secure and happy they can be in the setting. Spatial organization both communicates values and structures interactions. Educators' awareness of design possibilities and designers' awareness of educational means for reaching developmental goals are needed before we can design settings that support high-quality care.

REFERENCES

Abbott-Shim, M., & Sibley, A. (1987). *Assessment profile for early childhood programs: Manual administration*. Atlanta: Quality Assist.

American Public Health Association and the American Academy of Pediatrics. (1991). *Caring for our children—National health and safety performance standards; guidelines for out-of-home child care programs*. Washington, DC: American Public Health Association.

Aronson, S. (1991). *Health and safety in child care*. New York: HarperCollins.

Bailey, D., Harms, T., & Clifford, R. (1983). Matching changes in preschool environments to desired changes in child behavior. *Journal of the Division for Early Childhood*, 7, 61–68.

Bredekamp, S. (Ed.). (1988). *Developmentally appropriate practices in early childhood programs serving children from birth through age 8*. Washington, DC: National Association for the Education of Young Children.

Cryer, D., Harms, T., & Bourland, B. (1987a). *Active learning for infants*. Menlo Park, CA: Addison-Wesley.

Cryer, D., Harms, T., & Bourland, B. (1987b). *Active learning for ones*. Menlo Park, CA: Addison-Wesley.

Cryer, D., Harms, T., & Bourland, B. (1988a). *Active learning for twos*. Menlo Park, CA: Addison-Wesley.

Cryer, D., Harms, T., & Bourland, B. (1988b). *Active learning for threes*. Menlo Park, CA: Addison-Wesley.

Donowitz, L. (Ed.). (1991). *Infection control in the child care center and preschool*. Baltimore: Williams & Wilkins.

Enseki, C., & Ostroff, E. (1983). *Introductory workshops in adaptive environmental design workbook*. Boston: Adaptive Environments, Massachusetts College of Art.

Frost, J., & Klein, B. (1983). *Children's play and playgrounds*. Austin, TX: Playscapes International.

Greenman, J. (1988). *Caring spaces, learning places: Children's environments that work*. Redmond, WA: Exchange Press.

Harms, T., & Clifford, R. M. (1980). *The early childhood environment rating scale*. New York: Teachers College Press.

Harms, T., & Clifford, R. M. (1989). *The family day care rating scale*. New York: Teachers College Press.

Harms, T., Cryer, D., & Clifford, R. M. (1990). *Infant/toddler environment rating scale*. New York: Teachers College Press.

Johnson, L. (1987). The developmental implications of home environments. In C. S. Weinstein & T. G. David (Eds.), *Spaces for children: The built environment and child development* (pp. 139–157). New York: Plenum.

Johnson, L., & Dineen, J. (1981). *The kin trade.* Toronto: McGraw-Hill Ryerson.

Johnson, L., Shack, J., & Oster, K. (1980). *Out of the cellar and into the parlour.* Ottawa, Ontario: Canada Mortgage and Housing Corporation.

Kotch, J. (1990, Dec.). *Reduction in transmission of infectious disease in child care settings.* Grant #MCJ-37111. Final report submitted to the Maternal & Child Health Research Program, Maternal & Child Health Bureau, HRSA, PHS, USDHHS. Chapel Hill, NC: Dept. of Maternal & Child Health, University of North Carolina at Chapel Hill.

Kotch, J., Loda, F., McMurray, M., Harms, T., & Clifford, R. (1991). *Parent's reports of injuries among children in day care centers.* Chapel Hill, NC: University of North Carolina at Chapel Hill, School of Public Health and Medicine.

Lovell, P., & Harms, T. (1985). How can playgrounds be improved? A rating scale. *Young Children, 40*(3), 3–8.

Moore, G. (1987). The physical environment and cognitive development in child-care centers. In C. S. Weinstein & T. G. David (Eds.), *Spaces for children: The built environment and child development* (pp. 41–72). New York: Plenum.

Moore, G. T., Lane, C. G., Hill, A. B., Cohen, U., & McGinty, T. (1979). *Recommendations for child care centers.* Milwaukee, WI: School of Architecture and Urban Planning.

National Association for the Education of Young Children. (1984). *Accreditation criteria and procedures.* Washington, DC: Author.

Olds, A. R. (1979). Designing developmentally optimal classrooms for children with special needs. In S. J. Meisels (Ed.), *Special education and development: Perspectives on young children with special needs* (pp. 91–138). Baltimore: University Park Press.

Prescott, E. (1987). The environment as organizer of intent in child-care settings. In C. S. Weinstein & T. G. David (Eds.), *Spaces for children: The built environment and child development* (pp. 72–83). New York: Plenum.

Revara, F., DiGuiseppi, C., Thompson, R., & Calonge, N. (1989). Risk of injury to children less than 5 years of age in day care versus home care settings. *Pediatrics, 84*(6), 1011–1016.

Runyan, C., Gray, D., Kotch, J., & Kreuter, M. (1991). Analysis of U.S. child care safety regulations. *American Journal of Public Health, 81,* 981–985.

Sacks, J., Smith, J. D., Kaplan, K., Lambert, D., Sattin, R., & Sikes, R. K. (1989). The epidemiology of injuries in Atlanta day care centers. *JAMA, 262*(12), 1641–1645.

Wasserman, R., Dameron, D., Brozicevic, M., & Aronson, R. (1989). Injury hazards in home day care. *Journal of Pediatrics, 114,* 591–593.

Weinstein, C. (1987). Designing preschool classrooms to support development. In C. S. Weinstein & T. G. David (Eds.), *Spaces for children: The built environment and child development* (pp.159–185). New York: Plenum.

CHAPTER 11

Child Care: A Look to the Future

Bernard Spodek
Olivia N. Saracho

Some early childhood educators make no distinction between child care and other forms of early childhood education. Others see these as different but overlapping services to children. How one conceives of the relationship between child care and early education often determines one's position on standards for child care programs, basic requirements for early childhood personnel, and a host of other issues in the field.

CHILD CARE AND EARLY EDUCATION

If one looks at the history of child care in the United States and the history of early childhood education, it is possible to identify distinct streams of services for young children. At times these streams converge, so that little if any difference can be seen between them. At other times the streams are separate and distinct. The question is: Is there any difference between child care services and early education programs? There may be no simple "yes" or "no" answer.

Interestingly, no distinction was made between child care and early education in one of the earliest programs for young children in America. Robert Owen, a British industrialist, created the infant school to ameliorate the conditions of the working class in the early nineteenth century. Owen's social and educational ideas attracted the attention of Americans, and both fee-paying and charitable infant schools were established from New England through the Middle Atlantic states (May & Vinovskis, 1977). Bronson Alcott, a schoolteacher and later social reformer, established one of these infant schools in Boston in 1828. This infant school was supported by the clergy in Boston because it not only educated young children but also freed their mothers to seek gainful employment (Shepard, 1937).

The infant school movement was short-lived in America. Part of the difficulty was that it competed with the "common school," as public elementary schools were then called. Part of the problem lay in Alcott's collection and publication of young children's versions of the Gospel and in his enrollment of a black child in his infant school. Charles Strickland argues forcibly that the death of infant education in the United States was also the result of the "fireside education" movement and the cult of domesticity. This movement argued for the education of young children at home at their mothers' knees. Only mothers, it was felt, could provide the training needed to enhance the moral development of young children. Mothers were expected to stay home with their young children who, in turn, would be protected from the outside world during the tender years of development (Strickland, 1982).

Froebel's kindergarten arrived in the United States in 1856. It became the dominant model of early childhood education as fee-paying kindergartens were established along with charitable kindergartens for the poor. Kindergartens slowly became a part of the public schools beginning in the 1870s, and slowly they were reconstructed to serve primarily five-year-old children. Even as late as 1965, however, less than half the five-year-old children in the United States attended either private or public kindergartens (King, 1975). Early kindergartens served children in half-day programs, providing parent education during the other half-day (Weber, 1969). The structure of the kindergarten supported the importance of the role of mothers in caring for and educating young children. Thus its philosophy did not run counter to that of the fireside education movement. It also did not allow mothers to work while their children were educated and cared for outside the home.

In contrast, child care centers were not originally seen as educational institutions. First established in 1854 in New York, day nurseries, as they were then called, were first established as charitable agencies (Kahan, 1989). Often they were established by settlement houses or other philanthropic institutions to help the children of poor and immigrant mothers. Interestingly, one of the first programs established by Jane Addams in Chicago's Hull House, one of the first American settlement houses, was a kindergarten. The next year, responding to the needs of its clients, Hull House established a day nursery. It has continued to offer child care services in Chicago, often in cooperation with other social agencies.

In the 1920s the nursery school curriculum was integrated into the day nursery to create the day care center. This integration reconstructed day care from a child-minding service to a program for the education and care of young children. Since that time an educational program has been an expected part of the service offered in child care centers. Indeed, children's development is considered at risk if they are denied an educational program while they are attending a child care center.

Originally, primarily children of the poor were served by child care programs. Given the changes in American society in recent decades — a continual increase in the number of working mothers, and especially mothers of young children — child care today is a program for children of all socioeconomic backgrounds. Programs for the care and education of young children are an essential need of children around the world.

A knowledge of the history of child care in America, as Alice Honig demonstrates in Chapter 2, is essential in understanding the way in which child care services are provided to young children today. This knowledge is also essential in understanding the attitude of Americans toward child care. Although much of the concern about child care addresses the needs of preschool children in child care centers — a setting parallel to that of other early childhood programs — not all of it does. A significant portion of child care services is provided in family day care — the "other" form of care, as Susan Kontos has characterized it. Such care is similar in some ways to that offered in centers, but it is also different in significant ways: Children are not placed into organized groups, a curriculum is not offered, and few personnel requirements are placed on these caregivers. As Carollee Howes points out, there is no basis to consider one form of care better than the other in relation to child outcomes; they are merely different from each other.

Another form of care that is different from early childhood education is the before- and after-school care that is provided for school-aged children. These children may be in kindergarten or elementary classes. Unlike personnel in preschool child care centers, caregivers in these programs are seldom characterized as "teachers," nor do these programs seem to parallel school programs. Although some of these programs are extensions of preschool child care programs, many of them are sponsored by schools, libraries, and other community agencies. Often they represent a collaboration of several agencies. Programs offered in these non-child care center operations are seldom the same as those offered in center-based care for preschool-aged children. School-age child care programs seldom reproduce the curriculum of the school. Though help with homework might be provided, the programs are generally either supplemental or recreational in nature. They may be considered educational in nature, but not school oriented.

Thus child care for young children represents a diverse set of services, similar in some ways to early childhood education programs but different in others. The more we understand the nature of child care, the better we will be at providing appropriate services and using them to serve the needs of young children and their families.

CURRENT ISSUES IN CHILD CARE

This volume has identified many of the major issues related to caring for young children. These include issues related to child care clients, sponsors, programs, staffing, and standards of quality. Each of these areas presents dilemmas for the field.

Defining Child Care Clients

Typical early childhood programs are primarily concerned with serving the needs of children. When parent programs are offered they are viewed as a way to make the children's programs more effective. One of the contradictions of child care as early childhood education is that child care serves the needs of parents. The education of the children is often seen as a secondary concern. In the 1970s, when child care services were expanding, one of the issues was whether to support the expansion of child care services when the limited funds available might lead to a lessening of standards. The needs of parents were set in opposition to the needs of children.

Ellen Galinsky and Bernice Weissbourd envision a type of child care service that avoids this dilemma, in which the family is seen as the client of early childhood programs. Although the child care agency may not be able to provide all the services needed by the family, it can identify agencies that could provide whatever services are needed and act as a coordinator of services. Thus, neither the child nor the parent is put at risk by the provision of child care; the needs of all members of the family are addressed by such a program. Family-centered child care is a new concept that has the potential to change how child care centers and family agencies operate.

Although family-centered child care is not cheap, as noted in Chapter 4, it is cost-effective in the long run. The examples presented provide evidence of its effectiveness. These examples also suggest that such a service cannot be supported by user fees alone, but require a collaboration of several sponsors and might be dependent on public money for its development.

Identifying Child Care Sponsors

The great expansion of child care services in the 1970s saw a major change in child care sponsors. In the past, child care centers were operated primarily by not-for-profit community agencies—churches, social welfare agencies, and the like—as well as by individual entrepreneurs. The most visible change that has taken place in the field has been the establishment of large corporations devoted to creating chains of fully owned or franchised child care centers. Corporations have entered the child care field in other ways as well. A number of corporations have created child care centers for children of their employees or have supported child care information systems to help their employees identify child care resources.

More recently, another form of sponsor has entered the field— public school systems. More than a decade ago, public school systems began to receive recommendations that they open their schools to child care services. In many cases this was a response to the number of empty classrooms available in public schools, a condition that no longer exists. Although the majority of school systems still do not provide child care, many have begun to do so. In many cases the schools have allowed outside agencies to offer programs in their schools. Some systems have begun sponsoring programs on their own (Mitchell, Seligson & Marx, 1989).

Concern about the sponsorship of child care centers is not merely a concern for the cost of care. As Carollee Howes has noted, sponsorship of child care is also linked to its quality. Many in the child care field have been afraid that the increased involvement of public schools would diminish the role of private companies in the provision of child care services. Howes suggests that we need to look more closely at the quality of the services offered by these private providers. If we continue to find a strong relationship between type of program sponsor and child care quality and outcomes, then we need to be more concerned with the interests of the children and look more closely at the standards that are being established or place limits on private for-profit child care providers.

Determining the Content of Child Care Programs

It is not enough to establish child care programs where the need exists. We need to concern ourselves with the content of the educational programs offered. The term "educare" has been used to characterize the combining of education and child care into a single service for children. If the field is serious about making this combination a reality rather than simply a goal, child care centers need to carefully address the issue of the quality and kind of educational programs they will offer. There has been a call for these centers to provide developmentally appropriate programs for young children (Bredekamp, 1987), but they also need to be educationally worthwhile, considering the values and knowledge systems embedded in society (Spodek, 1988). Programs need to reflect a concern for the development of language, social, and cognitive skills. Increasingly we have come to understand, as Patricia Ramsey notes in Chapter 6, that a multicultural perspective must be embedded in programs for all children. Not only are many of the children enrolled in child care programs from multicultural backgrounds, but we live in a multicultural society with increasingly more intimate international relations. The education of all children must reflect this multicultural perspective.

Improved programs require improved educational settings. Thelma Harms, in Chapter 10, suggests criteria for establishing such settings. High-quality child care settings along with well-prepared interactive teachers can support strong early childhood programs in a context of health and safety.

Increasing numbers of young children are being enrolled in child care programs, and a higher proportion of these children will have special educational needs. Now that P.L. 99-457, the extension of the Education of All Handicapped Children Act, has become a reality, all programs serving children (at least from the age of three on) will be required to serve children with handicapping conditions. Although the resources needed to serve these children should be available within each community, increased responsibility for serving these children adequately will be placed on child care centers. As the nature of the clientele of these centers changes, the services provided will also have to change.

Dealing with Staffing Issues

Paula Jorde Bloom's chapter addresses the issues related to staffing child care centers. The qualifications of child care personnel are generally lower than those for early childhood teachers in public schools. The salaries are also lower. There is a general feeling that standards for child care staff need to be raised. There is also a belief that compensation and working conditions must improve.

Staff qualifications are usually embedded in state child care licensing regulations. Unfortunately, there has been no move to raise the standards of such regulations, either in relation to staff qualification or in other ways. Child care is labor-intensive; the largest expense is staff salaries. One of the dilemmas is that if staff salaries increase, the cost of care increases. In not-for-profit centers, this may lead to a reduction of services. In for-profit centers, this would lead to a price increase for parents (Willer, Hofferth, Kisker, Divine-Hawkins, Farquhar & Glantz, 1991). The result is that child care personnel continue to subsidize the cost of child care with their own low salaries, limited benefits, and poor working conditions.

Establishing Child Care Standards

Although most regulations in the United States are concerned with basic protection, they also seek to assure justice and equality. Regulation represents a floor of quality needed to protect children in programs. This standard is the basis for licensing and is enforceable by law (Morgan, 1982). Other levels of quality can be established by accreditation, which is usually a voluntary procedure that identifies centers meeting a higher standard than licensing. Child care centers are regulated by the state agencies that license them. The Center Accreditation Program of the Academy of Early Childhood Programs accredits programs that meet its standards and apply for accreditation. Only a minority of child care centers are accredited.

The licensing requirement for child care centers stands in contrast to the regulation (or lack thereof) of day care homes. There are, however, a number of exceptions to the licensing requirements for child care centers in many states. Centers that are operated by school systems, state agencies, or religious institutions may be exempt from such licensing. However, only a small minority of child care homes — Susan Kontos suggests between 11% and 15% — are licensed. Because licensing all family day care homes would be a burdensome task, registration is suggested as an alternative. This voluntary process is used in 16 states today.

A LOOK TO THE FUTURE

Looking to the future of child care in America requires that we extrapolate trends from current and past events. This is always a risky task. Goals need to be identified, but these goals may change as social conditions change. The National Research Council of the National Academy of Sciences recently published a report that identified three significant goals for an improved child care system: (1) improved quality in child care, (2) greater accessibility to child care for families, and (3) increased affordability for low- and moderate-income families (Hayes, Palmer & Zaslow, 1990). Certainly these are desirable goals, but they will not be achieved unless there are serious social initiatives in the future.

Perhaps the way to look to the future of child care in America is to return to the trends that Roger Neugebauer presented in the first chapter of this volume. Neugebauer suggested that children will continue to be enrolled in child care programs as mothers of young children continue to participate in the work force. There is no indication that this trend will diminish, and many have suggested that it will increase. It should be expected that child care centers will remain the care of choice.

The increased political popularity of child care is also expected to continue. Issues such as child care, health care, and education have become the "sexy issues" of the decade (Ifill, 1991). Whether child care will continue to be a sexy issue and whether its attractiveness will translate into increased financial support remain to be seen.

It is clearly evident that early childhood education has increasingly become a part of the public schools. Kindergarten attendance has now become the norm in the United States, and increasing numbers of school districts are providing all-day kindergarten programs and prekindergarten programs. But the all-day kindergarten represents only a full school day, not the extended day of child care. Although child care arrangements can be found in public schools in a minority of states, these arrangements are still the exception rather than the rule. There seems to be enough carryover from the fireside education movement of the past to keep Americans from accepting child care as a public responsibility as they have accepted education. In addition, budget difficulties and classroom shortages currently plaguing public school systems in many states will keep these systems from providing child care in the foreseeable future.

The trend for child care agencies to see parents as their clients will continue to grow. The move toward family-centered child care can offer an extended service to children and their parents, expanding the traditional conceptions of child care. The provision of this service will depend on the increased availability of funds as well as on the willingness of traditional child care agencies to accept greater responsibilities for a variety of programming initiatives.

Although Neugebauer sees a trend toward increased quality in child care, one must add a word of caution to that view. Studies have shown that the levels of education of child care personnel have decreased over the past decade or two. There has also been a trend for states to exempt certain kinds of child care centers from licensing standards. This would suggest a decrease in standards rather than an increase. Although the National Association for the Education of Young Children's *Developmentally Appropriate Practices* (Bredekamp, 1987) has been one of the most popular publications of that organization, all sorts of early childhood practices have been justified by reference to it. Although the book has set a standard of practice, it has not yet been translated into improved practice. A great deal more than a single book is required for that. Child care settings will need to be improved along with teaching practices. As Carollee Howes has indicated, these seem to be closely related to the sponsorship of child care programs. If this is the case, we will need an increase in the proportion of not-for-profit and publicly supported child care programs to increase the quality of child care in America.

The trend that Neugebauer finds missing, and the issue that Bloom addresses in Chapter 9, is the move to upgrade the wages and benefits of child care teachers. Providing better working conditions and higher salaries will have to go hand in hand with upgrading the qualifications of child care teachers. Unfortunately, the income of teachers and caregivers is decreasing rather than increasing. The average salary of teachers in child care centers has decreased by almost 25%, when adjusted for inflation, between the mid 1970s and 1990.

Teachers with higher levels of preparation and a greater commitment to their field will provide a more competent and more stable group of child care personnel. Only with an increase in the quality of child care personnel will we see an increase in the quality of child care services.

The look to the future is a mixed one, neither all positive nor all negative. But futures are not established by fate; they are created by individuals. Thus, the future of child care in America is dependent on what we make of it. Parents, professionals, politicians, and the lay public will have to work together to create a future for child care. Let us hope that this future is a good one, because the future of our culture depends on the quality of its child care services as much as it depends on the quality of its schools and its families.

REFERENCES

Bredekamp, S. (Ed.). (1987). *Developmentally appropriate practices in early childhood programs serving children from birth through age 8* (exp. ed.). Washington, DC: National Association for the Education of Young Children.

Hayes, C. D., Palmer, J. L., & Zaslow, M. J. (Eds.) (1990). *Who cares for America's children: Child care policy for the 1990s.* Washington, DC: National Academy Press.

Ifill, G. (1991, Nov. 18). Female lawmakers wrestle with new public attitudes on "women's" issues. *New York Times*, p. A9.

Kahan, E. D. (1989). *Past caring: A history of U.S. preschool care and education for the poor, 1820–1965.* New York: National Center for Children in Poverty, School of Public Health, Columbia University.

King, I. A. (1975). *Preprimary enrollment: October, 1974.* Washington, DC: US Government Printing Office.

May, D., & Vinovskis, M. (1977). A ray of millennial light: Early education and social reform in the infant school movement in Massachusetts. In T. Harevian (Ed.), *Family and kin in urban communities* (pp. 62–69). New York: New Viewpoints.

Mitchell, A., Seligson, M., & Marx, F. (1989). *Early childhood programs and the public schools: Between promise and practice.* Dover, MA: Auburn House.

Morgan, G. (1982). Regulating early childhood programs in the eighties. In B. Spodek (Ed.), *Handbook of research in early childhood education* (pp. 375–398). New York: Free Press.

Shepard, O. (1937). *Pedlar's progress: The life of Bronson Alcott.* Boston: Little, Brown.

Spodek, B. (1988). Conceptualizing today's kindergarten curriculum. *Elementary School Journal, 89*(2), 203–211.

Steinfels, M. O. (1973). *Who's minding the children? The history and politics of day care in America.* New York: Simon & Schuster.

Strickland, C. A. (1982). Paths not taken: Seminal models of early childhood education. In B. Spodek (Ed.), *Handbook of research in early childhood education* (pp. 321–340). New York: Free Press.

Weber, E. (1969). *The kindergarten: Its encounter with educational thought in America.* New York: Teachers College Press.

Willer, B., Hofferth, S. L., Kisker, P., Divine-Hawkins, P., Farquhar, E., & Glantz, F. B. (1991). *The demand and supply of child care in 1990: Joint findings from the national child care survey 1990 and a profile of child care settings*. Washington, DC: National Association for the Education of Young Children.

About the Editors and the Contributors

K. Eileen Allen is professor emeritus from the University of Kansas. Prior to her appointment there she was coordinator of early childhood education and research in the Child Development Research Center at the University of Washington in Seattle. She has worked with normally developing and atypical young children, their parents, and their teachers throughout her professional life. In 1981 she was selected as a Congressional Science Fellow by the Society for Research in Child Development and spent the year in Washington, D.C., as a legislative aide to Congressman Don Bonker on child and family issues. Her two most recent books are *Developmental Profiles: Birth through Six*, with L. Marotz (Delmar, 1989), and *Mainstreaming in Early Childhood Education*, 2d ed. (Delmar, 1992).

Paula Jorde Bloom is associate professor at National-Louis University in Evanston, Illinois, where she directs a graduate program in early childhood leadership and advocacy. She received her Ph.D. from Stanford University, has taught preschool and kindergarten, and served as administrator of a campus laboratory school. Her current research interests are in the area of organizational climate and occupational stress as related to indices of job satisfaction. Among her recent publications are *Avoiding Burnout: Strategies for Managing Time, Space, and People* (Gryphon House, 1982), *Living and Learning with Children* (Gryphon House, 1981), *A Great Place to Work: Improving Conditions for Staff in Young Children's Programs* (NAEYC, 1988), and, with M. Sheerer and J. Britz, *Blueprint for Action: Achieving Center-Based Change through Staff Development* (Gryphon House, 1991).

Ellen Galinsky is co-president of the Families and Work Institute, a nonprofit clearinghouse on work and family life that conducts research on business, government, and community efforts to help employees balance their job and family responsibilities. She is a past president of the National Association for the Education of Young Children and serves on the Advisory Committee to the New York State Permanent

Interagency Committee on Early Childhood Programs. Ms. Galinsky has published widely in academic journals and magazines. Her books include *The New Extended Family: Day Care that Works* (Houghton-Mifflin, 1977), *The Six Stages of Parenthood* (Addison-Wesley, 1987), *The Preschool Years* (Random House, 1988), *The Corporate Reference Guide to Work-Family Programs* (Families and Work Institute, 1991), *Beyond the Parental Leave Debate* (Families and Work Institute, 1991), and *Education Before School* (Committee on Economic Development, in preparation).

Ellen Gannett is associate director of the School-Age Child Care Project, a national action/research and technical-assistance project located at Wellesley College Center for Research on Women. She holds degrees from Lesley College, the University of Massachusetts, and the Merrill-Palmer Institute. She directed a Boston area school-age child care program and has been on the faculty of Massachusetts Bay Community College and Wheelock College. Ms. Gannett authored the School-Age Child Care Project's publication, *City Initiatives in School-Age Child Care* (Wellesley College, 1989), and a chapter in the book *Employer-Supported Child Care: Investing in Human Resources* (Auburn House, 1984). She also coauthored another Project publication, *School-Age Child Care: A Public Policy* (Wellesley College, 1984).

Thelma Harms is director of curriculum development at the Frank Porter Graham Child Development Center and an adjunct associate professor in the School of Education at the University of North Carolina at Chapel Hill. She earned a doctorate in early childhood education at the University of California, Berkeley. Previously, Dr. Harms was head teacher at the Harold E. Jones Child Study Center Preschool Program, University of California-Berkeley. Dr. Harms is first author of three widely used program assessment instruments, the *Early Childhood Environment Rating Scale* (Teachers College Press, 1980), the *Family Day Care Rating Scale* (Teachers College Press, 1989) and the *Infant/Toddler Environment Rating Scale* (Teachers College Press, 1990) as well as coauthor of several other curriculum publications and an early childhood video training series, *Raising America's Children*. Her work on environment and curriculum has been translated and is used abroad in many countries.

Alice Sterling Honig received her Ph.D. from Syracuse University, where she is now professor of child development. For 12 years she was program director for the Children's Center and the Family Development Research Program for low-income teen mothers and their infants and young children. She is currently president-elect of the International Association for Infant Mental Health. Dr. Honig has been on the editorial board of numerous journals, including the *Early Childhood Research Quarterly* and *Young Children*, and currently serves as the North American editor for *Early Child Development and Care*. Among the books that Dr. Honig has written or edited are *Playtime Learning Games for Young Children* (Syracuse University Press, 1982), *Risk Factors in Infancy* (Gordon & Breach, 1986), *Parent Involvement in Early Childhood Education* (NAEYC, 1979), and, with J. R. Lally, *Early Parenting and Later School Achievement* (Gordon & Breach, 1990) and *Infant Caregiving: A Design for Training* (Garland, 1992).

Carollee Howes is professor of developmental studies in the Graduate School of Education at the University of California, Los Angeles. She received her Ph.D. in developmental psychology from Boston University. Her research interests include the antecedents and beginning constructions of peer friendships and social competence and children's social development within infant child care. Her most recent books are *Peer Interaction in Young Children*, *The Social Construction of Pretend*, and *Forming Relationships: Children in Child Care*.

Susan Kontos is associate professor in the Department of Child Development and Family Studies at Purdue University. She received her Ph.D. in child development from Iowa State University. Her research focuses on family and child care influences on children as well as on early intervention. She is associate editor of the *Early Childhood Research Quarterly* and author of *Family Day Care: Out of the Shadows and into the Limelight* (NAEYC, 1992), a research monograph.

Roger Neugebauer is the publisher of *Child Care Information Exchange*, a magazine for directors of child care centers, and founder of the Director's Network. He is also on the governing board of the National Association for the Education of Young Children and the National Association of Child Care Resource and Referral Agencies. Mr. Neugebauer has a master's degree in day care administration from Lesley College. Prior to his involvement in the child care profession he worked for the federal Departments of Housing and Urban Development and Health, Education, and Welfare.

Patricia G. Ramsey is associate professor of psychology and education and director of the Gorse Child Study Center at Mount Holyoke College. She received her Ed.D. in early childhood education from the University of Massachusetts and is a former preschool teacher. Dr. Ramsey has published a number of articles on multicultural education and children's social development. She is the author of *Teaching and Learning in a Diverse World: Multicultural Education for Young Children* (1987) and *Making Friends in School: Promoting Peer Relations in Early Childhood* (1991), both published by Teachers College Press, and coauthor of *Multicultural Education: A Source Book*, published in 1989 by Garland Press.

Olivia N. Saracho (Editor) is professor of education in the Department of Curriculum and Instruction at the University of Maryland. She completed her Ph.D. in early childhood education at the University of Illinois in 1978. Previously, she taught Head Start, preschool, kindergarten, and elementary classes in Brownsville, Texas, and was director of the Child Development Associate Program at Pan American University. Her current research and writing focus on cognitive style, academic learning, and teacher education in relation to early childhood education. Dr. Saracho's most recent books are *Cognitive Style and Early Education* (Gordon & Breach, 1990); *Professionalism and the Early Childhood Practitioner*, edited with Bernard Spodek and Donald J. Peters (Teachers College Press, 1988); and *Foundations of Early Childhood Education* (Prentice-Hall, 1987, 1991), with Bernard Spodek and Michael J. Davis. Dr. Saracho is coeditor of the *Yearbook in Early Childhood Education* series and coeditor of Volume 1, *Early Childhood Teacher Education*, and Volume 2, *Issues in Early Childhood Curriculum*.

Michelle Seligson is director of the School-Age Child Care Project, a national action/research and technical-assistance project located at Wellesley College Center for Research on Women, where she is also associate director. She holds degrees from Simmons College and the Harvard Graduate School of Education. She has coauthored several publications, including *School Age Child Care: An Action Manual* (Auburn House), *School Age Child Care: A Policy Report*, (Wellesley College), *Child Care and Equal Opportunity* (U.S. Civil Rights Commission, 1980), *No Time to Waste: An Action Agenda for School Age Child Care*, and *Early Childhood Programs and the Public Schools: Between Promise and Practice* (Auburn House, 1989).

Bernard Spodek (Editor) is professor of early childhood education at the University of Illinois, where he has taught since 1965. He received his doctorate in early childhood education from Teachers College, Columbia University, then joined the faculty of the University of Wisconsin-Milwaukee. He has also taught nursery, kindergarten, and elementary classes. His research and scholarly interests are in the areas of curriculum, teaching, and teacher education in early childhood education. Dr. Spodek has lectured extensively in the United States, Australia, Canada, China, England, Israel, Japan, Mexico, and Taiwan. From 1976 to 1978 he was president of the National Association for the Education of Young Children, and from 1981 through 1983 he chaired the Early Education and Child Development Special Interest Group of the American Educational Research Association. He is widely published in the field of early childhood education. Dr. Spodek's most recent books are *Educationally Appropriate Kindergarten Practices* (National Education Association, 1991); *Professionalism and the Early Childhood Practitioner*, edited with Olivia N. Saracho and Donald J. Peters (Teachers College Press, 1988); *Foundations of Early Childhood Education* (Prentice-Hall, 1987, 1991), with Olivia N. Saracho and Michael J. Davis; and *Today's Kindergarten: Exploring Its Knowledge Base, Expanding Its Curriculum* (Teachers College Press, 1986). Dr. Spodek is coeditor of the *Yearbook in Early Childhood Education* series and coeditor of Volume 1, *Early Childhood Teacher Education*, and Volume 2, *Issues in Early Childhood Curriculum*.

Bernice Weissbourd founded Family Focus in 1976, a not-for-profit organization providing comprehensive community-based programs for parents of children through three years of age. In 1981 she initiated the Family Resource Coalition, a national organization representing programs, academicians, and policymakers in the family support field and, in 1989, she and T. Berry Brazelton cofounded Parent Action, a nationwide advocacy group for parents. She is also a lecturer at the School of Social Service Administration, University of Chicago. Ms. Weissbourd is past president of the American Orthopsychiatric Association, former vice president of the National Association for the Education of Young Children, and a congressional appointee to the National Commission on Children. She is a contributing editor to *Parents* magazine and has authored and edited numerous publications, including *America's Family Support Programs* (Yale University Press, 1987), "Family Resources and Support Programs: Changes and Challenges in Human Services" in *Families as Nurturing Systems: Support Across the Life Span* (Haworth Press, 1991), and "Family Resources and Support Programs: Promoting Family Well-Being" in the *Handbook of Infant Mental Health* (Guilford Press, in press).

Index